THE LIBRARY
OF
BIBLICAL STUDIES

Edited by

Harry M. Orlinsky

THE FORMS OF HEBREW POETRY

THE FORMS

OF

HEBREW POETRY

CONSIDERED WITH SPECIAL REFERENCE
TO THE CRITICISM AND INTERPRETATION
OF THE OLD TESTAMENT

BY

GEORGE BUCHANAN GRAY

D.Litt., D.D.

PROFESSOR OF HEBREW AND OLD TESTAMENT EXEGESIS IN MANSFIELD COLLEGE
AND SPEAKER'S LECTURER IN BIBLICAL STUDIES IN THE UNIVERSITY OF OXFORD

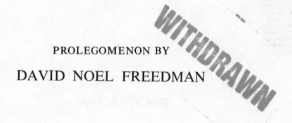

PROLEGOMENON BY

DAVID NOEL FREEDMAN

KTAV PUBLISHING HOUSE

1972

FIRST PUBLISHED 1915

NEW MATTER

© COPYRIGHT 1972
KTAV PUBLISHING HOUSE, INC.

SBN 87068-064-1

MANUFACTURED IN THE UNITED STATES OF AMERICA
LIBRARY OF CONGRESS CATALOG CARD NUMBER: 67-11892

CONTENTS

CHAPTER VII

CHAPTER VIII

INDEX I

INDEX II

PROLEGOMENON

George Buchanan Gray was born in 1865. His education was not typical of nineteenth-century England in that he was not initially a product of the "Oxbridge" establishment. He studied at private schools in Dorset and Exeter, matriculated at London University where he read Greek and Latin, and received his A.B. in 1886. Since his father was a Congregational minister, Gray chose to pursue his interest in Semitic languages and literature at Mansfield College, a non-Conformist hall at Oxford. On completion of his studies, in which he won many distinctions, he was appointed, first, tutor and then Professor of Hebrew and Exegesis of the Old Testament at Mansfield, where he remained for the rest of his life. During the thirty years of his professional career, he wrote numerous articles and eight books, including commentaries on Numbers, I Isaiah, and Job in the prestigious ICC series and a Critical Introduction to the Old Testament (the latter two in collaboration with his senior colleague, S. R. Driver). His final book, *Sacrifice in the Old Testament,* was published posthumously, after his sudden death in November, 1922. G. R. Driver has characterized him as follows, "On critical questions his judgment was shrewd and sane; he distrusted extreme views and advanced cautiously to his conclusions, but, so soon as he was sure of his ground, he could not be shaken."

A bibliography of Gray's works is found in *Sacrifice in the Old Testament* (Oxford, 1925), pp. ix-xi—happily now reissued by KTAV in the *Library of Biblical Studies* (1971; the bibliography on pp. xlvii-xlix), with a Prolegomenon by Baruch A. Levine.

In preparing his classic volume on the *Forms of Hebrew Poetry,*
Gray stated his aim as follows: "It is . . . to survey the forms of
Hebrew poetry, to consider them in relation to one another, and
to illustrate their bearing on the criticism and interpretation of the
Old Testament" (pp. v-vi). He goes on to say that he has no new
theory of Hebrew meter to present; and at the same time he does
not fully accept any past or current theory. His views throughout
are characterized by a cautious pragmatism: he affirms the existence of metrical principles in Hebrew poetry, but questions whether
enough is yet known to substantiate the "regular symmetrical
forms" which other scholars claim to have identified in the poetry
of the Old Testament.

The introductory chapter is devoted to a discussion of the formal
aspects of Hebrew poetry. In Gray's view, the principal components
are parallelism and meter, with strophe as a third but less important factor. The point of departure is the first systematic treatment of formal elements in Hebrew poetry by Robert Lowth whose
lectures *De Sacra Poesi Hebraeorum Praelectiones Academicae*
appeared in 1753; they were followed by more extended studies
in 1778 in connection with his translation of Isaiah. According to
Gray, Lowth's contribution was twofold: "He for the first time
clearly analysed and expounded the parallelistic structure of Hebrew poetry, and he drew attention to the fact that the extent of
poetry in the Old Testament was much larger than had generally
been recognized, that in particular it included the greater part of
the prophetic writings" (pp. 6-7). Since that time no one dealing
seriously with the subject has questioned either the existence or
general characteristics of parallelism as described by Lowth, or
that it is a central and basic component of Hebrew poetry.

In the remainder of the chapter, Gray reviews the evidence
available in Jewish and Christian tradition concerning the nature
of Old Testament poetry. Philo and Josephus, Origen, Eusebius,
and Jerome all refer to Hebrew poetry, and describe its structure
in terms derived from classical Greek metrics. Among a variety
of inexact statements, Eusebius alone claims that Psalm 119 consists of hexameters of sixteen syllables. Gray's main point is that
formal knowledge of the structure of Hebrew poetry does not seem

to have been preserved beyond the second century C.E. if indeed that long. At the same time parallelism, that central feature of such poetry, continues to be characteristic of Jewish poetry well into if not beyond the first century C.E., whether composed in Hebrew or Aramaic and translated into Greek or Latin, or directly in Greek.

Chapter II, "Parallelism: A Restatement," deals in depth with the main subject of Lowth's analysis. After discussing the theoretical and practical distinctions between prose and poetry and the applicability of parallelism and meter to these differences, Gray concludes that parallelism is the only reliable criterion for making an effective determination. As he says, "Parallelism is unmistakable, metre in Hebrew literature is obscure: the laws of Hebrew metre have been and are matters of dispute, and at times the very existence of metre in the Old Testament has been questioned" (p. 47).

He then proceeds to a detailed discussion of the different kinds of parallelism. Lowth distinguished three: synonymous, antithetic, and synthetic. Concerning the first two, Gray has little to say, but points out that the third category, serving as a catchall, has proved to be a vulnerable point in Lowth's exposition. Some of his examples under this third heading exhibit partial parallelism, since the second unit repeats part of the sense of the first, but also adds something new. For this type of couplet (or bicolon), Gray prefers the term "incomplete parallelism" (p. 49). Actually they are variations or by-forms of the first two headings: synonymous and antithetic.

For the other examples under the third heading, Gray readily agrees that the component lines are synthetically related, but without any discernible parallelism. In other words, the term as used by Lowth is extended to material in which there is no sense of parallelism at all; it has become in fact a metrical designation indicating that the two units are parallel in structure. The question is whether the use of the term is justified in such situations, or whether it is not misleading to use it in a radically different sense to describe the changed situation.

In line with his proposed classification of the phenomena under the headings: complete and incomplete parallelism, Gray offers numerous examples of both with appropriate translations and annotations. With regard to Gen. 49:12 (p. 61) we may suggest the rendering (cf. The New Jewish Version, 1962):

> Darker than wine are his eyes,
> and whiter than milk are his teeth

in place of

> Red-are his-eyes with-wine
> and-white-are his-teeth with-milk.

(Cf. *Studies in Ancient Yahwistic Poetry* [AYP], pp. 137, 161.)

To indicate the character and degree of parallelism Gray employed letters of the alphabet to designate the separate terms in the different cola: a . b . c , etc., in the first line, and a′ . b′ . c′ in the corresponding line (pp. 59-60). This system, with some modifications is now universally employed by scholars.

In discussing possible variations of the basic schemes:

$$a . b \text{ and } a . b . c$$
$$a′ . b′ \quad\quad a′ . b′ . c′$$

Gray points to

$$a . b$$
$$b′ . a′$$

and various rearrangements of a . b . c , some of which result in

$$a′ . b′ . c′$$

chiastic patterns (e.g., a . b . c, etc.).

$$c′ . b′ . a′$$

Gray does not use the technical term, apparently failing to recognize this significant literary device.

Gray goes on to describe parallelism of paired terms, indicated, e.g., as

$$a 2 . b$$
$$a′ 2 . b′$$

As Gray points out, incomplete parallelism offers much greater variety of patterns: e.g., a . b or a . b

$$c . b′ \quad a′ . c$$

With three or more terms, the number of possible variations increases geometrically. Gray distinguishes two broad classes of incomplete parallelism: with or without compensation (p. 74). Such schemes as

$$a \cdot b \cdot c \quad \text{or} \quad a \quad \cdot b \cdot c$$
$$a' \cdot b' \qquad\qquad a'2$$

are incomplete without compensation, whereas a $\cdot$ b $\cdot$ c or

$$a' \cdot d \cdot c'$$

a $\cdot$ b $\cdot$ c are incomplete parallelism with compensation. The

$$a'2 \cdot b'$$

latter subdivision would now be designated a ballast variant (see n. 8 below).

Gray then illustrates the value of such an analytical procedure in dealing with bicola where failure to recognize examples of partial parallelism has resulted in wrong division of the lines, and misunderstanding of the text. These errors are further compounded by mutilation of the passage, disguised as emendation: striking examples from the work of W. R. Harper and C. A. Briggs are offered in evidence.

In Chapter III, Gray discusses Parallelism and Rhythm in the Book of Lamentations. Again his point of departure is Lowth, who treated the Book both in his *Lectures* and *Isaiah*. He pointed to the special features which distinguish the first four chapters from the fifth, especially the falling rhythm and the paucity of parallelism in the former. Budde advanced beyond Lowth in analyzing the exact nature of the "unequal division of the rhythmical periods" and the extent to which this pattern occurs outside of Lamentations (p. 91). With regard to the rhythm, commonly designated *kinah*, Budde stipulated that normally the first unit consists of three words or stresses, and the second of two. Variations are possible, but the division is never equal: if the first element has only two words, these are heavier than the corresponding pair.

Lamentations 5 on the other hand consists of balanced lines, with a 3:3 pattern. Seventeen of the twenty verses show strict parallelism between at least one term in each colon. Of the remaining verses, two lack parallelism (vss. 8, 16), while two others seem to be parallel to each other (vss. 9-10). The last (vs. 5) is too obscure to classify.

Gray then returns to a description of chaps. 1-4 which are separate poems in the form of alphabetic acrostics: the first three chapters have three line acrostics: in the first two each three-line stanza begins with a different letter of the alphabet in ascending order from *aleph* to *taw*. In the third, 'each line of the stanza begins with the same letter. Chapter 4 is a two-line acrostic of the same type as chaps. 1 and 2.

Gray points out that the normal line consists of five words or stresses as against six in chap. 5. He argues from this that the common form of complete parallelism a . b . c / a' . b' . c' does not occur at all in chaps. 1-4; complete parallelism in any form is rare, especially by comparison with chap. 5 in which it is quite frequent.

There follows a discussion of the distinction between "rhythmical parallelism" and "parallelism of thought" on the basis of observations by DeWette and Budde. This distinction, essentially a contrast between form and content, has colored the debate over Hebrew poetry almost throughout its history. Scholars have argued on both sides, in favor of the primacy of one factor over the other, but it must finally be recognized that both are present in Hebrew poetry, often functioning in concord, occasionally in conflict with each other.

Citing Lam. 3, Gray makes the point that parallelism, whether sectional or subsectional (i.e., between bicola or cola) is quite rare, and hence the metrical scheme is sustained by "mere rhythmical parallelism" (p. 102). In chap. 2 on the other hand, parallelism of thought is well-nigh universal, especially between sections (bicola); subsectional parallelism is rare.

His analysis and interpretation of 2:2 deserve discussion. He divides the verse and renders as follows (p. 106):

billa' '^{a}dōnāy lō' hāmal	The Lord hath destroyed unsparingly
'ēt kol-n$^{e'}$ōt ya'^{a}qōb	all the homesteads of Jacob;
hāras b$^{e'}$ebrātō	He hath pulled down in his wrath
mibṣ^{e}rē bat-y^{e}hūdāh	the strongholds of Judah;

higgīaʻ lāʼāreṣ ḥillēl	He hath brought to the ground,
	ḥath profaned |
mamlākāh wᵉśārēhā	the realm and its princes.

While the text is satisfactory and the translation makes sense, there are certain difficulties with Gray's arrangement and analysis of the sections. The division in the third line is awkward, and contrary to the Massoretic punctuation. The second line hardly conforms to the normal *ḳinah* pattern. In addition we should expect a closer linkage between the expressions *mbṣry bt-yhwdh* "the strongholds of Judah" and *hgyʻ lʼrṣ* "he hath brought to the ground" (again following the arrangement in MT) than Gray would allow. I suggest the following:

a) blʻ ʼdny lʼ ḥml	The Lord devoured, he showed
	no mercy—
b) ʼt kl-nʼwt yʻqb	All the dwellings of Jacob
hrs bʻbrtw	he tore down in his wrath
c) mbṣry bt-yhwdh	the fortresses of Daughter-Judah
hgyʻ lʼrṣ	he brought down to the earth—
d) ḥll-m mlkh wśryh	He slew her king and her princes.

The key to this analysis is the recognition of the extended parallelism between the two central sections of the verse (*b* and *c*). In similar fashion units *a* and *d* balance. Thus the verbs *hrs* and *hgyʻ* are parallel terms, both referring to the destruction of buildings. A striking illustration is to be found in the roughly contemporary utterance of Ezek. 13:14, "And I will destroy (*whrsty*) the wall . . . and I will bring it down to the earth (*whgʻtyhw* . . . *ʼl-hʼrṣ*) . . ." Another example from the same period is Isa. 25:12 ". . . and the fortress . . . he brought down to earth . . ." (*wmbṣr . . . hgyʻ lʼrṣ*). Cf. also Isa. 26:5. Similarly the verbs *blʻ* and *ḥll* are to be taken as parallel. I derive *ḥll* from the root "to pierce, slay" rather than "to profane." In view of the reading of the LXX and the parallel expression in 2:9 *mlkh wśryh*, I think we must read the same here: the initial *mem* of *mmlkh* should then be taken as an enclitic with the preceding verb *ḥll*.

On the basis of the proposed analysis, we note that the three-line unit divides into two equal parts, after *b'brtw*. A similar structure may be observed in 2:10 which Gray also discusses (p. 107).

yāsᵉbū* lā'āreṣ yiddᵉmū	They sat on the ground dumb— |
ziqnē bat-ṣiyyon	the elders of Sion;
heʿelū ʿāpār ʿal-rō'šām	Lifted up dust on their head, |
hāgᵉrū śaqqīm	were girded with sackcloth;
hōrīdū lā'āreṣ rō'šān	They lowered to the ground their head— |
bᵉtūlōt yᵉrūšālayim	the virgins of Jerusalem.

*We read *yāsᵉbū* instead of MT *yēsᵉbū,* in view of the other perfect forms at the beginning of cola in this verse. Many other stanzas in this chapter also begin with verbs in the perfect form: vss. 2, 3, 4, 5, 7, 8, 9, 11, 15, 16, 17, 18, 21.

Gray observes correctly the intricate pattern of parallels in the verse. Thus the poet compares the elders with the virgins while contrasting their actions. The former raise dust upon their heads, the latter lower their heads to the ground. Going beyond Gray, we note the chiastic structure which serves to emphasize the point:

zqny bt-ṣywn ——————— h'lw 'pr 'l-r'šm
hwrydw l'rṣ r'šn ——————— btwlt yršlm

We also suggest that the major division in the verse comes in the middle, after *r'šm:* everything before that refers to the "elders of Daughter-Zion," everything after it refers to the "virgins of Jerusalem." In particular, it is the "virgins" who gird themselves with sackcloth. This analysis produces a more exact balance between the parts, and emphasizes the parallel structure in the description of the two groups: the old men sit (*yšbw*) and lift up dust (*h'lw*); the virgins gird sackcloth (*hgrw*) and lower their heads (*hwrydw*). The juxtaposition of Qal and Hiphil verb forms seems deliberate. It may be added that the distinctions are poetic rather than realistic, and that the two groups chosen are intended to be representative of the surviving population, of whom all the actions described would be typical. Grammatically the clause *hgrw śqym* could take the "elders" as subject, or the "virgins" or both.

Gray concludes that parallelism is not a dominant feature in these chapters (2 and 4). But as compared with chaps. 2 and 4, chap. 1 exhibits parallelism, whether sectional or subsectional, even less frequently. Given the relative paucity of parallelism throughout the first four chapters, a question arises concerning the rhythmic character of these chapters. A regular rhythm may well be the product of consistent use of parallelism; thus the pattern a . b . c / a′ . b′ . c′ would normally produce a 3:3 rhythm. But how does one account for rhythmic regularity when parallelism is a minor element (i.e., incomplete) or absent altogether? The persistence of a distinctive pattern in the first four chapters of Lamentations requires a theory of Hebrew meter to account for the phenomenon. The pattern may be described as a sequence of lines in which there are five words or stress-groups, with a characteristic pause or break after the third. This is what is meant by *ḳinah* meter or rhythm. Unfortunately, as Gray points out, the pattern is not consistent throughout, and in chap. 1 must compete for dominance with another pattern, a more balanced meter which may be characterized as 2:2 instead of the 3:2 of *ḳinah* rhythm. In fact there are a number of other variations from the presumed normal *ḳinah* pattern, but such passages generally are emended to make them conform to one or the other rhythm described. In our judgment Gray has oversimplified the problem, and we have suggested a different and we believe a more objective approach to the phenomenon, the fact of which is widely acknowledged. How to describe, analyze, and control the exact data remain to be considered. In our opinion there was a standard line length (which we can measure in total number of syllables, rather than stresses), which can be determined statistically, as well as a normal range above and below the mean. Measured in this fashion, the separate poems in chaps. 1-3 are practically identical in structure and share a common metrical or rhythmic pattern. In other words, the problem of mixed meter in chap. 1 as over against chaps. 2 and 3, and the related question concerning 2:2 lines as a legitimate variant of the standard 3:2 lines do not seem to have the urgency they once did. The variations are stylistic rather than metrical or quantitative, and well within the overall range which obtains in chaps. 2 and 3, as well as 1.

In Chapter IV, Gray turns to the other main topic: Hebrew rhythm. As he says, "... parallelism is but one law or form of Hebrew poetry, and ... it leaves much to be explained by some other law or form" (p. 123). He goes on to say that, "Some such rhythmical principle, whether or not its nature can ever be exactly and fully explained, seems to govern much of the present text of the Old Testament ..." (p. 124). To this affirmation there would be widespread agreement, though sharp divergences emerge as soon as the attempt is made to explain or describe that principle more exactly. Gray makes a series of very judicious comments about the difficulties facing the scholar in any attempt at metrical analysis. Given the uncertain state of the present text we could hardly expect to find a precise metrical pattern preserved in it. But if we emend freely, at least in part on the basis of a metrical theory, then we have in effect proved our prejudice; and someone else, emending along other lines, could establish an entirely different metrical pattern.

In developing his views about Hebrew rhythm, Gray begins predictably with parallelism, and affirms that parallelism naturally produces a coincidence between rhythmical periods and sense divisions. He goes further and argues that "parallelism is, broadly speaking, incompatible with anything but 'stopped-line' poetry" (p. 127). This is a plausible conclusion, and applies to sections rather than subsections; it also leaves out of consideration non-parallelistic poetry, where the same criteria do not apply.

Gray then draws a fateful analogy between Hebrew and old Anglo-Saxon poetry (pp. 128 ff.). He quotes extensively from G. Saintsbury's *A History of English Prosody* to sketch the principal characteristics of Anglo-Saxon verse: the division of the line into halves, with two accented syllables in each half-line (three of the four being alliterated). The number of unaccented syllables varies widely between half-lines and from line to line. According to Gray, Hebrew poetry shares in several features: "(1) The isolated verse in Anglo-Saxon corresponds to the parallel distich in Hebrew; (2) the strong internal pause in Anglo-Saxon to the end of the first parallel period of the Hebrew distich; (3) there is a correspondingly great irregularity in the number of syllables in successive distichs of Hebrew" (p. 130). As a qualification of the last point, it should be mentioned that there is a greater approximation to regularity in the length of lines in *Piers Ploughman,* which Gray is using as the basis of his comparison (pp. 129-30). (Our own studies and statistical tables on Lamentations and other acrostic poems indicate that the same is true of a number of the Hebrew poems considered by Gray.)

The critical question according to Gray is whether Anglo-Saxon and Hebrew poetry agree as to the constant quantity of stressed syllables in a verse, and the constant ratio of stressed syllables in the two parts of a verse. Part of the difficulty in answering the question is that, as Gray says, "In many Hebrew lines we cannot immediately see for certain either which, or how many, are the stressed syllables . . ." (p. 131). We may add the theoretical consideration that Hebrew may not have had stresses in the commonly assumed sense at all in the early period.

Before proceeding with the question of stress-counting Gray takes up the broader problem of basic rhythmic variety in Hebrew poetry. He distinguishes two broad classes or types of rhythm: *balancing rhythm* and *echoing rhythm.* Thus in Lam. 5 we have lines in which the two parts match (*balancing rhythm*), while in Lam. 4, the lines are unbalanced, the first part being longer than the second (*echoing rhythm*) (p. 133). Nevertheless, exceptions to the norm occur in both poems, so that balancing lines are to be found in chap. 4 and echoing lines in chap. 5.

Gray then seeks to determine the criteria of measurement by which balance and echo are to be distinguished. The first proposal is that all syllables be counted.

A second possibility is to count metrical values, weighing long and short syllables as in Greek and Latin poetry. Thus the number of syllables in a Latin hexameter varies, but the sum is always equivalent to six spondees.

The third is based on the number of stressed words or syllables in each subsection. If they are equal then the line is balanced, if there is a larger number in the first part, then it is echoed.

Gray dismisses the first two without further discussion, and concentrates further attention on the third. As I have suggested elsewhere, this decision was unfortunate, and both of the other hypotheses should have been re-examined. In the study of several poems I have tried to weigh the relative merits of all three systems. While there are difficulties in all of them, there are also positive values. Further investigation is surely warranted.

Gray, however, deals only with the stressed-syllable system, and suggests a number of problems which arise in connection with it. For example, is there any limit to the number of unaccented syllables between accented syllables, or does a secondary stress or counter-tone occur if the number exceeds a certain standard, say three or four? Put another way, may a word bear more than one accent or stress, or does the general correlation of one word, one stress hold throughout? On the other hand, do one-syllable particles like *l'* or *ky* take a stress or are they absorbed by neighboring words? As Gray points out, none of these questions can be answered with certainty, but any rigid rule is likely to be wrong. Some flexibility is necessary in dealing with the different phenomena, but the greater the flexibility and the more applicable, the less real utility any system has, since finally it may come down to mere sanction of whatever happens to be the case.

After discussing briefly possible contributions to the elucidation of these problems from the study of Massoretic punctuation and Assyrian poetry, Gray turns to the proposals of E. Sievers, which constitute a detailed and systematic approach to the whole range of metrical issues. His rules are: 1) the number of unstressed syllables attached to a stressed syllable may never exceed four and in most cases three. So every word with more than five syllables must have two stresses; 2) the stressed syllable regularly follows the unstressed syllables associated with it, and no more than one unstressed syllable may follow a stressed syllable (pp. 143-44). Hence Hebrew meter is essentially anapestic, i.e., two unstressed syllables followed by a stressed syllable, though with substantial variations in practice. Gray's conclusion about Sievers' views is that they remain unproved in spite of the erudition and mass of data which Sievers brings to bear on the subject. Gray's comment is pertinent: "The degree of uncertainty which the theory would remove is largely counter-balanced by the insecurity of the basis on which it rests" (p. 147). After examining specific cases in which Sievers alters the pronunciation of Biblical Hebrew:

mainly to reduce the number of unstressed syllables, but occasionally to introduce some to avoid the harsh-sounding sequence of two stressed syllables, Gray summarizes Sievers' contribution to the subject as follows: Hebrew poetry is basically anapestic (or iambic) rather than dactylic (or trochaic) in character; there should be some overall balance in total length between parallel units.

At the end of the chapter, Gray proposes a rule of his own: with respect to rhythmically ambiguous terms, he suggests that parallel expressions tended to receive the same treatment; if one was stressed, the other was, and vice versa. He then applies the rule to a number of controversial examples with plausible results. But the arguments are hardly conclusive, and alternate proposals deserve consideration as well. His most detailed discussion is reserved for Lam. 1:1 which on the face of it seems to have an aberrant metrical structure: 3:3, 2:2, 2:2.

'ēkāh yāš^{e}bāh bādād	How doth she sit solitary, |
hā'īr rabbātī 'ām	—the city (once) great in population!
hāy^{e}tāh k^e'almānāh	She is become like a widow, |
rabbātī baggōyīm	she that was great among the nations:
śārātī bamm^{e}dīnōt	She that was mistress over provinces, |
hāy^{e}tāh lāmas	she hath been (set) to forced labour.

Budde thought that *h'yr* in vs. 1a^2 was suspect since a 3:2 meter was desiderated. But Sievers argued that *rbty 'm* should receive only one stress, and therefore preserved the text. Gray defends Sievers' view, arguing at length that *rbty 'm* is a closed unit differing in force from *rbty // śrty* in 1bc. The argumentation on both sides, however, seems to me to be special pleading in favor of a metrical scheme which is assumed to be normative. To remove *h'yr* on metrical grounds (there are no other) would be arbitrary in the extreme, and Sievers and Gray are right in rejecting that proposal. Their defense of the text, however, is forced, and the metrical distinctions too fine to be sustained by the data. Thus 1a would normally be construed as 3:3 except for the notion that such a meter is impermissible in this poem. It is hard to believe that

Israelite poets drew such a sharp line. Other criteria, not easily defined, must have played a role in determining metrical structure; but in view of the plethora of doubtful and ambiguous cases, it does not appear that the stressed-syllable count was decisive.

In Chapter V, Gray discusses varieties of rhythm, and then goes on to the subject of strophes. He asserts at the start that there are only two major types of rhythm: balancing, in which the lines or subsections are of equal length, and echoing, in which the second is shorter than the first. He claims that a third type, in which the first part is shorter than the second, is extremely rare and does not warrant the detailed treatment given to the others. Nevertheless, with commendable caution he defends its occurrence against those who would exclude it entirely, and gives several examples.

Under the main headings, Gray lists the following rhythmic types: *balanced*—2:2, 3:3, and 4:4; *echoing*—3:2, but 4:3 occurs as well, though it often breaks down into 2:2:3 which does not convey the same impression as 3:2. There is a certain amount of mixed meter, which may well be deliberate, though the situation is complicated by the presence of apparent corruptions in the text. He summarizes as follows: "1) The typical echoing rhythm is 3:2; with this 2:2 alternates, sometimes occasionally, sometimes as in Lam. 1, frequently; other distichs of unequal lines, 4:3 or 4:2, are at best much rarer alternatives. 2) Of the fundamental balancing rhythms 2:2 and 4:4 are closely allied and interchange, and by expansion a further natural and occasional variant is 2:2:2. 3) But this last-mentioned alternative to 2:2 or 4:4 constitutes a link with the third fundamental balancing rhythm, viz. 3:3; for 3:3 and 2:2:2 are but different ways of dividing the same higher unity, viz. the six-stress period, which may yet again divide into 4:2 or 2:4 . . ." (pp. 184-85).

Gray concludes the chapter with a discussion of strophes or stanzas and their occurrence in Hebrew poetry. On the whole there is not much evidence for this practice and what there is is not necessarily convincing. An obvious starting point is the alphabetic acrostics and in Lam. 1, 2, and 4 there is compelling evidence for verse-paragraphs delimited by the successive letters of the alphabet and of equal length throughout the poems. In other acrostics, e.g., Lam. 3 and Ps. 119, no such pattern emerges, however. In some poems, a repeated refrain occurs, which marks off sections or stanzas of the poem. In some poems these units are of approximately equal length, in others they are not. Then there are poems, which naturally divide into verse paragraphs of approximately equal length, though there are no formal indications of this division in the text. At the same time, there are many poems in which such paragraphs are very unequal in length, and still others where the lines of demarcation are difficult to determine, if they exist at all. Attempts to discover greater symmetry in the structuring of verse-paragraphs of unequal or irregular length, have proved unsuccessful though the effort has been made with great industry and ingenuity by men like Fr. Köster ("Die Strophen, oder der Parallelismus der Verse der hebräischen Poesie untersucht," *Theologische Studien und Kritiken* [= *TSK*], IV [1831]), and D. H. Müller (*Die Propheten in ihrer ursprünglichen Form* [1896]; *Strophenbau und Responsion* [1898]).

Chapter VI, entitled "The Bearing of Certain Metrical Theories on Criticism and Interpretation," is devoted largely to a critique of the published views of Sievers and Duhm. With respect to Sievers' elaborate demonstration that the books of Genesis and Samuel are poetic in structure sharing rhythmic patterns already attested in the poetic books (*Metrische Studien:* II. *Die hebräische Genesis* [1904-5]; III. *Samuel* [1907]), Gray effectively criticizes Sievers' ambitious attempt as both unproven and improbable, pointing especially to the excessive amount of emendation to which Sievers resorts in order to sustain his theory. Even more destructive of Sievers' theories is the observation that if we begin with a variety of metrical patterns allowing for lines of different lengths, accept run-on lines as a matter of course, allow a wide range of variations and exceptions—not counting emendations—then anything becomes metrical, and it is impossible to distinguish prose from poetry. Once parallelism in both form and sense, and paired cola and larger units are abandoned, then there is little left in the way of criteria to determine the presence of poetry apart from the assertion that it is there. What remains from the wreckage of these monumental schemes is nevertheless considerable. That authentic poems are embedded in the prose of Genesis and Samuel (and the other narrative books of the Pentateuch and Former Prophets) cannot be doubted; now in addition to obvious examples such as Gen. 49; I Sam. 2:1-10; II Sam. 1:19-27; 22; 23:1-7, many other passages can be so identified, especially in speeches and dialogue which lend themselves more easily to poetic presentation. There are, as well, narrative passages which have the rhythm of poetry; and we may recognize the survival in the present prose accounts of an older metrical version or source from which the material has been derived. On the whole, Gray's sober conclusions have stood the test of time, and his views, rather than those of Sievers, have prevailed.

The same can be said also of his judgment against Duhm. Here his quarrel is with the attempt to impose a rigid regularity on the meter of a poem both with respect to distichs (or bicola) and strophes (or stanzas). Duhm is not alone in this camp (Briggs is another with whom Gray crosses swords), but he is an outstanding representative of the surgical school of Hebrew poetry. Gray concedes immediately that the texts of the Prophets, Psalms, and Job, with which Duhm deals, are corrupt, and that not much help is to be had from the versions, the LXX in particular. Hence some room must be allowed for conjectural emendation; but when this procedure is followed in the interests of a metrical theory, then the results are more likely to be harmful than helpful. Gray's words on the subject deserve the most careful and respectful consideration: "But there is need for the greatest possible caution in using a metrical theory as the sole reason for emendation; for one Hebrew metre can be changed into another with fatal ease; drop the verb, or some other parallel term that the sense will spare from the second line of a 3:3 distich, and the result is a very dissimilar 3:2; and, conversely, in a 3:2 distich prefix an infinitive absolute to the verb of the second line and a distich 3:3 is the result" (p. 225).

Gray then discusses examples of Duhm's arbitrary procedures in various parts of Isaiah, but reserves his sharpest criticism for Duhm's treatment of the oracles of Jeremiah. Here in addition to the insistence on regularity in meter and strophe, Duhm maintains that Jeremiah composed in only one meter. The result is catastrophic: very little of the extant book is left to the prophet, and that little is roughly handled. Such practice is a parody of serious scholarship, and has tended to bring the study of Hebrew prosody into disrepute. Over the years Gray's steadying influence has been felt and there is a growing body of opinion that conjectural emendation must be more closely regulated than in the past, if any consensus is finally to be achieved, and that such changes are to be resisted even more rigorously when inspired by metrical considerations. Nevertheless the spirit of Duhm is still abroad in the lands. While deploring the mutilating effects on the text of their labors, we may agree that scholars so inspired stimulate response and reaction, and in their way they contribute to progress in the field.

Gray sums up his inquiry into the nature of Hebrew poetry in the closing pages of the chapter: "The main forms of Hebrew poetry are two—parallelism and rhythm, to which, as a third and occasional form, we may add strophe" (p. 236). Of the two main forms parallelism is most closely connected with sense. The two basic forms of rhythm are balancing and echoing. Anything more than this is fraught with uncertainty. Nevertheless more precision in measurement is desirable, even necessary, so a system of counting stressed syllables serves this purpose. Lines or distichs are defined "by the number of stressed syllables in them. The exact number of unstressed syllables that may accompany a stressed syllable may be uncertain but is certainly not unlimited" (p. 238). We have been able to show that there is a certain regularity and predictability in counting all syllables and that such a method overcomes or avoids some of the subjectivity as well as the seemingly endless and futile debate over how to determine and count stressed syllables.

We subscribe enthusiastically to Gray's final word on the subject: "The best service to the future of Old Testament studies, so far as these can be affected by the examination of those formal elements with which alone these discussions have attempted to deal, will be rendered, I believe, by those who combine with that further study of Hebrew metre which is certainly needed, for it is a subject which still presents many obscurities and uncertainties, an unswerving loyalty to the demands of that other and more obvious form or characteristic of Hebrew poetry which is known as parallelism" (pp. 239-40).

Gray has appended two lengthy studies of specific poems of the Bible (Chapter VII, "The Alphabetic Poem in Nahum," and Chapter VIII, "The Alphabetic Structure of Psalms IX and X") which were originally published elsewhere (*Expositor,* Sept. 1898 and Sept. 1906). In these, Gray has endeavored to practice what he preaches so well, and by and large he has done so. Nevertheless, much time has passed since he did his work, and much has been learned about classical Hebrew and its Northwest Semitic relatives. It would take us too far afield to examine these studies in detail or offer a comprehensive critique. The problems remain very much as Gray described—how to achieve effective results without on the one hand canonizing an admittedly corrupt text (but just where, and in what way), or on the other emending a perfectly sound text (but not immediately intelligible for a variety of other reasons) into something equally appealing and wrong. Many of the other features and devices of Hebrew poets, along with their counterparts in neighboring societies, must be recognized and given their due place in the further studies of which Gray speaks before the reasonable goals which scholars set for themselves in the way of understanding, translation, and interpretation can be reached. If they ever are, then a major part of the credit for such an achievement must be accorded to George Buchanan Gray.

This reprinting of G. B. Gray's classic study, *The Forms of Hebrew Poetry,* provides an excellent opportunity not only to acknowledge his noteworthy contribution to the subject and to appraise his views in the light of the present state of our knowledge, but also to make a few suggestions about research in the future.[1] As stated above, Gray's book first appeared when the scholarly world was being shaken by the brilliant, often conflicting, and sometimes erratic metrical theories of the German specialists Bickell, Ley, Budde, and above all Sievers, to say nothing of the radical and disturbing results achieved by men like Duhm in the analysis of prophetic oracles and Briggs in his treatment of the Psalms. In the face of such an onslaught, Gray supplied a much-needed note of caution in his sober evaluation of the new

developments. Partly by appealing to the older tradition in the
study of Hebrew poetry initiated by Bishop Lowth of Oxford,[2]
and partly by subjecting the newly proposed methods and conclusions to a rigorous, systematic analysis, Gray defined for his day
the substantial foundations upon which the study of Hebrew poetry
could be built, as well as the limits within which such study
could successfully be prosecuted. His work was not notably revo-
lutionary or even novel, but by selecting and adapting wisely
among the various principles and techniques then available, he
constructed an eclectic and flexible system which served as a
framework for the classification and interpretation of the phenomena. In general his findings have proved durable, and scholars
have proceeded substantially along the lines he marked out.

Toward the end of the volume (pp. 236-40), Gray listed, in
order of importance, three basic factors in Hebrew poetic structure: 1) *parallelism,* which he regards as the central and crucial
feature; 2) *rhythm,* which is defined in terms of the number of
stressed syllables in the characteristic Hebrew verse-line (i.e.,
distich or bicolon); and 3) *strophe,* or stanza, which although
clearly discernible in certain compositions, is not a regularly repeated or consistently identifiable phenomenon.

Basing his study of parallelism on the famous work of Lowth,
and taking into account the contributions of his successors, Gray
analyzed and classified once again the various types of parallelism,
adding a significant measure of clarity and precision to the description of this universally recognized aspect of Hebrew poetry.
Certainly his categories of complete and incomplete parallelism
are an improvement over previous efforts at classification. Furthermore, he exposed the weakness of Lowth's catchall third category, synthetic parallelism, which all too often disguised or concealed the plain fact that a substantial number of lines of biblical
poetry have no parallelism at all. If we now combine these important observations by Gray, we can construct a table or grid on
which to plot the whole of biblical poetry with respect to the
presence or absence of parallelism. The graph would run from
zero (no parallelism) through all the gradations of incomplete
parallelism to 100 (complete parallelism); it would then be possible to classify lines and poems according to the degree and

distribution of parallelism. Such a table would show at the same time that parallelism could not be regarded as the sole or even sufficient criterion of Hebrew verse, if only because of the large number of lines which have no parallelism. Since, as Gray and others have pointed out correctly, these lines often share a common rhythm or meter with others in the same poem which, however, have parallel elements, it then becomes clear that the overriding consideration in such cases is rhythm rather than parallelism.

If in fact rhythm, with all its deliberate variety and irregularity, is the fundamental criterion of Hebrew verse, then parallelism may be regarded as a stylistic device, the use of which has been influenced, in part at least, by metrical considerations. Thus the poet could use parallel expressions to fill out a line according to the metrical requirements. Such a factor could explain both the presence and the absence of parallelism, as well as the degree or extent of its use in given lines. Viewed in this fashion, the poem expresses the author's thoughts in lines of predetermined length. In those cases in which the poet's thought as expressed coincides in length with the metrical requirement, there will be no parallelism, whereas in those cases in which the basic expression comes short of the requirement, parallel terms would be added to make up the deficiency. In this way we can explain the occurrence of lines without parallelism, with complete parallelism, and with varying degrees of parallelism in the same poem, and having the same rhythm or meter. We are not offering this hypothesis as an analysis of the psychology of the poet, or a probable method of composition, but only as a logical description of the phenomena.

Once it is recognized that parallelism is not a necessary characteristic of Hebrew poetry, and that many lines do not have this feature, it is interesting to observe how the poet deals with this potentially prosaic element. In some cases, the line stands as is, indistinguishable from prose constructions, reflecting either the poverty of poetic imagination or the fact that the dividing line between poetry and prose is not a sharp one; it is also possible that we have an intrusive component not an original part of the poem. In other cases, the poet simply rearranges the parts, often in a provocative way, producing grammatical and syntactical anomalies very different from normal prose practice. Since Gray deals with only one aspect of this important phenomenon, and that tangentially, it may be worthwhile to explore it here, if only briefly, and to cite a few pertinent examples.

One device, often ignored or minimized as an inexact form of parallelism, involves the use, in parallel constructions, of complementary rather than synonymous terms; occasionally because the line of demarcation is not a sharp one, we should speak of overlapping terms. The difference remains, and has important implications for the analysis and interpretation of given texts. That Gray reckons with this factor, is shown by his interpretation (pp. 20-21) of the complementary terms "day" and "night" in Ps. 42:4,9. Taken together they describe continuous time in its totality. In Ps. 72:1-2 there is a series of paired terms which are complementary or overlapping rather than equivalent or synonymous. We may render the verses as follows:

$^{\prime e}$lōhīm mišpāṭēkā l^{e}melek tēn	O God, give your justice to the king
w^{e}ṣidqāt^{e}kā l^{e}ben-melek	And your righteousness to the king's son.
yādīn 'amm^{e}kā b^{e}ṣedeq	He will judge your people with righteousness
wa'^{a}niyyēkā b^{e}mišpāṭ	And your humbled ones with justice.

The terms *mšpṭ* and *ṣdq* are not equivalent or synonymous, but complementary. Together they describe the nature and process of the divine administration of justice (vs. 1), which serves as a model for the king (vs. 2). Similarly *mlk* and *bn-mlk* are not identical or interchangeable terms (i.e., they are not meant to say the same thing). It hardly needs to be pointed out that not all kings were kings' sons, and contrariwise, kings' sons do not always become kings. The case described here is of a king who was a king's son, and succeeded to the throne of his father; the poet thus emphasizes the stability and legitimacy of the royal line. The proposed interpretation would help to explain the rubric which identifies the king of the Psalm as Solomon rather than David (who, of course, was not a king's son). In vs. 2, the paired terms we wish to consider are '*mk* and '*nyyk*. While the terms are obviously not synonymous, they are nevertheless related. The second defines a special group ("the poor/afflicted") within the first ("the people"). The king is expected to dispense equitable justice to all the people, but the test of his administration will be his treatment of the oppressed, who cannot defend themselves and have no other champion (cf. vs. 12). The sense of the passage would be: "He will judge your people, your afflicted ones in particular, with righteousness and justice." That the principal concern of the poet is with the treatment of the poor and afflicted is amply attested in vss. 4 and 12-14. While we must allow for a certain ambiguity or multiplicity of meaning in the intention of the poet, we contend that the combination '*mk*/'*nyyk* in vs. 2 is equivalent to the construct chain '*nyy-'m* in vs. 4 (which is the normal way of expressing the thought involved).

A similar pattern is to be observed in vs. 9, which may be rendered as follows:

l^{e}pānāw yikr$^{e'}$ū ṣiyyīm   Before him the desert-dwellers bow down,

w$^{e'}$ōy^{e}bāw 'āpār y^{e}laḥēkū   And his enemies lick the dust.

It is clear that the verbal units (*lpnyw ykr'w* and '*pr ylḥkw*) are complementary and describe sequential actions. The noun-subjects (*ṣyym* and '*ybyw*) are not parallel terms, and their relationship, if any, is not immediately apparent. A number of scholars, including those responsible for the RSV, have found the situation sufficiently disturbing to resort to emendation: *ṣārīm* "foes" for *ṣiyyīm* (it is not necessary to read *ṣārāw*, since the suffix attached to '*ōy^{e}bāw* can serve both nouns). Slight as the emendation is, and appealing as is the resultant reading, it is at the same time unnecessary and unwarranted. The context (vss. 8-11) shows that the poet wishes to emphasize the submission of distant lands and peoples to the king, including not only the coastal areas (vs. 10a) but also the desert regions (Sheba and Seba, vs. 10b). Hence a reference to desert-dwellers in vs. 9 is entirely in order. It only remains to recognize that 'ybyw defines a specific group within the larger category of ṣyym, "the desert-dwellers who are his enemies" or "his enemies among the desert-dwellers." The verse may be interpreted as follows: The desert-dwellers, his enemies, bow down and lick the dust before him.

Amos 2:6b reads:

'al-mikrām bakkesep ṣaddīq   Because they sell the righteous for money

wᵉ'ebyōn ba'ᵃbūr na'ᵃlāyim   And the poor for a pair of sandals.

Both sets of paired terms are to be considered. In spite of arguments to the contrary, and later developments in language and social theory, the terms ṣdyq and 'bywn are not parallel or equivalent. Rather they define and limit each other so as to isolate a single group in society to be distinguished from three others, namely, the righteous poor in contrast to the wicked rich, and the other pair, the righteous rich and the wicked poor. Inevitably the chief concern of the prophet was with the two anomalous groupings: the righteous poor and the wicked rich.[3] The existence of these seemed inconsistent with the prevailing theology, whereas the persistence of the other groups illustrated the divine righteousness in the management of human affairs. Here the prophet calls attention to the anomaly, pointing out that the Israelites make no distinction between righteous (or innocent) and wicked (or guilty), but sell the poor into slavery without discrimination. It seems clear that the prophet accepts the legal stipulation concerning the sale of persons into slavery to satisfy outstanding debts, but protests about the way the law is applied to catch innocent victims. In addition, the prophet raises a serious question about the size of the debt for which these people are sold. The amount of "money" (ksp) in the first colon is defined by the "pair of sandals" (n'lym) in the second; the reference is not to the value of the persons sold, but to the amount of the debt for which they are sold. According to the prophet, there is something gravely wrong with a system in which the innocent poor (i.e., through no legally definable fault of their own) are sold into slavery to satisfy debts no greater than the price of a pair of sandals.

Another example is to be found in Ps. 135:5, which reads,

kī 'ᵃnī yāda'tī kī-gādōl Yhwh	For I know that Yahweh is great,
wa'ᵃdōnēnū mikkol-'ᵉlōhīm	And our Lord than all gods.

The RSV resolves the difficulty in the second line by supplying the necessary element of comparison: ". . . and that our Lord is above all gods." But it is surely preferable to recognize the double-duty function of *gādōl* in the first colon, and read: "and that our Lord is greater than all the gods." Next to be noted is that in *Yhwh w'dnynw* we have the breakup of a stereotyped expression: *Yhwh 'dnynw* "Yahweh our Lord" which occurs in the opening and closing lines of Ps. 8 (vss. 2 and 10).[4] Finally we observe that the poet has successfully rearranged the words of a simple declarative statement to produce a poetic couplet. Written as prose the sentence would be:

kī 'ᵃnī yāda'tī kī-gādōl mikkol-	For I know that our Lord Yahweh
'ᵉlōhīm Yhwh 'ᵃdōnēnū	is greater than all the gods.

Still another example of rearrangement is to be found in Ps. 140:10, which reads:

rō'š mᵉsibbāy	The poison of those who surround me,
ᶜᵃmal śᵉpātēmō yᵉkassēmō[5]	The mischief of their lips—let it cover them.

A literal rendering, while correctly representing the individual words of the sentence, does not bring into sharp focus the poet's thought. Since he has already described his enemies as poisonous snakes with venom on their lips (vs. 4), his intention here is to propose a suitable punishment for these human serpents, namely that they should drown in their own poisonous spittle. Reassembling the component parts, we render: "As for those mischief-makers who surround me (i.e., those who surround me with mischief), may the poison of their lips overwhelm them."

Another difficult passage may suitably be discussed here. Lam. 3:41 reads as follows:

niśśā' l^ebābēnū 'el-kappayim   Let us lift our hearts and hands
'el-'ēl baššāmayim   to God in heaven!   (RSV)

The translation ignores the problem posed by the preposition '*l* in
the first colon. Other prepositions are used in the LXX ("upon")
and the Vulgate ("with") to smooth out the relationship between
the nouns "heart" and "hands." In analyzing the structure of the
bicolon, it is clear that *lbbnw* and *kpym* are parallel expressions;
and this impression is strengthened by the fact that each term is
directly followed by the preposition '*l*. In order to make this
structural feature apparent, we redivide the line as follows:
niśśā' l^ebābēnū 'el   We lift our heart to—
   kappayim 'el-'ēl baššāmayim   Our hands to El in the sky.
Needless to say, the first person plural suffix with "heart" applies
as well to "hands." In this passage, the repetition of the preposition enhances the parallelism of the terms involved, as well as
pointing up their syntactic relationship to the object, El. At the
same time, it produces a grammatical anomaly so far as normal
prose procedures are concerned.

   Another possibility, though less appealing, is to read the '*l* after
lbbnw as the divine name '*ēl* 'El', as in the next colon. In that
case, the preposition '*l* after *kpym* must be understood as functioning before El in the first colon as well. The rendering would
be:
               We lift our heart to El
               our hands to El in the sky.

Although there has always been a wide spectrum of opinions, and
the subject continues to be much debated, Gray reflected—if he
did not establish—the prevailing view of his day (and probably
of ours) that rhythm is important, that it is regular and repeated
within broad limits, that it is discernible and that its governing
principles are definable. He shied away from those at one extreme who denied that there is meter in Hebrew poetry, and from
the rigorists at the other, who insisted that Hebrew meter is
quantitative and metronomically regular. Gray held, along with
many colleagues before and after him, that Hebrew meter is best

defined by the number of stressed syllables in a line or distich, these occurring in a variety of regular and repeated patterns: e.g., 3:3, 2:2, 3:2, etc. He distrusted more elaborate quantitative theories, though he conceded the possibility that the number of unstressed syllables, at least in the aggregate, also figured in the determination of line length. While rejecting Sievers' detailed hypotheses about the sequence and ratio of stressed and unstressed syllables in lines of Hebrew poetry, Gray believed that there were probable practical limitations (both minimal and maximal) as to the total number of unstressed syllables in a line, or between stressed syllables. But his primary concern was with patterns of stressed syllables; in this respect he considered Hebrew poetry to be comparable to Anglo-Saxon poetry.

In spite of the fact that Gray's basic views on meter have prevailed, and that they are held in one form or other by a majority of scholars, I believe that they are one-sided and inadequate. It is important to emphasize, as Gray does (pp. 10 ff.), that we have no information on this subject from the poets themselves or their audiences; and the earliest sources in which the matter is discussed (e.g., Josephus) reflect interpretations of the phenomena rather than authentic traditions. We do not know what principles of meter or rhythm the Hebrew poets acknowledged as authoritative or how they went about meeting the formal requirements. What we are necessarily concerned about, therefore, is an analysis that describes the phenomena adequately, that most faithfully reflects what is actually before us. Without denying either the importance of stressed syllables for determining rhythm, or the possible application of a more precise quantitative system to Hebrew verse, we are persuaded that unstressed syllables played a role in Hebrew poetry along with stressed syllables, and that counting the total number of syllables in lines and larger units produces a more reliable picture of the metrical structure than any other procedure now in use.

On pp. 135-36 Gray discusses all three approaches to the problem of Hebrew meter. Using Lam. 5:3 as an example, he points out that although the syllable count is 8:8, the meter according to a stress-syllable system is unbalanced at 3:2.

y^{e}tōmīm hāyīnū 'en[6] 'āb   Orphans were we, without father,
'immōtēnū k^e'almānōt   (And) our mothers (were) as
                                    widows[.][7]

He also notes that the prevailing rhythm of Lam. 5 is balanced, with lines following a 3:3 pattern. While he insists on describing vs. 3 as unbalanced, 3:2, it would appear to be more accurate to say that the line is balanced syllabically, and in this respect conforms to the dominant pattern.[8] There may be only two stresses in vs. 3b, but such a variation may not affect the basic rhythm at all. The same situation occurs in vs. 14, where we read:

z^{e}kēnīm miššaʿar šābātū   The elders have disappeared from
                                    the gate,
baḥūrīm minn^{e}gīnātām   The young men (have ceased)
                                    from their music.

Once again the stress pattern is apparently 3:2, but the syllable count is 8:8 (if we take the segolate šaʿar in vs. 14a as mono-syllabic).[9] While recognizing the stylistic variation in matching two words against three, we would nevertheless insist that this is not a change in rhythm, which remains balanced (8:8). As already indicated this is the prevailing pattern in Lam. 5. At least half of the lines (distich or bicolon) have 16 syllables, usually divided 8:8 (vss. 3, 4, 5, 14, 16, 20), though occasionally 9:7 (vss. 9, 19), or 7:9 (vss. 11, 12); 10:6 occurs once (vs. 2). Other lines range in length from 12 to 22 syllables, but the mean and average remain at 16. Verse 2 is instructive because the line, unlike vss. 3 and 14, is actually unbalanced. Not only is the stress-syllable pattern clearly 3:2, but the total-syllable count is 10:6 confirming the unbalanced character of the bicolon. At the same time, the total line length is the same as the others, an effect achieved by lengthening the first half of the line, while shortening the second:

naḥ$^{(a)}$lātēnū[10] nehepkāh   Our inheritance has been turned over
   l^{e}zārīm   to strangers,
bāttēnū l^{e}nokrīm   Our homes to aliens.

We do not wish to dispute Gray's contention that the three lines under discussion have a stress-syllable pattern of 3:2, but we question whether it is appropriate to group them together as having the same rhythmic structure. According to our view, based on a total syllable count, vss. 3 and 14 have a balanced rhythm and are therefore to be grouped with vss. 4, 5, 16, 20 (all 8:8), although these are properly counted 3:3 according to the stress-syllable system. Verse 2, however, is unbalanced with a 10:6 count, indicating a deliberate shift from the frequent 8:8 pattern. The persistence of the total of 16 syllables indicates that the basic unit was the full line (distich or bicolon), and that it was considered a legitimate variation to move the caesura or line division from the center of the line toward one side or the other in an unbalanced construction. Needless to say, these stylistic subtleties or refinements cannot be isolated or even recognized if we are limited to a stress-syllable system. Since the surviving text can hardly be described as errorless, and has certainly undergone both accidental and deliberate changes in the course of transmission, the fact that in its present state it exhibits a high degree of metrical regularity is very impressive. That can hardly be the result of changes introduced into the text, and hence it is likely that the original composition was somewhat more symmetrical and precise in its rhythm. Occasionally, variant readings still attested in the manuscripts or the versions will supply a clue to the more original and metrical reading; more rarely a persuasive conjecture will do the same. It is sufficient for our purposes to uncover the basic patterns without attempting to restore or reconstruct the supposed original.

Other examples of metrical subtleties revealed by a total-syllable count, as contrasted with a stress-syllable count, may be drawn from early poems, e.g., the Song of the Sea (Exod. 15),[11] and David's Lament over Saul and Jonathan (II Sam. 1).[12] In Exod. 15:4 we read:

mark^{e}bōt par^{c}ōh w^{e}ḥēlō	The chariots of Pharaoh and his army
yārāh bayyām	He hurled into the sea;
ūmibḥar šālīšāw	And the choicest of his officers
tubb^{ec}ū b^{e}yam-sūp	Were drowned in the Reed Sea.

The stress-syllable count is clearly 3:2 / 2:2. Since the prevailing pattern in this poem is 2:2 / 2:2 (/ 2:2), (cf. vss, 6, 7, 9, 10, 11, 12, 13, 15, 16a, 17, 18), with occasional lines of 3:3 (cf. vss. 8bc, 14 16b), the text of vs. 4 is often emended (usually by dropping w^{e}ḥelo),[13] to produce the expected 2:2 / 2:2. If, however, we use a total-syllable count, the picture is somewhat different. The verse as a whole has 24 syllables, with the major division at *bym* exactly in the middle: the two clauses match at 12 syllables each, and are parallel to each other in structure and content. The only difference between them (aside from the stress-syllable count) is in the placement of the minor pause or caesura. In the first bicolon it comes after *wḥylw* which results in an unbalanced division of the cola: 8:4 according to syllable count. In the second bicolon, the division comes in the middle, resulting in a syllable count of 6:6. In view of the data, the present text is to be defended, rather than emended, on metrical grounds. We may add that the 8:4 pattern in 4a is to be regarded as a permissible variant of the more common 6:6 pattern. In verse 7 we find a similar situation. The total number of syllables is 24, with the major division exactly in the middle of the verse (*qmyk*), producing a pattern 12:12; the two bicola are parallel in structure and content. The minor divisions within the bicola are also in the middle, resulting in patterns of 6:6.

In our opinion, the relative importance of stressed syllables in contrast with unstressed syllables has been exaggerated; a count of all the syllables provides a better clue to the metrical patterns of the poems of the Hebrew Bible. There is no reason why the two procedures cannot be used jointly, to check results, and sharpen insights into the nature of the material.

Gray shows commendable caution in dealing with larger poetic units. That such stanzas or strophes existed may be inferred from the use of certain devices to mark off sections of a poem. The most obvious of these are refrains, that is lines repeated exactly or with slight modfications at regular intervals in the poem. They occur in the Psalter (e.g., Pss. 46, 67), and were used also by the prophets (e.g., Amos 1-2, 4; Isa. 9-10). Difficulties arise when the attempt is made to deduce the principles governing stanza formation, or to define the structure of the strophes set off by the refrains. All too often the stanzas do not have a regular structure, nor do they conform to a standard pattern. There is always the possibility that the extant text is not intact, and that it has suffered losses through scribal error, or has gained accretions by accident or editorial design. Displacement and rearrangement are also to be reckoned with, but to restore a supposed original and symmetrical structure is a hazardous procedure.

Inclusion in its basic form is characterized by the exact repetition of key words or phrases. When these are extended to clauses or entire verse-lines, they are equivalent to refrains, which serve to define the limits of the poem or the stanzas within it. A more complex and less easily recognized form of inclusion (or envelope construction) does not involve the repetition of terms, but rather the resumption or completion of a thought. It is as though the poet deliberately split a bicolon or couplet, and inserted a variety of materials between the opening and closing halves of that unit to form a stanza. The notion that a grammatical unit may begin at one point in a composition and be continued somewhere else is novel to say the least. Proposed examples must be tested thoroughly, and in any case are not likely to convince all scholars. It may be added that such a view of poetic structure implies, if it does not require, a degree of literary sophistication not usually associated with oral composition or the poets of ancient Israel. Nevertheless the subject deserves attention, and the isolated example offered here may be a harbinger of others not yet detected.

It has been observed that the prophet Hosea often links Egypt and Assyria in parallel construction when speaking of Israel's imminent doom and threatened exile: e.g., 7:11, 9:3; 11:5, 11; 12:2.[14] In 8:9 we have a typical reference to Assyria:

kī-hēmmāh ʿālū[15]	For behold they will go up
ʾaššūr	to Assyria.

There is no parallel to this colon in vs. 9, but in vs. 13 we read:

hēmmāh miṣray(i)m yāšūbū	Behold they will return to Egypt.

The latter has no parallel in vs. 13 or its vicinity, but it is clear that the two cola complement each other impressively. Thus we note the repetition of the particle *hmh*,[16] the balancing alternation of the perfect (*'lw*) and imperfect (*yšwbw*) forms of the verb, and the chiasm in *'lw 'šwr* and *mṣrym yšwbw;* the syllable count is 7:7. It would occasion no surprise to find these well-matched cola side by side in a poem, but they are four verses apart. Assuming that the positioning of these cola was deliberate, it is inescapable that they form an envelope or framework around a major poetic unit.[17]

In his search for the key to Hebrew metrics, Gray devoted considerable attention (Chaps. III, VII, VIII) to the acrostic poems of the Old Testament. Since they are by no means typical of Hebrew poetry generally, it may be doubted whether they provide a suitable base on which to formulate principles governing the nature of the metrical systems employed by the biblical poets. Furthermore the fact that acrostic poems have a rather rigid structure may have encouraged greater independence on the part of the poet in working out internal configurations so that a wider range of variation results, partly from the desire to avoid monotony, than would otherwise be the case.[18] The great virtue of acrostic poems is that lines or stanzas are regularly marked off by words beginning with successive letters of the alphabet. Thus in the Book of Lamentations, the first four chapters are regular acrostics, while the fifth chapter follows the same pattern but without making use of the alphabetic device itself. In the first three chapters, three-line stanzas are the rule; in chaps. 1 and 2 each stanza begins with a successive letter of the alphabet, whereas in chap. 3, each of the three lines of the stanza begins with the same letter of the alphabet. Thus the first word of the first stanza of each of the poems begins with the letter *'ālef;* in the case of chap. 3, the second and third lines of the stanza also begin with *'ālef.* The first word of the second stanza begins with *bēt;* again in chapter three, the second and third lines also begin with *bēt.* Chapter 4 follows the same pattern as chaps. 1 and 2, except that the stanzas have two lines instead of three.

Thanks to this feature, students can determine line and stanza length with a considerable degree of objectivity and accuracy. Since the Book of Lamentations is a relatively homogeneous corpus so far as subject matter and perspective are concerned, it is possible to assemble sufficient data for statistical purposes to describe the typical or standard metrical unit, as well as the range of deviation from the norm. It should also be possible to devise criteria to establish the limits of acceptability, beyond which deviations could be identified as the result of error or editorial modification.

Unless we are to assume gross wholesale corruption of the text, we must recognize that there is considerable variation in the length of lines and stanzas, whatever counting system is used. The evidence for such widespread corruption is negligible, and the assumption is based largely on certain metrical theories about the material. The combination of theories and assumptions is self-defeating, as the reasoning is circular, and results in the creation of a variety of new texts with matching metrical systems. On the contrary there is every reason to believe in the essential soundness of the preserved text, especially in Lamentations, because the editors and scribes had the same acrostic pattern in front of them to help keep the poetic structure intact.

For the reasons given, a statistical approach is likely to yield better results for metrical analysis than the virtuoso handling of individual lines which has characterized much of the work to date. In fact, the range of variation is rather limited, and sufficient data seem readily available from Lamentations to fix line and stanza patterns within relatively narrow limits. The writer hopes to publish elsewhere a detailed statistical analysis of the acrostic poems in Lamentations and elsewhere in the Hebrew Bible. It will suffice to summarize the results here:

Poem	Syllables	Lines	Average
Lamentations 5	362	22	16.5
Proverbs 31	360	22	16.4
Psalm 25	362	22	16.5
Psalm 34	351	21	16.7
Psalm 37	719	44	16.3
Psalm 111	169	11	15.4

Poem	Syllables	Lines	Average
Psalm 112	169	11	15.4
Psalm 119	2,870	176	16.3
Psalm 145	400	22	18.2

The other group, including Lam. 1-4 exhibits the following pattern:

Lamentations 1	865	67	12.9
Lamentations 2	863	67	12.9
Lamentations 3	868	66	13.2
Lamentations 4	609	44	13.8

There seem to be at least two different structures for acrostic poems in the Bible, with the major group having lines, or bicola, averaging around 16 and ½ syllables. A special group represented by Lam. 1-4 has a shorter line of 13-14 syllables. In the poems there is a wide range of variation in the length of lines and stanzas.[19] The deviations form their own patterns, as we have observed, and the end product was strictly controlled by factors of overall length, and a strong sense of balance.

In his discussion of the widespread practice of emending the biblical text through alteration, excision, addition, and rearrangement on the basis of metrical considerations, Gray focussed attention on the arbitrary and subjective character of many of the proposals made by scholars of his day. The destructive results of such scholarship have become only too apparent in the years since, and scholars on the whole are now more careful in dealing with the Hebrew text. The chief danger in invoking the formula *metri causa* lies in the necessarily circular reasoning which is used to support proposed emendations. Since there are no external criteria for determining the meter, it must be derived or calculated from the existing text. Then the same text is corrected or improved on the basis of the meter which was derived from it. The more tightly drawn the reasoning the more vicious the circle.

Conjectural emendations, whatever their basis or source, are inevitably suspect, and few have survived critical scrutiny. Those which are based upon metrical factors are peculiarly vulnerable, and should be avoided assiduously. Apart from the fact that there has been too much activity of this sort with unconvincing results, there are two important reasons for pursuing a different strategy in dealing with the biblical text:

1. Metrical analysis is now entering a new statistical phase, and can provide an adequate often detailed description of the phenomena. We can henceforth be reasonably confident about overall patterns and structures, as well as the numerical limits within which the poets operated; but in the nature of the case these cannot help us decide specific questions about particular lines or words. As we have seen, there are standard deviations from presumed norms, i.e., they are part of the poet's bag of tools, to be used at his option. It would be practically impossible to determine on metrical grounds when such variations were the result of error or later editorial change, and when they were part of the original poet's plan. Earlier approaches to the question of meter were often monotonously mechanical, and the structures on the basis of which emendations were made too rigidly repetitive.

2. Emendations inevitably reflect the state of scholarship at the time the emendations are proposed, and hence have an inhibiting effect on the advancement of knowledge, and the discovery of new features of the language. Emendation often eliminates or obscures devices deliberately used by the poet but not readily recognized by scholars trained in the formal grammar and syntax of Hebrew prose. Much of the progress in analyzing and interpreting the more difficult poetic passages in the Hebrew Bible has been achieved through decipherment of literary materials in cognate languages, especially Ugaritic, and the application of these new data to biblical poetry. The identification of the same and related phenomena in the biblical text has helped to clarify obscure passages, without recourse to drastic or wholesale emendation. Increasingly, new and more refined techniques for dealing with the text are being developed which give promise of achieving more economic, convincing, and satisfying results.

In all this, we do not question the importance or validity of the emendatory process as a scholarly enterprise or obligation. Certainly we do not imply that the preserved Hebrew text is intact. Admittedly numerous errors have occurred in the transmission of the text, as well as deliberate editorial and scribal changes. The difficulty lies in locating, defining, and then correcting them. All too often, the prescribed cure is only another form of the disease, sometimes more virulent. In the case of divergent readings in·Hebrew manuscripts or the versions, it is clear that choices must be made. But in the absence of direct manuscript evidence, extreme caution should be exercised, and emendation should be avoided if at all possible. While the Massoretes were fallible, they were also faithful to the tradition. So even changes in vocalization, or the redivision of words and phrases should be justified with care. Recourse to more drastic procedures should be recognized as a last and desperate resort. Conjectural emendations are more likely to be remembered as exercises in scholarly ingenuity than as serious contributions to the recovery of the original reading.

There is every reason to believe that many of the remaining problems in the poetry of the Bible will yield to the vigorous but controlled application of the new methods, disciplined by a rational respect for the extant text, and extreme caution in conjecture. There is always the expectation of new discoveries of literary materials which will enhance our knowledge of the language of the Bible, and the cultural tradition from which it came.

An Annotated Bibliography on Hebrew Poetry
from 1915 to the Present[20]

Contributions to the study of Hebrew poetry in the period since Gray have been so numerous that a general bibliography such as this cannot hope to be exhaustive. Scholarly discussions in this period have ranged from the smallest unit, even single words, to the complexity of entire Books. The present bibliography is intended to be representative of the various scholars who have contributed to the elucidation of the larger problems of the form, structure, and nature of this poetry. Most of these works deal with the Psalms and the ancient poems embedded in the historical works, although there are some authors whose chief interest has been the prophetic Books. Those articles which deal only with the exegesis of short pericopes, without application of phenomena to the larger questions, have been excluded. While this limitation is admittedly subjective, it is necessary for two reasons: 1) the sheer bulk of such material, and 2) the fact that most such articles are primarily concerned with problems other than poetic ones.

German authors contemporary with Gray continued to write well into the twenties, and for this reason several of these older writers are represented in this bibliography; these include R. Kittel, Budde, Duhm, and Sellin. Except for Kittel's work on the Psalms, the major contributions of these men to the discussion of Hebrew poetry came at the turn of the century, or even earlier, and are not listed here.

However, another German scholar contemporary with Gray published his work on the Psalms well after 1915. This was Hermann Gunkel, associated above all with the development of *Gattungskritik* (form criticism) in the Old Testament. The *Einleitung in die Psalmen* (1933), published the year after his death by his pupil, Begrich, was not only one of his major works, but has influenced every writer on Hebrew poetry to the present day. For many years Gunkel's work was available only in German, but now general readers and beginning students can study Gunkel's ideas in a translation of his article, "The Psalms," which originally appeared in *Die Religion in Geschichte und Gegenwart*. Although this is far from the detailed study of his larger work, it presents Gunkel's classification of Psalms material by literary type, and is easily understood.

Hebrew metrics have had a great fascination for German scholars, though they are not alone in this interest. While the majority of writers listed in the first two sections of the bibliography have accepted the metrical theories of Sievers, several German writers have proposed a system of alternating stressed and unstressed syllables, resulting in "iambic" and "trochaic" feet. Four, or sometimes three, of these feet combine to form a colon, so that the normal pattern for the bicolon in Hebrew poetry is said to be 4+4 or 4+3. Hölscher's modifications of this system, originally proposed by Bickell, have been accepted in large part by Segert and Mowinckel. Hölscher's 1920 article in *BZAW* laid the complete groundwork for this system; but today it is not as accessible to readers as the later articles of Segert and Mowinckel, particularly since the latter two have had works translated into English.

Sigmund Mowinckel, a Norwegian, is undoubtedly the most prolific of the "German" writers of the more recent period. Working chiefly with the poetry of the Psalms, he has built on the groundwork laid by Gunkel in form criticism and by Hölscher in metrical theories. His metrical theories, hammered out in a series of articles in *ZAW* and *Studia Theologica,* can be found in his larger works as well—in *Psalmenstudien* and *The Psalms in Israel's Worship.* Mowinckel is quite conservative in his metrical studies, and has been extremely cautious in applying Ugaritic data to Hebrew poetry. This attitude is reflected in both *Real and Apparent Tricola* and in his essay on Psalm criticism, written in the fifties. The latter article, especially, is directed to a criticism of Albright's position and a reiteration of his own.

A somewhat different metrical theory has been proposed by Hans Kosmala. In two articles in *VT,* he has worked out a critical method for dealing with poetic material, based on balanced word units in the bicolon. Working on the assumption that there have been many glosses added to the original poems, Kosmala seeks to eliminate these and retrieve the original structure of bicola in which each colon has the same word unit length. Although there are affinities with statements by Mowinckel about the coincidence of words and stress units (feet), Kosmala accepts bicola of much greater, and more varying lengths than recognized by Mowinckel. Another innovator is Arvid Bruno. He has rendered the greater part of the Hebrew Bible as poetry, proceeding from Genesis to Kings and on into the Prophets and Writings, thus outdoing even the redoubtable Sievers. The main difficulty with such an undertaking is that very soon it becomes necessary to remake the Bible or redefine the concept of poetry, or mix the two.

The second group of writers in the bibliograpy has been influenced by the German tradition in the study of Hebrew poetry, but has drawn from other sources as well. In general these authors belong to the main stream of continental scholarship and subscribe to the basic principles of a stress-counting system of Hebrew metrics. This was the tradition within which Gray himself worked. (Many German writers might also be described in this way, but for convenience they have been listed separately.) Each of these scholars contributes to the study of Hebrew poetry what he has discerned, filling out a framework which is widely accepted today.

Prominent among these writers has been T. H. Robinson. All four of the works cited in this bibliography give a complete view of Robinson's understanding of Hebrew poetry. He is a clear writer, and quite specific in his analysis of poems, without excessive use of technical jargon, an almost irresistible temptation in this field. His thinking has not altered radically over the years, and many of his earlier statements are distinctly echoed in the two later essays. However, these later articles also show Robinson's awareness of the importance of the Ras Shamrah discoveries for the understanding of Hebrew poetry, although he does not undertake the project himself.

While German writers have concentrated chiefly on the metrical form of the bicolon, writers within this second group have been interested as well in the larger units, the organization of bicola into "strophes" or "stanzas." This problem receives cursory treatment from German scholars, but has fared better from scholars in this group, as can be seen by the titles of works by Meek, Montgomery, Condamin, Kraft, and Skehan, though in other respects the methods employed by these writers vary considerably.

Other authors have concentrated on the literary techniques and devices used by Hebrew poets. These include much more than various types of parallelism, although each in his way has endeavored to repair the recognized weaknesses of the catchall category of Lowth, "synthetic" parallelism. The techniques explored include the break-up of stereotype phrases (Melamed), numerical sequence (Weiss), and formulaic language (Culley and Hillers).

The interest in the literary devices used to convey poetic imagery and form has been termed "rhetorical criticism" by James Muilenburg, and he has been joined by many others in developing this subject. Although he nowhere gives a precise definition of all the factors involved in such "rhetorical criticism," each of his articles delineates specific areas: the use of key words to begin and end, or divide, a poem; the use of conventional language, or chiasm and inclusio, and of potent words of imagery. In short, it is a type of literary criticism that seeks to penetrate the mind of the poet by analyzing his linguistic usage. Holladay similarly has explored Jeremiah's language in the attempt to understand the structure and composition of this complex book.

Two other writers have recently devoted more attention to the study of poetic imagery itself. Kelly has explored the symbolism of Psalm 46, using insights from Eliade, a leading figure in the field of comparative religion. Alonso-Schökel has included a long section on poetic imagery and symbolism in his large and systematically organized work on Hebrew poetry. The "philosophy" or nature of poetry is of special interest to him, and the opening chapters of his book are concerned with this subject, rarely dealt with by other writers.

The third group of scholars have in common a great appreciation of the importance of Ugaritic studies for the understanding of Hebrew poetry. Several of the works listed in this section do not deal with biblical poetry at all, or only peripherally, but they provide the necessary background in the language and literature of Ras Shamrah for students in the field. These include the articles by Aistleitner, Driver, and Ginsberg (literature), and Gordon and Young (linguistics). John Gray's book, *The Legacy of Canaan,* undertakes a survey of Ugaritic materials and their relation to the Old Testament.

The increasing value of Ugaritic studies for the study of Hebrew poetry over the past forty years can be clearly seen in the work of W. F. Albright. A small portion of his articles, chosen for this bibliography, illustrate this growth. Aware of the potential significance of the Ras Shamrah discoveries from the beginning, Albright demonstrated their importance in a series of brilliant articles on classic Hebrew poetry, including the Oracles of Balaam, the Psalm of Habakkuk, and Psalm 68. In his latest major work, *Yahweh and the Gods of Canaan,* chap. 1, Albright outlines a new typological sequence dating of early Hebrew poetry, a significant breakthrough in the analysis of this formidable corpus.

In addition to contributing to the study of Hebrew poetry himself, Albright has influenced the careers of a large number of other scholars, including many of his own students. Among these are Cross and Freedman, who have collaborated on a number of articles as well as publishing individually. *Studies in Ancient Yahwistic Poetry,* part of their earliest venture together, shows the influence of Albright both in the application of Ugaritic and Phoenician parallels to Hebrew linguistic phenomena, and in the systematic attempt to analyze the text in the light of the history of Hebrew orthography. Similarly, their joint article in 1948, "The

Blessing of Moses," already shows an interest in syllable counting as an observable phenomenon which can aid in describing the structure of a poem. The use of syllable counting, and its implications for interpreting metrical and strophic patterns can be traced in Freedman's later articles, and in the introduction to this volume.

The most prolific—and the most controversial—writer in this field presently is Mitchell Dahood. His works are too numerous for exhaustive listing, but those chosen are a comprehensive selection of his work. The first seven articles are illustrative of his application of Ugaritic poetic and linguistic phenomena in specific cases. The articles on lexicography, beginning with Aleph, and spread out over seven years in *Biblica,* with more to come ('Ayin was reached in 1969), are a *vade mecum* for students and scholars in Ugaritic-biblical studies. "Ugaritic Studies and the Old Testament" provides a resumé of Dahood's views, considered radical by many, concerning the importance of Ugaritic materials for the Old Testament. Finally, the three-volume work on Psalms offers both laymen and specialists the chance to study Dahood's methods applied on a major scale to biblical poetry. The development of his thinking is clearly reflected in these volumes: thus Volume II is at once more radical and more carefully argued and documented than Volume I. The Introduction to Volume II elaborates on the difference, the result partly of the critics' reactions, and of his own further studies. In Volume III the conversation is continued, as well as the development of his latest views. Volume III also contains the outline of a new poetic grammar in which the linguistic data are collected and classified. These volumes are difficult and consistently controversial; they reflect the most extensive application of Ugaritic studies to the Old Testament to date.

"GERMAN" TRADITION

Begrich, Joachim
"Der Satzstil im Fünfer," in *Gesammelte Studien zum AT*. Munich, 1964, pp. 132–167.
"Zur hebräischen Metrik," *Theologische Rundschau*, 4 (1932), pp. 67–89.

Bruno, D. Arvid
Die Bücher Genesis-Exodus: Eine rhythmische Untersuchung. Stockholm, 1953.
Die Bücher Josua. Richter. Ruth: Eine rhythmische Untersuchung. Stockholm, 1955.
Die Bücher Samuel: Eine rhythmische Untersuchung. Stockholm, 1955.
Die Bücher Könige: Eine rhythmische Untersuchung. Stockholm, 1955.
Jesaja: Eine rhythmische und textkritische Untersuchung. Stockholm, 1953.
Jeremia: Eine rhythmische Untersuchung. Stockholm, 1954.
Die Psalmen: Eine rhythmische und textkritische Untersuchung. Stockholm, 1954.
Der Rhythmus der ältest Dichtung: Eine Untersuchung über die Psalmen I-LXIII. Leipzig, 1930.

Budde, Karl, *Der Segen Mose's*. Tübingen, 1922.

Duhm, Bernard. *Die Psalmen erklärt*. Tübingen, 1922.

Dus, Jan. "Die altisraelitische amphiktyonische Poesie," *ZAW*, 75 (1963), pp. 45–54.

Fohrer, Georg. "Über den Kurzvers," *ZAW*, 66 (1954), pp. 199–236.

Gábor, Ignaz. *Der hebräische Urrhythmus*. *BZAW*, 52 (1929).

Gunkel, Hermann. *The Psalms*. Facet Books, biblical series 19, Philadelphia, 1967. (Translation by Thomas Horner from Vol. 1, 2nd ed. of *Die Religion in Geschichte und Gegenwart*.)

Gunkel, Hermann and J. Begrich. *Einleitung in die Psalmen*. Göttingen, 1933.

Hölscher, Gustav. "Elemente arabischer, syrischer, und hebräischer Metrik," *BZAW*, 34 (1920), pp. 93–101.

Horst, Friedrich. "Die Kennzeichen der hebräischen Poesie," *Theologische Rundschau*, 21 (1953), pp. 97–121.

Kosmala, Hans. "Form and Structure in Ancient Hebrew Poetry," *VT*, 14 (1964), pp. 423–445; 16 (1966), pp. 152–180.

Kittel, Rudolph. *Die Psalmen.* Leipzig, 1922.

Krszyna, Henryk. "Literarische struktur von Os. 2:2–17," *Biblische Zeitschrift,* n.s., 13 (1969), pp. 41–59.

Kunz, Lucas. "Zur Liedgestalt der ersten fünf Psalmen," *Biblische Zeitschrift,* n.s., 7 (1963), pp. 261–270.

Lund, Eimar. "Eine metrische Form im AT," *Acta Orientalia,* 17 (1939), pp. 249-303.

Maecklenburg, Albert. "Einführung in die Probleme der hebräischen Metrik," *Wiener Zeitschrift für die Kunde des Morgenlandes,* 46 (1939), pp. 1–46.

Möller, Hans. "Der Strophenbau der Psalmen," *ZAW,* 50 (1932), pp. 240–256.

Mowinckel, Sigmund
   Psalmenstudien. Oslo, 1921–1924.
   "Zum Problem der hebräischen Metrik," in *Bertholet-Festschrift,* 1950. pp. 379–394.
   The Psalms in Israel's Worship. New York, 1962. (Translation by D. R. Ap-Thomas of *Offersang og sangoffer,* Oslo, 1951.)
   "Der metrische Aufbau von Jes. 62:1–12 und die neuen sog. Kurzverse," *ZAW,* 65 (1953), pp. 167–187.
   "Zur hebräischen Metrik II," *Studia Theologica,* 7 (1954), pp. 54–85, 166.
   "Psalm Criticism Between 1900 and 1935 (Ugarit and Psalm Exegesis)," *VT,* 5 (1955), pp. 13–33.
   "Marginalien zur hebräischen Metrik," *ZAW,* 68 (1956), pp. 97–123.
   Real and Apparent Tricola in Hebrew Psalm Poetry. Oslo, 1957.

Prijs, L. "Der Ursprung der Reimes im Neuhebräischen," *Biblische Zeitschrift,* n.s., 7 (1963), pp. 33–42.

Sauer, Georg. "Erwägungen zum Alter der Psalmendichtung in Israel," *Theologische Zeitschrift,* 22 (1966), pp. 81–95.

Schmidt, Hans. "Das Meerlied Ex. 15:2–19," *ZAW,* 49 (1931), pp. 59–66.

Segert, Stanislav.
   "Vorarbeiten zur hebräischen Metrik," *Archiv Orientalni,* 21 (1953), pp. 481–542; 25 (1957), pp. 190–200.
   "Die Methoden der althebräischen Metrik," *Communio Viatorum,* 1 (1958), pp. 233–241.
   "Problems of Hebrew Prosody," *VT Supplement,* 7 (1960), pp. 283–291.

Sellin, Ernst. "Das Deboralied," *Festschrift Otto Proksch.* Leipzig, 1934, pp. 149–166.

"TRADITIONAL"

Alonso-Schökel, Luis. *Estudios de Poética Hebrea.* Barcelona, 1963.

Barnes, W. E. *The Psalms with Introduction and Notes,* 2 vols. London, 1931.

Blenkinsopp, J. "Ballad Style and Psalm Style in the Song of Deborah; A Discussion," *Biblica,* 42 (1961), pp. 61–76.

Boling, Robert G. " 'Synonymous' Parallelism in the Psalms," *JSS,* 5 (1960), pp. 221–255.

Bullough, Sebastian. "Question of Metre in Psalm I," *VT,* 17 (1967), pp. 42–49.

Carmignac, Jean. "Etude sur les procédés poétiques des Hymnes," *Revue de Qumran,* 2 (1960), pp. 515–532.

Causse, Antonin. *Les plus vieux chants de la Bible.* Paris, 1926.

Condamin, Albert. *Poèmes de la Bible. Avec une introduction sur la strophique hébraïque.* 1933.

Culley, Robert C. *Oral Formulaic Language in the Biblical Psalms.* Toronto, 1967.

Dhorme, Edouard P. *La poésie biblique.* Paris, 1931.

Fensham. Frank C. *'n Ondersoek na die geskiedenis van die interpretasie van die Hebreeuse poësie* (includes English summary). Stellenbosch, 1966.

Good, Edwin M. "Hosea and the Jacob Tradition," *VT,* 16 (1966), pp. 137–151.

Hillers, D. R. "Convention in Hebrew Literature; the Reaction to Bad News," *ZAW,* 77 (1965), pp. 86–90.

Kelly, Sidney. "Psalm 46: A Study in Imagery," *JBL,* 89 (1970), pp. 305–312.

Kraft, Charles F.
> *The Strophic Structure of Hebrew Poetry as Illustrated in the First Book of the Psalter.* Chicago, 1938.
>
> "Some Further Observations Concerning the Strophic Structure of Hebrew Poetry," *A Stubborn Faith,* ed. E. C. Hobbs. Dallas, 1956. pp. 62–89.

Loader, J. A. "Qohelet 3:2–8; a Sonnet in the Old Testament," *ZAW,* 81 (1969), pp. 240–242.

Meek, T. J. "Hebrew Poetic Structure as a Translation Guide," *JBL,* 59 (1940), pp. 1–9.

Melamed, E. Z. "Break-up of Stereotype Phrases as an Artistic Device in Biblical Poetry," *Scripta Hierosolymitana,* VIII (1961), pp. 115–153.

Montgomery, J. A. "Stanza Formation in Hebrew Poetry," *JBL,* 64 (1945), pp. 379–384.

Newman, Louis I. and William Popper. *Studies in Biblical Parallelism.* Berkeley, 1918.

Oesterley, W. O. E. *Ancient Hebrew Poems.* New York, 1938.

Piatti, T.

"I carmi alfabetici della Bibbia chiave della metrica ebraica?" *Biblica,* 31 (1950), pp. 281–315, 427–458.

"Una nuova interpretazione metrica testuale, esegetica, del Cantico di Debora," *Biblica,* 27 (1946), pp. 65–106, 161–209, 434.

Rankin, Oliver S. "Alliteration in Hebrew Poetry," *JTS,* 31 (1930), pp. 285–291.

Ridderbos, N. H. "Kennmerken der Hebreeuwse poëzie," *Gereformeerd Theo. Tijdschrift,* 55 (1955), pp. 171–183.

Robinson, T. H.

"Some Principles of Hebrew Metrics," *ZAW,* 54 (1936), pp. 28–43.

The Poetry of the Old Testament. London, 1947.

"Basic Principles of Hebrew Poetic Form," in *Bertholet-Festschrift,* 1950, pp. 438–450.

"Hebrew Poetic Form: The English Tradition," *VT Supplement, I* (1953), pp. 128–149.

Skehan, Patrick W.

"Strophic Structure in Psalm 72 (71)," *Biblica,* 40 (1959), pp. 302–308.

"Strophic Patterns in the Book of Job," *CBQ,* 23 (1961), pp. 125–142.

Slotki, Israel W.

"The Song of Deborah," *JTS,* 33 (1932), pp. 341–354.

"Longer and Shorter Versions of Ancient Hebrew Poems," *AJSL,* 50 (1933), pp. 15–31.

Stampfer, Judah. "On Translating Biblical Poetry: Isaiah Ch. 1 and 2:1–4," *Judaism,* 14 (1965), pp. 501–510.

Towner, W. Sibley. "Poetic Passages of Daniel 1–6," *CBQ,* 31 (1969), pp. 317–326.

Weiss, Meir

"Wege der neuen Dichtungswissenschaft in ihrer Anwendung auf die Psalmenforschung," *Biblica,* 42 (1961), pp. 255–302.

"The Pattern of Numerical Sequence in Amos 1–2," *JBL,* 86 (1967), pp. 416–423.

Wevers, John W. "A Study in the Form Criticism of Individual Complaint Psalms," *VT,* 6 (1956), pp. 80–96.

"RHETORICAL CRITICISM"

Gottwald, Norman K. "Poetry, Hebrew," in *Interpreter's Dictionary of the Bible,* Vol. III. New York, 1962. pp. 829–838.

Holladay, W. L.

"Prototype and Copies: A New Approach to the Poetry-Prose Problem in the Book of Jeremiah," *JBL,* 79 (1960), pp. 351–367.

"Style, Irony, and Authenticity in Jeremiah," *JBL,* 81 (1962), pp. 44–54.

"Chiasmus, the Key to Hosea 12:3–6," *VT,* 16 (1966), pp. 53–64.

"The Recovery of Poetic Passages of Jeremiah," *JBL,* 85 (1966), pp. 401–435.

Muilenburg, James.

"A Study in Hebrew Rhetoric: Repetition and Style," *VT Supplement,* I (1953), pp. 97–111.

"Form Criticism and Beyond," *JBL,* 88 (1969), pp. 1–18.

"The Terminology of Adversity in Jeremiah," in *Translating and Understanding the Old Testament,* ed. H. T. Frank and W. L. Reed. Nashville, 1970, ch. II.

"CANAANITE (UGARITIC) STUDIES AND HEBREW POETRY"

Aistleitner, J. *Die mythologischen und kultischen texte aus Ras Shamra.* Budapest, 1959.

Albright, William F.

"The Earliest Forms of Hebrew Verse," *JPOS,* 2 (1922), pp. 69–86.

"The North-Canaanite Poems of Al'êyân Ba'al," *JPOS,* 14 (1934), pp. 1–40.

"The Oracles of Balaam," *JBL,* 63 (1944), pp. 207–233.

"The Old Testament and the Canaanite Language and Literature" *CBQ,* 7 (1945), pp. 5–31.

"The Psalm of Habakkuk," *Studies in Old Testament Prophecy,* ed. H. H. Rowley, Edinburgh, 1950.

"Some Remarks on the Song of Moses in Deut. 32," *VT,* 9 (1959), pp. 339–346.

Yahweh and the Gods of Canaan. London, 1968.

Andersen, F. I.

"A Lexicographical Note on Ex. 32:18," *VT,* 16 (1966), pp. 108–112.

"A Short Note on Psalm 82:5," *Biblica,* 50 (1969), pp. 393-394.

"Orthography in Repetitive Parallelism," *JBL,* 89 (1970), pp. 343-344.

Cross, Frank M. "Song of the Sea and Canaanite Myth, *"Journal for Theology and the Church,* 5 (1968), pp. 1-25.

Cross, Frank M. and David Noel Freedman
"The Blessing of Moses," *JBL,* 67 (1948), pp. 191-210.
Studies in Ancient Yahwistic Poetry. Baltimore, 1950.
"A Royal Song of Thanksgiving: II Samuel 22-Psalm 18," *JBL,* 72 (1953), pp. 15-34.
"The Song of Miriam," *JNES,* 14 (1955), pp. 237-250.

Dahood, Mitchell
"Canaanite-Phoenician Influence in Qoheleth," *Biblica,* 33 (1952), pp. 30-52, 191-221.
"The Divine Name *'Ēlî* in the Psalms," *TS,* 14 (1953), pp. 452-457.
"Enclitic MEM and the Emphatic LAMEDH in Psalm 85," *Biblica,* 37 (1956), pp. 338-340.
"Some Aphel Causatives in Ugaritic," *Biblica,* 38 (1957), pp. 62-73.
"Some Northwest-Semitic Words in Job," *Biblica,* 38 (1957), pp. 306-320.
"The Value of Ugaritic for Textual Criticism," *Biblica,* 40 (1959), pp. 160-170.
"The Linguistic Position of Ugaritic in the Light of Recent Discoveries," in *Sacra Pagina,* Vol. I *(Miscellanea Biblica Congressus Internationalis Catholici de re Biblica,* ed. J. Coppens, *et. al.*), pp. 267-279.
"Hebrew-Ugaritic Lexicography, I-VII," *Biblica,* 44-50 (1963-1969), 44: pp. 289-303; 45: pp. 393-412; 46: pp. 311-332; 47: pp. 403-419; 48: pp. 421-438; 49: pp. 355-369; 50: pp. 337-356.
"Ugaritic Studies and the Old Testament," *The Bible Today,* 12 (1964), pp. 780-786.
Ugaritic-Hebrew Philology: Marginal Notes on Recent Publications (Biblica et Orientalia 17), Rome 1965.
Psalms I, II, III (Anchor Bible Vols. 16, 17, 17a), New York, 1966-1970.
"Vocative LAMEDH in the Psalter," *VT,* 16 (1966), pp. 299-311.
"A New Metrical Pattern in Biblical Poetry," *CBQ,* 29 (1967), pp. 574-579.

Donner, Herbert. "Ugaritismen in der Psalmenforschung," *ZAW,* 79 (1967), pp. 322-350.

Driver, G. R. *Canaanite Myths and Legends.* Edinburgh, 1956.

Freedman, David Noel
"Archaic Forms in Early Hebrew Poetry," *ZAW,* 72 (1960), pp. 101-107.

"The Song of the Sea" in *A Feeling of Celebration* (A Tribute to James Muilenburg), San Anselmo, 1967, pp. 1-10.

"Structure of Job 3," *Biblica,* 49 (1968), pp. 503-508.

"Structure of Psalm 137," *Albright Festschrift* (1971).

"Strophe and Meter in Exodus 15," *J. M. Myers Festschrift* (1971).

"Psalm 29: A Structural Analysis," *HTR* (1972); in collaboration with Mrs. Christine Hyland.

Gevirtz, Stanley. *Patterns in the Early Poetry of Israel.* Chicago, 1963.

Ginsberg, H. L., in *Ancient Near Eastern Texts,* ed. J. B. Pritchard, 2nd ed. pp. 129-155. Philadelphia, 1955.

Gordon, Cyrus. *Ugaritic Textbook.* Rome, 1965.

Gray, J. *The Legacy of Canaan: The Ras Shamra Texts and Their Relevance to the Old Testament.* Leiden, 1957.

Hanson, Paul D. "The Song of Heshbon and David's Nir," *HTR,* 61 (1968), pp. 297-320.

Held, Moshe. "The Action-Result (Factitive-Passive) Sequence of Identical Verbs in Biblical Hebrew and Ugaritic," *JBL,* 84 (1965), pp. 272-282.

Patton, J. H. *Canaanite Parallels in the Book of Psalms.* Baltimore, 1944.

Pope, Marvin H. "Marginalia to M. Dahood's *Ugaritic-Hebrew Philology,*" *JBL,* 85 (1966), pp. 455-466.

Rin, Svi. "Ugaritic-Old Testament Affinities," *Bib. Z.,* n.s., 7 (1963), pp. 22-23.

Rin, Svi and Shifra Rin. "Ugaritic-Old Testament Affinities II," *Bib. Z.,* n.s., 11 (1967), pp. 174-192.

Young, G. D. "Ugaritic Prosody," *JNES,* 9 (1950), pp. 124-133.

> David Noel Freedman
> San Francisco Theological Seminary
> San Anselmo, Calif.

May, 1971

NOTES

[1] An excellent summary and accompanying bibliography are to be found in Otto Eissfeldt's *The Old Testament: An Introduction* (trans. P. R. Ackroyd; New York: Harper and Row, 1965), pp. 57-64, with additional comments on pp. 731-32.

[2] Lowth's *De Sacra Poesi,* etc., (1753), was translated by G. Gregory as *Lectures in the Sacred Poetry of the Hebrews* (1835).

[3] This group is to be identified in Isa. 53:9, where we read:

wayyittēn 'et-rᵉšā'īm qibrō   And his grave was made with the wicked

wᵉ'et-'āšīr bōmātō (lQIsᵃ)   And his sepulcher with the rich.

Although *'šyr* is often emended to *'ōśē rā'* or the like, there is no textual or other basis for it. The terms "wicked" and "rich" qualify each other in defining the group who are at the opposite pole from Amos' "righteous poor."

[4] For discussion of this phenomenon, references, and other examples, see M. Dahood, *Psalms I* in *The Anchor Bible* (New York: Doubleday and Co., 1966), pp. xxxiv-xxxv, and Index of Subjects, p. 325, under "Breakup of stereotyped phrases." Cf. also *Psalms II* (1968), Index of Subjects, p. 390, under "Breakup of composite divine names."

[5] In accordance with the Qere. The Kethib (*ykswmw*) has the plural form of the verb which probably reflects the double subject: *r'š* and *'ml.* The general sense is not affected, however.

[6] The Qere has *wᵉ'ēn* for Kethib *'yn* . The readings may in fact be the same, the only difference being orthographic. When the first of two words in sequence ended with the same letter with which the next word began, the letter was sometimes written only once. Cf. I. O. Lehman, "A Forgotten Principle of Biblical Textual Criticism Rediscovered," *JNES*, XXVI (1967), pp. 93-101; W. Watson, "Shared Consonants in Northwest Semitic," *Biblica,* 50 (1969), pp. 525-33. See also Dahood, *Psalms II,* p. 81 for discussion and additional bibliography. A contrary position is presented by A. R. Millard in " '*Scriptio Continua*' in Early Hebrew: Ancient Practice or Modern Surmise?" *JSS,* XV (1970), pp. 2-15. In the present case we follow the Kethib since it is not clear whether or how such elliptical spelling affected the syllable count. The same possibility occurs in v. 7 where the Kethib has *ḥṭ'w 'ynm* but the Qere reads *ḥāṭᵉ'ū wᵉ'ēnām* .

[7] We have given Gray's rendering. However, notice should be taken of certain stylistic features which affect the interpretation of the passage. Recognition of the chiastic pattern

ytwmym ⟍ ⟋ hyynw
'mwtynw ⟋ ⟍ k'lmnwt

helps to focus attention upon the double-duty particle *k-* which qualifies *ytwmym* as well as *'lmnwt* . We would translate the verse as follows:

We became as orphans without a father
    our mothers as widows.

It is also possible to interpret *k-* as the emphatic particle rather than the preposition of comparison, and read the verse as affirming the equation as a fact:

We became orphans
    our mothers indeed, widows.

In either case *ytwmym* and *'lmnwt* should be regarded as having the same status in the declaration. If we are orphans, our mothers are widows; if they are like widows, then we are like orphans.

[8] It is a good example of what C. H. Gordon calls a ballast variant. Cf. his *Ugaritic Textbook* (Rome, Pontifical Biblical Institute, 1965), §13.116 (pp. 135-37).

[9] I hope to discuss elsewhere the conventions for syllable counting; cf. the discussion by W. Holladay, "Form and Word Play in David's Lament over Saul and Jonathan," *VT*, XX (1970), pp. 157-59.

[10] The *ḥatef pataḥ* after laryngeals is a secondary development, and is not included in the syllable count.

[11] Cf. Cross and Freedman, "The Song of Miriam," *JNES*, XIV (1955), pp. 237-50. A detailed study of the meter and strophic structure of Exod. 15 will appear in the forthcoming J. M. Myers *Festschrift*. A provisional treatment is to be found in "The Song of the Sea," *A Feeling of Celebration* (*Festschrift* in honor of Professor James Muilenburg; San Anselmo, Calif., 1967), pp. 1-10. For a somewhat different arrangement, see Cross, "The Song of the Sea and Canaanite Myth," *God and Christ: Existence and Province* (*Journal for Theology and the Church* [=*JTC*], 5 [1968]), pp. 1-26.

[12] Pending the publication of a study of the Lament of David in the Geo Widengren *Festschrift*, see an earlier provisional study of the poem, Cross and Freedman, *AYP*, pp. 43-50. Cf. also, Gevirtz, *Patterns in the Early Poetry of Israel*, pp. 72-96, and Holladay, *VT*, XX (1970), pp. 153-89.

[13] We treated the passage as conflate in Cross and Freedman, *JNES*, XIV (1955), pp. 241-44; cf. also Cross, *JTC*, 5 (1968), p. 13. n. 44.

[14] An echo of this pattern is to be seen in Lam. 5:6.

[15] In spite of the perfect form, the verb seems to have future force.

[16] While *hmh* is normally taken as the 3rd m. pl. pronoun, it is more likely to be the interjection, "Lo! Behold!" equivalent to Ugaritic *hm/hmt*, cf. Dahood, *Psalms I*, Index, p. 320, and *Psalms II*, Index, p. 383. A good example of similar usage is to be found in Deut. 33:7.

wᵉhēm ribᵉbōt 'eprayim	Now behold the myriads of Ephraim,
wᵉhēm 'alpē mᵉnaššeh	Now behold the thousands of Manasseh.

See Cross and Freedman, *JBL*, LXVII 1948), pp. 195, and 207, n. 62.

[17] This phenomenon has been dealt with in an article on the structure of Ps. 29 which has been prepared by a student, Mrs. Christine Hyland, with my assistance, and which is scheduled to appear in *HTR* (1972).

[18] Of the five poems in Lamentations, chap. 5 is the most regular from a metrical standpoint; at the same time it is the only one without the alphabetic pattern.

[19] Except for the short poems, Pss. 111 and 112, which have a narrow range of variation.

[20] The annotated bibliography was prepared by Mrs. Bonnie Kittel of the Graduate Theological Union, under my supervision and with my assistance.

PREFACE

It is impossible to go far at the present day in any serious attempt to interpret the prophetical books, or the books commonly called poetical, or certain other parts of the Old Testament, without being faced by questions relating to the forms of Hebrew poetry. I was myself compelled to consider these questions more fully than before when I came to prepare my commentary on *Isaiah* for the " International Critical Commentary," and in the introduction to that commentary I briefly indicated the manner in which, as it seemed to me, the more important of these questions should be answered. But it was impossible then and there to give as full an exposition of the subject as it requires. In the present volume I have ampler scope. Yet I must guard against a misunderstanding. Even here it is not my purpose to add to the already existing exhaustive, or at least voluminous, discussions of Hebrew metre. My aim is different: it is rather to survey the forms of Hebrew poetry, to consider them in relation to one another, and to illustrate their bearing on the criticism and interpretation of the Old Testament.

I have no new theory of Hebrew metre to set forth ; and I cannot accept in all its details any theory that others have elaborated. In my judgment some understanding of the laws of Hebrew rhythm has been gained : but much still remains uncertain. And both of these facts need to be constantly borne in mind in determining the text or interpreting the contents of Hebrew poetry. Perhaps, therefore, the chief service which I could expect of the discussion of Hebrew metre in this volume is that it may on the one hand open up to some the existence and general nature of certain metrical principles in Hebrew poetry, and that it may on the other hand warn others that, in view of our imperfect knowledge of the detailed working of these principles, considerable uncertainty really underlies the regular symmetrical forms in which certain scholars have presented the poetical parts of the Old Testament.

The first six chapters of the volume are an expansion of a course of University lectures delivered in the spring of 1913. They were published in the *Expositor* of May, June, July, August, September, October and December of the same year, and are now republished with some modifications and very considerable additions. The two last chapters, though written earlier, are in the present volume rather of the nature of an Appendix, being special studies in the reconstruction of two mutilated acrostich poems. These also originally appeared in the *Expositor*, the former (Chapter VII.) in September 1898, the latter (Chapter VIII.) in September 1906. Except for the omission of a paragraph which would have been a needless repetition now that the two discussions appear together, and for a few slight or verbal alterations, and for additions which are clearly indicated, I have preferred to republish these chapters as they were originally written. They were both, and more especially the former, written before I saw as far, or as clearly, as I seem to myself at least now to do, into the principles of Hebrew metre : but additional notes here and there suffice to point out the bearing of these more fully appreciated principles on the earlier discussions, which remain for the most part unaffected, largely, I believe, because in the first instance I followed primarily the leading of parallelism, and parallelism is likely for long to remain a safer guide than metre, though metre may at times enforce the guidance of parallelism, or act as guide over places where parallelism will not carry us.

A word of explanation, if not of apology, is required for the regularity with which I have added translations to the Hebrew quoted in the text. In many cases such translation was the readiest way of making clear my meaning; in others it is for the Hebrew student superfluous, and parts of the book can scarcely appeal to others than Hebrew students. But a large part of the discussions can be followed by those who are but little familiar or entirely unfamiliar with Hebrew. For the sake of any such who may read the book, and to secure the widest and easiest use possible for it, I have regularly added translations, except in the latter part of Chapter IV., where they would have been not only superfluous, but irritating to Hebrew students, and useless to others.

My last and pleasant duty is to thank the Rev. Allan Gaunt for his kindness in reading the proofs, and for offering various suggestions which I have been glad to accept.

G. BUCHANAN GRAY.

CHAPTER I

INTRODUCTORY

CHAPTER I

FAILURE to perceive what are the formal elements in Hebrew poetry has, in the past, frequently led to misinterpretation of Scripture. The existence of formal elements is now generally recognised ; but there are still great differences of opinion as to the exact nature of some of these, and as to their relation to one another ; and large questions or numerous important details of both the lower and higher criticism and of the interpretation of the Old Testament are involved in these differences. An examination of the forms of Hebrew poetry thus becomes a valuable, if not indeed a necessary, means to the correct appreciation of its substance, to an understanding of the thought expressed in it, in so far as that may still be understood, or, where that is at present no longer possible, to a perception of the cause and extent of the uncertainty and obscurity.

More especially do the questions relating to the two most important forms of Hebrew poetry

—parallelism and metre—require to be studied in close connexion with one another, and indeed in closer connexion than has been customary of late. I deliberately speak at this point of the *question* of parallelism and metre ; for, on the one hand, it has been and may be contended that parallelism, though it is a characteristic of much, is never a form of any, Hebrew poetry, and, on the other hand, it has been and still is sometimes contended that metre is not a form of Hebrew poetry, for the simple reason that in Hebrew poetry it did not exist. Over a question of nomenclature, whether parallelism should be termed a form or a characteristic, no words need be wasted ; the really important question to be considered later on is how far the phenomena covered by the term parallelism can be classified, and how far they conform to laws that can be defined. A third form of some Hebrew poetry is the strophe. This is of less, but still of considerable importance, and will be briefly considered in its place ; but rhyme, which is not a regular feature of Hebrew poetry, and poetical diction need not for the purposes of the present survey be more than quite briefly and incidentally referred to.

The first systematic treatment of any of the formal elements of Hebrew poetry came from Oxford. There have been few more distinguished occupants of the chair of Poetry in that university than Robert Lowth, afterwards Bishop of London,

and few lectures delivered from that chair have
been more influential than his *De Sacra Poesi
Hebraeorum Praelectiones Academicae*. These lectures were published in the same year (1753) as
another famous volume, to wit, Jean Astruc's
*Conjectures sur les mémoires originaux dont il
paroît que Moyse s'est servi pour composer le
livre de la Genèse*. It is as true of Astruc as of
Lowth that " in theology he clung to the traditional orthodoxy "; [1] yet Astruc was the first
to apply a stylistic argument in a systematic
attempt to recover the original sources of a portion
of the Pentateuch, and Lowth, by his entire
treatment of his subject, marks the transition
from the then prevailing dogmatic treatment of
the Old Testament to that treatment of it which
rests on the recognition that, whatever else it
may be, and however sharply distinguished in
its worth or by its peculiarities from other literatures, the Old Testament is primarily literature,
demanding the same critical examination and
appreciation, alike of form and substance, as
other literature. Owing to certain actual characteristics of what survives of ancient Hebrew
literature, documentary analysis has necessarily
played an important part in modern criticism of
the Old Testament; and if, narrowing unduly
the conception of Old Testament criticism, we
think in connexion with it mainly or exclusively

[1] T. K. Cheyne, *Founders of Old Testament Criticism*, p. 3.

of documentary analysis and questions of origin, Astruc may seem a more important founder of Modern Criticism than Lowth. But in reality the general implications of Lowth's discussion of Hebrew poetry, apart from certain special conclusions reached by him to which we shall pass immediately, make his lectures of wider significance than even Astruc's acute conjectures ; and we may fairly claim that, through Lowth and his two principal works, both of which were translated into German, the *Lectures* by Michaelis, the *Isaiah* by Koppe, Oxford, in the middle of the eighteenth century, contributed to the critical study of the Old Testament and the appreciation of Hebrew literature in a degree that was scarcely equalled till the nineteenth century was drawing to its close.

It is a relatively small part of Lowth's lectures that is devoted to those forms or formal characteristics of Hebrew poetry with which we are here concerned : of the thirty-four lectures one only, the nineteenth, is primarily devoted to that form with which Lowth's name will always be associated, though the subject of parallelism was already raised in the third lecture. The maturer and fuller discussion of this and kindred topics was first published in 1778 as a preliminary dissertation to the translation of Isaiah. Briefly summed up, Lowth's contribution to the subject was twofold : he for the first time clearly

analysed and expounded the parallelistic structure of Hebrew poetry, and he drew attention to
the fact that the extent of poetry in the Old
Testament was much larger than had generally
been recognised, that in particular it included
the greater part of the prophetic writings.

The existence and general characteristics of
parallelism as claimed by Lowth have never been
questioned since, nor the importance for interpretation of recognising these; nor can it be questioned, once the nature of parallelism is admitted,
that parallelism occurs in the Prophets as well
as in the Psalms, and in many passages of the
Prophets no less regularly than in many Psalms.
If, then, *on the ground of parallelism*, the Psalms
are judged to be poetry, the prophetic writings
(in the main) must also be regarded as poetry;
and, if, on the ground of parallelism, a translation
of the Psalms is marked, as is the Revised Version,
by line divisions corresponding to the parallel
members of the original, a translation of the
Prophets should also be so marked; and by
failing so to mark the prophetic poetry, and
thereby introducing an unreal distinction between
the form of the Psalms and the form of the prophetic writings, the Revised Version conceals
from those who use it one of the most important
and one of the surest of the conclusions which
were reached by Lowth in his discussion of
Hebrew poetry.

Whether after all parallelism is itself a true *differentia* between prose and poetry in Hebrew, may be and will be discussed ; but it will be useful before proceeding to a closer examination either of parallelism or of other alleged *differentiae* between prose and poetry, to recall the earlier scattered and unsystematic attempts to describe the formal elements of Hebrew poetry.

It has always been recognised that between mediaeval Jewish poetry and the poetry of the Old Testament there is, so far as form goes, no connexion ; nor, indeed, any similarity beyond the use, especially by the earliest of these mediaeval poets such as Jose ibn Jose and Kaliri, of acrostic, or alphabetic schemes such as occur in Lamentations i.-iv. and some other poems [1] in the Old Testament. The beginnings of mediaeval Jewish poetry go back to the ninth or tenth century A.D. at least ; it arose under the influence of Arabic culture, though it may also have owed something to Syriac poetry ; it flourished for some centuries in the West, and particularly in Spain. This poetry was governed by metre and rhyme ; [2] and the metre was quantitative. The same period was also, and again owing to the influence of Arabic culture, an age

---

[1] Enumerated below, p. 244 f.

[2] The introduction of rhyme into Hebrew poetry is attributed to Jannai ; rhyme was also employed by Kaliri. Both Jannai (probably) and Kaliri were Palestinians, and both lived in or before the ninth century A.D. : see Graetz, *Gesch. des Judenthums*, v. 158, 159.

of Jewish grammarians and philologists. These recognised the difference between the old poetry and the new, but contributed little to an understanding of the forms of the older poetry beyond a tolerably general acquiescence in the negative judgment that that older poetry was not metrical. In any case, no living tradition of the laws of the older Hebrew poetry, the poetry of the Old Testament, survived in the days of the poets Chasdai (A.D. 915–970), Solomon ibn Gabirol (1021–1058, or 1070), Judah hal-Levi (born 1085); of the grammarians and philologists, of whom some were poets also, Dunash ibn Labrat (c. 920–990), Menahem ibn Saruk (c. 910–970), Abu'l-Walid (eleventh century), Ibn Ezra, and the Kimhis (twelfth century). The older poetry had long been a lost art. Whatever these mediaeval scholars say of it has, therefore, merely the value of an antiquarian theory ; and however interesting their theories may be, they need not detain us longer now.

But there exist a few far earlier Jewish statements on the formal elements of the poetry of the Old Testament which run back, not indeed to the time of even the latest poems within the Old Testament, but to a time when, as will be pointed out in detail later on, poetry of the ancient Hebrew type was still being written. Statements from such a period unquestionably have a higher degree of interest than those of the

mediaeval Jewish scholars. Whether as a matter
of fact they point to any discernment of the real
principles of that poetry, and whether they do
not betray at once misconceptions and lack of
perception, is another question. At all events,
it is important to observe that while the authors
of these statements were Jews, the readers with
a view to whom they wrote were Greeks. So far
as I am aware, there is no discussion of metre,
or parallelism, or in general of the formal elements
of Hebrew poetry, in the Rabbinical writings, that
is to say in Jewish literature written in Hebrew
or Aramaic, until after the gradual permeation
of Jewish by Arabic scholarship from the seventh
or eighth century A.D. onwards. We owe the
earliest statements on Hebrew poetical forms to
two Jews who wrote in Greek—to Philo and to
Josephus.

Philo's evidence is slight and indirect as to
the poetry of the Old Testament. In the *De
vita Mosis* i. 5 he asserts that Moses was taught
by the Egyptians " the whole theory of rhythm,
harmony and metre " (τήν τε ῥυθμικὴν καὶ ἁρμονικὴν
καὶ μετρικὴν θεωρίαν); but he nowhere states that
the poems attributed to Moses in the Pentateuch
are metrical. Of Jewish poetry of a later age he
speaks more definitely, if the *De vita contem-
plativa* is correctly attributed to him, and if the
sect therein described was a Jewish sect. It is
asserted in this tract (cc. x. xi.) that the thera-

peutae sang hymns "in many metres and tunes,"
and in particular in iambic trimeters.

The three statements of Josephus on the
subject are much more specific and definite. Of
Moses he says, in reference to Exodus xv. 2 ff.,
that "he composed a song to God . . . in hexameter verse" (ἐν ἐξαμέτρῳ τόνῳ) ;[1] and again,
in reference to Deut. xxxii., that Moses read to
the Israelites "a hexametrical poem" (ποίησιν
ἐξάμετρον), and left it to them in the holy book.[2]
Of David he says that "he composed songs and
hymns in various metres (μέτρου ποικίλου), making
some trimetrical, others pentametrical."[3]

These exhaust the direct testimony of Jews,
who lived while poetry similar to that in the Old
Testament was still being written, to the metrical
character of that poetry. It is possible that we
have an indirect testimony to more specific
Jewish statements or theories in certain of the
patristic writers. It will be sufficient here to
refer to what is said by Origen and Eusebius and
Jerome ;[4] all these scholars belong to a period
before the new style of poetry adopted by the
mediaeval Jews had begun to be written, though
perhaps none of them belong quite to the age
when the older poetry was still practised as a
living art.

[1] *Ant.* ii. 16. 4.   [2] *Ant.* iv. 8. 44.   [3] *Ant.* vii. 12. 3.
[4] The passages from these and other patristic writers have been
brought together and discussed by J. Döller (*Rhythmus, Metrik und
Strophik in der bibl.-hebr. Poesie*, Paderborn, 1899 ; see pp. 18-35).

Origen's reference to the subject of Hebrew metre is to be found in a scholion on Psalm cxviii. 1 (LXX). He agrees with Josephus that Deuteronomy xxxii. is hexametrical, and that some of the Psalms are trimetrical ; but as an alternative metre used in the Psalter, he gives not the pentameter, as Josephus had done, but the tetrameter. At the same time he clearly recognises that Hebrew verses are different in character (ἕτεροι) from Greek verses. Ley finds two further statements in Origen's somewhat obscure words : (1) that the metrical unit (*den vollen Vers*) in Hebrew consists of two stichoi, not of a single stichos ; (2) that Hebrew metre was measured by the number of accented syllables.[1]

Eusebius refers to metre in Hebrew poems as follows : " There would also be found among them poems in metre, like the great song of Moses and David's 118th Psalm, composed in what the

[1] The scholion in question was published by Cardinal Pitra in *Analecta Sacra*, ii. 341, and reprinted thence by Preuschen in the *Zeitschrift für die AT. Wissenschaft*, 1891, pp. 316, 317 ; in the same *Zeitschrift* for 1892 (pp. 212-217) Julius Ley translated and commented on the scholion. The text being still none too well known or accessible, it may be well to reproduce it here. The words commented on are Μακάριοι οἱ ἄμωμοι ἐν ὁδῷ, οἱ πορευόμενοι ἐν νόμῳ κυρίου, and the scholion runs as follows :—οὕτω γε στίχος ἐστίν · οἱ γὰρ παρ᾽ Ἑβραίοις στίχοι, ὡς ἔλεγέ τις, ἔμμετροί εἰσιν · ἐν ἑξαμέτρῳ μὲν ἡ ἐν τῷ Δευτερονομίῳ ᾠδή · ἐν τριμέτρῳ δὲ καὶ τετραμέτρῳ οἱ ψαλμοί. οἱ στίχοι οὖν, οἱ παρ᾽ Ἑβραίοις, ἕτεροί εἰσιν παρὰ τοὺς παρ᾽ ἡμῖν. Ἐὰν θέλωμεν ἐνθάδε τηρῆσαι, τοὺς στίχους ποιοῦμεν. " Μακάριοι οἱ ἄμωμοι ἐν ὁδῷ, οἱ πορευόμενοι ἐν νόμῳ κυρίου." Καὶ οὕτως ἀρχόμεθα δευτέρου τοῦ ἑξῆς· ἰστέον τοίνυν ὅτι οἱ Ἕλληνες οἱ ἑρμηνεύσαντες πεποιήκασι τὸν παρ᾽ Ἑβραίοις στίχον ἐν τοιούτοις δύο (ὡς [ὁ] τοῦτο ἀντίγραφον γράψας οἱονεὶ πεποίηκε τὴν ἀρχὴν τοῦ στίχου μετ᾽ ἐκθέσεως) · τὸν δὲ δοκοῦντες δεύτερον, μὴ ὄντα δεύτερον, ἀλλὰ λεῖμμα τοῦ προτέρου μετ᾽ αἰσθήσεως· καὶ τοῦτο πεποίηκεν ἐπὶ ὅλου τοῦ ῥητοῦ.

Greeks call heroic metre. At least it is said (φασὶ γοῦν) that these are ʹhexameters, consisting of sixteen syllables ; also their other compositions in verse are said to consist of trimeter and tetrameter lines according to the sound of their own language." [1] The reference to Deuteronomy xxxii. and Psalm cxviii. (cxix.) and the specific metres mentioned are as in Origen ; but whether or not Origen suspected or asserted measurement by accented syllables, Eusebius clearly refers to a measurement by syllables, and thereby produces the impression that the Hebrew hexameter was of the same nature as the Greek : whereas Origen distinctly asserts that Hebrew metres are as compared with the Greek ἕτεροι. At the same time, the final words in Eusebius have something of the character of a saving clause.

Scattered over Jerome's writings are a larger number of specific statements, which may be summarised as follows :

1. Job iii. 2–xl. 6 consists of hexameters ; but the verses are varied and irregular.[2]

2. Job, Proverbs, the songs in Deuteronomy (i.e. Deut. xxxii.) and Isaiah, " Deuteronomii et Isaiae Cantica," are all written in hexameters or

---

[1] *Praep. Ev.* xi. 5. 5 : the translation given above is Gifford's.

[2] " Hexametri versus sunt, dactylo spondaeoque currentes ; et propter linguae idioma crebro recipientes et alios pedes non earumdem syllabarum, sed eorumdem temporum. Interdum quoque rhythmus ipse dulcis et tinnulus fertur numeris lege metri solutis," *Praef. in Job* (Migne, *Patr. Lat.* xxviii. 1082).

pentameters.[1]   Yet   elsewhere [2]   " Deuteronomii
Canticum " is said to be written in iambic tetrameters.

3. Psalms cx. and cxi. are iambic trimeters.[2]

4. Psalms cxviii., cxliv. and Proverbs xxxi.
10-31 are iambic tetrameters.[2]

5. Lamentations i. ii. are in " quasi sapphico
metro " ; but Lamentations iii. in trimeters.[2]

6. The prophets, though the text of them
is marked off by commas and colons, are *not*
metrical.[3]

But these statements occur in such connexions,
or are accompanied by such qualifying phrases,
as to indicate that Jerome did not intend them
to be taken too strictly, or as exactly assimilating
Hebrew poetry in respect of its measurements to
classical poetry. Thus, the hexameters in Job
are said to admit other feet in addition to dactyls
and spondees ; the " sapphic metre " of Lamentations i. ii. iv. is qualified as " quasi " ; and in
forestalling incredulity, such as the Emperor
Julian is said to have expressed, as to the existence
of metre in Hebrew literature, Jerome speaks of
the Hebrew poems as being " *in morem* nostri
Flacci "—*after the manner* of Horace.

There is one further important observation
to be made with regard to Jerome : the authori-

---

[1] " Quae omnia hexametris et pentametris versibus . . . apud suos
composita decurrunt," *Praef. in Chron. Eusebii* (Migne xxvii. 36).

[2] *Ep.* xxx. (ad Paulam) (Migne xxii. 442).

[3] *Praef. in Isaiam* (Migne xxviii. 771).

ties whom he cites for his statements are not his
own Hebrew teacher, but Philo, Josephus, Origen,
and Eusebius,[1] to the first two of whom Origen
in turn may refer indefinitely in his phrase
ἔλεγέ τις.

From this we may with some probability conclude (1) that Jerome's views of the nature of
Hebrew poetry do not represent those of Jewish
scholarship of his day ; but (2) that they are a
reproduction of the statements of Josephus, or
deductions made by Jerome himself from or in
the spirit of Josephus' statements. On whom
Eusebius relied for the statement (φασὶ γοῦν)
that the Hebrew hexameter contained sixteen
syllables we cannot say, but his informants were
scarcely Jewish contemporaries of his.

If, then, any theory or tradition of the metrical
character of the old Hebrew poetry formulated

[1] " If it seem incredible to any one that the Hebrews really have
metres, and that, whether we consider the Psalter, or the Lamentations
of Jeremiah, or almost all the songs of Scripture, they bear a resemblance
to our Flaccus, and the Greek Pindar, and Alcaeus, and Sappho, let
him read Philo, Josephus, Origen, Eusebius of Caesarea, and with the
aid of their testimony he will find that I speak the truth " : Preface to
the translation of Job (Fremantle's translation, p. 491) : Migne xxviii.
1082. This was written about A.D. 392 ; but Jerome had expressed
himself to much the same effect ten years earlier in a passage, partly
cited already in the original, in his Preface to the Chronicle of Eusebius :
" What can be more musical than the Psalter ? Like the writings of
our own Flaccus and the Grecian Pindar it now trips along in iambics,
now flows in sonorous alcaics, now swells into sapphics, now marches
in half-foot metre. What can be more lovely than the strains of
Deuteronomy and Isaiah ? What more grave than Solomon's words ?
What more finished than Job ? All these, as Josephus and Origen tell
us, were composed in hexameters and pentameters, and so circulated
amongst their own people."—Fremantle, p. 484 : Migne xxvii. 36.

by those who actually wrote it still survives, our primary source for it is Josephus. But does what Josephus says depend on a previously existing theory or tradition ? In all probability it does not. Josephus, in commending Hebrew poetry to his Greek readers, followed his usual practice of describing things Jewish in terms that would make a good impression on them. And so he calls Deuteronomy xxxii. hexametrical—a term which some modern scholars would still apply to it—but he gives his readers no clue to, even if he himself had any clear idea of, the difference between these hexameters and those of Greek and Latin poetry. Neither he nor any of the Christian scholars who follow him defines the nature of the feet or other units of which six, five, four, and three compose the hexameters, pentameters, tetrameters, and trimeters respectively of which they speak ; and, indeed, so loosely are these terms used that Jerome describes Deuteronomy xxxii. on one occasion as hexameter, and on another as tetrameter. Some modern scholars continue to use these same terms, but define more or less precisely what they mean by them ; and the Hebrew hexameters of the modern metrist have far less resemblance to a Greek or Latin hexameter than any of the numerous English hexameters with which English poets have at intervals experimented from the age of Elizabeth down to our own times. There is no reason for believing that Josephus, Origen, or Jerome really detected, or even thought that they detected, any greater similarity; Jerome's "quasi," Origen's ἕτεροι, cover, as a matter of fact, a very high degree of difference.

Early Jewish observations on Hebrew metre are neither numerous nor valuable ; but observations on the characteristic parallelism of Hebrew poetry seem to have been entirely non-existent earlier than the time of the mediaeval Jewish grammarians. Josephus was stimulated to discover or imagine metre in Hebrew poetry by his desire to commend it to the Greeks ; he had no such stimulus to draw attention to parallelism, for that corresponded to nothing in the poetry of Greece or Rome. And another cause worked against the recognition by the Jewish Rabbis of the part played by parallelism in Hebrew poetry. But before defining this cause it will be convenient to record the extent to which Lowth's analysis of parallelism was anticipated by the mediaeval Jews.

Dukes [1] drew attention to the fact that D. Ḳimḥi (c. A.D. 1160–1235) in his comment on Isaiah xix. 8 calls parallelism " a reduplication of the meaning by means of synonymous terms " (כפול ענין במלות שנות), and that Levi ben Gershon had called it an elegance (דרך צחות), and also noted the fact that the same style was customary

---

[1] *Zur Kenntnis der neuhebr. religiösen Poesie* (1842), p. 125.

with the Arabs. Schmiedl, in 1861,[1] drew attention to the still earlier use by Ibn Ezra (A.D. 1093–1168) of these same expressions as well as of some others with reference to parallelism. So far as I am aware, similar observations in writers earlier than Ibn Ezra have never yet been discovered.[2] Ibn Ezra's observations may be summarised as follows : it is an elegance of style, and in particular a characteristic of the *prophetic* style, to repeat the same thought by means of synonymous words.[3] Whether in regarding parallelism as peculiarly characteristic of the prophetic style (דרך הנביאות) Ibn Ezra anticipated Lowth's observation that Old Testament prophetic literature is, in the main, poetical in form, is doubtful : for the examples of parallelism given by Ibn Ezra are drawn, not from the prophetical books, but from the prophetic poems in the Pentateuch attributed to Jacob, Moses, and Balaam.

Far more important is Ibn Ezra's insistence that parallelism is a *form* of poetry, and that when a writer repeats his thought by means of synonymous terms he is not adding to the substance, but merely perfecting the form of what he had to say. This represents a reaction against

---

[1] In *Monatsschrift für Gesch. u. Wissenschaft des Judenthums*, p. 157.

[2] Cardinal Pitra was of opinion that Origen's scholion given above (p. 12 *n.*) recognised parallelism, but this is doubtful.

[3] Ibn Ezra cites as examples Genesis xlix. 6 a, b, Deuteronomy xxxii. 7 c, d, Numbers xxiii. 8.

a mode of exegesis that treated such repetition as an addition to the substance. It was this mode of exegesis, doubtless, that militated against the discernment of the real nature of parallelism by earlier Jewish scholars. How could interpreters who attributed importance to every letter and every external peculiarity of the sacred text admit that it was customary in a large part of Scripture to express the same thought twice over by means of synonymous terms ? If the fact that וייצר in Genesis ii. 7 is written with two yods, though it might have been written with one, was supposed to express the thought not only that God " formed " man, but that He formed him with two " formations," or " inclinations," to wit, the evil inclination and the good inclination, how could two parallel lines convey no fuller meaning than one such line standing by itself ? The influence of this exegetical principle lingers still ; at an earlier time it was far-reaching. For example, in Lamech's song (Gen. iv. 23), " the man " and " the young man " came to be treated not as what in reality they are, synonymous terms with the same reference, but as referring to two different individuals, one old and one young, who were, then, identified with the ancient Cain and the youthful Tubal-Cain.[1] Again, the reduplication of the same thought in

[1] See the commentary of Rashi (eleventh century A.D.) on Gen. iv. 23.

two parallel lines is not recognised in.

Therefore, the wicked shall not stand in the judgment,
  Nor sinners in the congregation of the righteous (Ps. i. 1).

Rabbi Nehemiah, a Rabbi of the second century A.D., said " the wicked mean the generation of the Flood, and the sinners mean the men of Sodom." [1]   If no other difference of reference could be postulated between two parallel terms or lines or other repetitions of a statement, it was customary to explain one of the present world and the other of the world to come.[2] " Day and night " is a sufficiently obvious expression for " continually " ; and a poet naturally distributed the two terms between two parallel lines without any intention that what he speaks of in the one line should be understood to be confined to the day, and what he speaks of in the second line to the night : thus, when a Psalmist says (xcii. 1),

It is a good thing . . .
To declare thy kindness in the morning
And thy faithfulness in the night,

what he means is that it is good to declare both the kindness and the faithfulness of God at all times. Yet even some modern commentators still continue to squeeze substance out of form by making Psalm xlii. 9 (8)—

By day will Yahweh command his kindness,
And in the night his song shall be with me—

---

[1] *Sanhedrin* x. 3.
[2] See e.g. *Sanhedrin* x. 3 for several examples of second-century exegesis of this kind.

mean more than that the Psalmist is the constant recipient of God's goodness ; and herein these modern commentators follow, in misconceiving the influence of form, the early Jewish interpreter Resh Lakish (third century A.D.) who explained the verse thus : " Every one who studieth in the Law in this world which is like the night, the Holy One, blessed be He, stretches over him the thread of grace for the future world which is like the day."

To sum up this part of our discussion : Jewish Rabbis in the second century A.D. misunderstood the parallelism that is characteristic of most of the poetry of the Old Testament, and, with the exception of Philo and Josephus, no Jews appear to have given any attention to any metrical laws that may also have governed that poetry ; [2] and

---

[1] Talmud B. *Ḥagigah* 12 b ; ed. Streane, p. 64. Another passage where some modern commentators have failed to see how much the real range of thought is defined by parallelism is Hos. ii. 5 a, b—
> Lest I strip her naked,
> And set her as on the day she was born.

These two lines are entirely synonymous. For the correct understanding of the second line the most important thing is to recall Job i. 21, " Naked came I out of my mother's womb " ; the two lines mean simply this : Lest I strip her to the skin so that she becomes as naked as a child just drawn from the womb. Such a note as Harper's in the *International Critical Commentary* (p. 227), which is partly based on Hitzig's, is not really interpretation : the lines do *not* mean that Israel is to become a nomadic people again. Strangely enough, the modern commentaries which I have consulted do not give the really pertinent reference to Job i. 21 : and it was not until I turned to Ḳimḥi that I found a commentator who did. He very correctly paraphrases the second line : I will cause her to stand naked as on the day of her birth, and regards it as repeating the meaning of the first line by synonymous terms (הענין כפול במלות שונות).

[2] It is possible enough that the practice of distinguishing certain poems (viz. those in Ex. xv., Deut. xxxii., Judg. v. and 2 Sam. xxii.) by spacing within the lines, a practice still regularly observed in printed

what Josephus says on that subject is expressed
in Greek terms, was written as part of his apology
for all things Jewish, and appears at most to
imply that Josephus had some perception of
difference of rhythm in different Hebrew poems.
The account he gives wears a rather more learned
air, but is in reality as vague and insufficient as
the account given to Dr. Dalman by some of
those who supplied him with his specimens of
modern Palestinian poetry.[1]

---

editions of the Hebrew Bible even when other poems such as Psalms
and Job are not so distinguished, goes back to this period. It is
certainly vouched for by sayings in both Talmuds (*j. Meg.* iii. 74, col.
2, bottom ; *b. Meg.* 16 b ; cp. *Shabbath,* 103 b, bottom), of which the
Jerusalem Talmud is commonly considered to have been completed
c. A.D. 350, the Babylonian *c.* A.D. 500 ; and by the time that the
tractate *Soferim* was written (probably *c.* A.D. 850), according to statements therein contained (*Soferim,* ed. Joel Müller, xiii. 1, p. xxi), it was
customary in accurately written MSS. to distinguish Psalms, Proverbs,
and Job in the same way ; and in some of the earliest existing MSS.
Psalms and Job as well as the four passages above mentioned are so
distinguished.   But it is difficult, not to say impossible, to derive from
these facts any theory of the nature of parallelism, or of the rhythm
of the lines so distinguished : on the contrary, the different divisions
of these poetical passages in different MSS., the failure to distinguish
at all such obvious poems as the blessing of Jacob in Gen. xlix., the
poems attributed to Balaam in Num. xxiii., xxiv., and the blessings of
Moses in Deut. xxxiii. (cp. Ginsburg's edition of the Hebrew Bible),
and the fact that the directions in the Talmud for writing certain
passages στιχηρῶς group together the poems in Ex. xv., Deut. xxxii.,
etc., and the lists of the kings of Canaan in Jos. xx. 9-24 and of the sons
of Haman in Esth. ix., rather suggest the absence of any clear theory
of either parallelism or rhythm.

[1] " In modern Arabic folk-poetry the purely rhythmical has begun
to drive out the quantitative principle so that a distinction may be
drawn between quantitative and rhythmical poems." . . .

" I have never been able to discover how the composers of this folk-
poetry go to work in the composition of these poems.   To the question
whether there was nothing at all in his lines that the poet numbered so
as to secure regularity (*Gleichmass*), I received from several different
quarters the reply, that nothing at all was numbered, that for the folk-

And yet, in the second century A.D., Hebrew
poetry of the type found in the Old Testament
had not yet become a long obsolete type, as it had
become when the new art of rhymed, metrical
poems without parallelism was brought to perfection in the tenth to the twelfth centuries ; contemporaries of Josephus were still employing
parallelism with as much regularity and skilful
variation as the best writers of the Old Testament
period ; and in all probability, in many cases at
least, rhythmical regularity of the same kind, and
as great, accompanied these parallelistic compositions, as is found in any of the Biblical poems.
But later than the second century A.D. only
meagre traces of parallelism of the types found
in the Old Testament, or of the same kind of
rhythms as are used there, can be found ;
and certainly, when the new Hebrew poetry
was created, it dispensed with parallelism—with
parallelism, at all events, as any constant feature
of the poems.

Without prejudging the question whether
parallelism in Hebrew necessarily constitutes or
implies poetical form, it will be convenient at
this point to take a survey of those parts of
ancient Jewish literature outside the Old Testament in which either parallelism is conspicuous,

---

poetry there was only one standard (*Mass*)—absolute caprice. No
doubt it may be supposed that the individual poet instinctively imitates
the form of some poem that is known to him."—G. H. Dalman, *Palästinischer Diwân*, pp. xxii, xxiii.

or other features are prominent which distinguish those parts of the Old Testament commonly regarded as poetry. Most of this literature, especially the latest of it, survives only in translation ; and, with regard to much of it, it is disputed whether it actually runs back to a Hebrew original at all. The exact date, again, of much of it is uncertain, and I shall, therefore, attempt no rigid chronological order of mention ; in general the period in question is from the third or second century B.C. to the second century A.D.

Of the apocryphal books it was clear even before the discovery of the Hebrew original that Ecclesiasticus (*c.* 180 B.C.) must have possessed all the characteristics of ancient Hebrew poetry ; and even the alphabetic structure of li. 13-30 had been inferred.[1] But Ecclesiasticus may well be older than some of the latest poems in the Old Testament.

The Hebrew original of the first book of Maccabees (*c.* 90 B.C.) has not yet been recovered : but, even through the translations, it is easy to detect certain passages to which the use of parallelism gives an entirely different character from the simple prose narrative of the main body of the work. Such passages are the eulogies of Judas (iii. 3-9) and Simon (xiv. 6-15) and also i. 25-28, 36 b-40, ii. 8-11 (13 a). Isolated distichs,

---

[1] By G. A. Bickell in the *Zeitschrift für katholische Theologie*, 1882, pp. 319 ff.

such as occur in ii. 44 and ix. 41, may be citations
from now lost poems, as vii. 17 is from a still
extant Psalm (lxxix. 2, 3). In ix. 20, 21 reference
is made to an elegy on Judas and the opening
words are cited. It is possible to infer the Hebrew
original of these words with practical certainty,
and to detect in

איך נפל הגבור | מושיע ישראל

> How hath the valiant man fallen,
> He that delivered Israel,

the opening of a poem constructed after the same
form [1] as elegies in the Old Testament.

In the book of Judith, which may have been
written about 150, or as some think about 80 B.C.,
we find a long poem of praise and thanksgiving ;
in part, it is a close imitation of earlier poems in
the Old Testament ; but its parallelistic, as was
also presumably its rhythmical, regularity is by
no means least where it is most independent, as,
for example, in the lines (xvi. 8-10)—

> She anointed her face with ointment,
> And bound her hair in a tire ;
> And she took a linen garment to deceive him,
> Her sandal ravished his eye,
> And her beauty took his soul prisoner,
> The scimitar passed through his neck,
> The Persians quaked at her daring,
> And the Medes at her boldness were daunted.

Not only the Apocrypha, but the Pseudepigrapha, contain much, the New Testament,

[1] See below, pp. 96 ff.

perhaps, a little, that was originally written in Hebrew and was poetical in form. Among these specimens of late Hebrew poetry we may certainly include the eighteen " Psalms of Solomon " (c. 50 B.C.)[1] and perhaps some of the most ancient elements of the Jewish liturgy, such as the "Eighteen Blessings " (c. A.D. 100), and the blessings accompanying the recitation of the Sh°ma' ; [2] possibly also the Magnificat and other New Testament Canticles.[3] Several of the apocalypses also include poems ; in those which he has edited more recently, Dr. Charles has distinguished the poetry from the prose by printing the former in regular lines. Without admitting that *all* parts thus distinguished by him or others possessed

---

[1] The parallelistic structure is indicated in my translation of these Psalms in *The Apocrypha and Pseudepigrapha of the Old Testament* (ed. R. H. Charles), ii. 631-652.

[2] The Hebrew text of these and of the " Eighteen " is conveniently brought together in W. Staerk, *Altjüdische liturgische Gebete* (Bonn, 1910). The rhythm is indicated in the notes and German translation in P. Fiebig, *Berachoth : Der Mischnatractat Gegensprüche*, pp. 26 ff.

[3] Dr. Burney has recently argued that the parable of the last Judgment in Matt. xxv. 31-46 was a Hebrew poem ; and his Hebrew translation from the Greek text of the Gospel, his metrical analysis of the poem and his English translation, as far as possible in the rhythm of his Hebrew reconstruction, deserve careful attention. See the *Journal of Theological Studies* for April 1913 (vol. xiv. 414-424).

Parts, but parts only, of Matt. xxv. 31-46 are thrown into parallel lines by Dr. Moffat also in *The New Testament : a new translation.* That parts only are so arranged in this passage is the more noticeable because in a considerable number of other, longer or shorter, passages in this translation of the New Testament an arrangement in lines is adopted. It is, however, tolerably clear that this line arrangement is not always intended to imply poetical form. And certainly, even for example in the parts of 1 Cor. xiii. which are so arranged, the form is not that of Hebrew parallelism ; in *vv.* 1-3 the formal effect is obtained by exact repetition of the same phrase (" but if I have no love "), not by repetition of the same thought by means of synonymous terms.

poetical form in the original, I think it may be safely said that such apocalypses as the Twelve Patriarchs, the Book of Jubilees, the Apocalypse of Baruch and IV. Esdras do each contain *some* such passages.

Now of these books or passages which show the same characteristics as the poetry of the Old Testament, some at least were written by men who were contemporary both with Josephus and also with those who after A.D. 70 founded that Jewish school at Jamnia of whose methods of exegesis (in the second century A.D.) examples have been given above. At the very time that the Rabbis were examining scripture with eyes blind to parallelism, other Jews were still writing poems that made all the old use of parallelism. This may be proved by reference to the Apocalypse of Baruch : for with regard to this book I believe that it may be safely asserted [1] (1) that it was written in Hebrew, (2) that it was written not earlier than *c.* A.D. 50, and therefore (3) that its author was in all probability a contemporary, though perhaps an elder contemporary, of Josephus and of the founders of the school of Jamnia. But this book contains a long passage (xlviii. 1-47) that is among the most regular and sustained examples of parallelism in the whole range of Hebrew literature ; a sufficiently large portion of it may be cited here to prove this ;

[1] Cp. R. H. Charles, *The Apocalypse of Baruch.*

the translation is in the main that of Dr. Charles ;
for the line division, which in one place (*v.* 14)
involves an important change of punctuation, I
am responsible.[1]

2 O my Lord, Thou summonest the advent of the times, and
they stand before Thee ;
Thou causest the power of the ages to pass away, and
they do not resist Thee :
Thou arrangest the method of the seasons, and they
obey Thee.
3 Thou alone knowest the goal of the generations,
And Thou revealest not Thy mysteries to many.
4 Thou makest known the multitude of the fire,
And Thou weighest the lightness of the wind.
5 Thou explorest the limits of the heights,
And Thou scrutinisest the depths of the darkness.
6 Thou carest for the number which pass away that they
may be preserved,
And Thou preparest an abode for those that are to be.
7 Thou rememberest the beginning which Thou hast made,
And the destruction that is to be Thou forgettest not.
8 With nods of fear and indignation Thou givest commandment to the flames,
And they change into spirits,[2]

---

1 The translation, without line division, referred to above is that in
R. H. Charles, *The Apocalypse of Baruch* (1896).   Since the above words
were written, Dr. Charles has published a revised translation with
division into parallel lines in *The Apocrypha and Pseudepigrapha of the
Old Testament* (Oxford, 1913), vol. ii. p. 504 f.   In this later translation
Dr. Charles has adopted the punctuation in *v.* 14, given above ; its
correctness, indeed, becomes obvious so soon as the sustained parallelism of the passage is recognised.   Verse 2 is now divided by Dr. Charles
into six lines : the division into three, as above, shows the parallelism
more clearly.

2 I suspect corruption in *v.* 8 a, b.   In the original text " flames "
was probably a parallel term to " spirits " (cp. Ps. civ. 4), and not, as
in the present text of the versions, that which changes into spirits.
Moreover, the two lines are likely to have been more nearly equal to
one another in length : the inequality between them presents a striking
contrast to what is found in the rest of the poem.

And with a word Thou quickenest that which was not,
And with mighty power Thou holdest that which has not
yet come.
[9] Thou instructest created things in the understanding of
Thee,
And Thou makest wise the spheres so as to minister in
their orders.
[10] Armies innumerable stand before Thee,
And they minister in their orders quietly at Thy nod.
[11] Hear Thy servant,
And give ear to my petition.
[12] For in a little time are we born,
And in a little time do we return.
[13] But with Thee, hours are as a time (?),
And days as generations.
[14] Be not therefore wroth with man ; for he is nothing ;
And take not account of our works ; [15] for what are we ?
For lo ! by Thy gift do we come into the world,
And we depart not of our own will.
[16] For we said not to our parents, " Beget us,"
And we sent not to Sheol, saying, " Receive us."
[17] What, then, is our strength that we should bear Thy wrath,
Or what are we that we should endure Thy judgment ?
[18] Protect us in Thy compassions,
And in Thy mercy help us.

The Apocalypse of Esdras (IV. Esdras) was
probably written shortly after A.D. 100, and
though it contains nothing quite so regular and
sustained as the passage just cited from the
Apocalypse of Baruch, a considerable number of
passages are printed both by Professor Gunkel [1]
and Mr. Box [2] as poetry, and, some (*e.g.* viii.
20-30) at least, with good reason.

[1] In E. Kautzsch, *Die Apokryphen und Pseudepigraphen des AT.*,
ii. 352-401 (cp. p. 349).
[2] G. H. Box, *The Ezra-Apocalypse* ; and also in *The Apocrypha and
Pseudepigrapha of the Old Testament* (ed. R. H. Charles), ii. 542-624.

Parallelism, then, certainly continued into the second century A.D. to be a feature in Hebrew poetry, or in Hebrew literature written in a form differing from ordinary prose. Whether poetry distinguished by the sustained use of parallelism was still composed after the second century is doubtful;[1] but in this connexion two recently recovered documents may be very briefly referred to.

[1] Certainly no literary work that is at present generally admitted to be later than the second century is marked by such sustained parallelism as we find in parts of the Apocalypse of Baruch, or by anything approaching it. But the Talmud contains a few snatches of occasional poetry one or two of which, at least, are characterised by parallelism and by something closely resembling rhythms found in the Old Testament. The most pertinent example is that attributed in *Moed Kaṭan* 25 b to an elegist (ספרנא) on the death of Ḥanin who is described as חתניה דבי נשיאה, which is interpreted by Levy (*Neuheb. Wörterbuch*, ii. 83 a) as meaning that Ḥanin was a son-in-law of R. Juda Nasi. The elegy alludes to the fact that Ḥanin died on the day that his son was born. It runs :—

שמחה לתוגה נהפנה | ששון ויגון נדבקו

בעת שמחתו נאנח | בעת חנינתו אבד חנינא

This may be rendered, though the last lines are not free from ambiguity (see Levy, *loc. cit.*):

Joy was turned into weariness,
  Gladness and sadness were united ;
When his gladness came, he sighed,
  When his favour came, he that was favoured, perished.

The parallelism is obvious ; and the rhythm of the first distich is 3 : 3 (see below, p. 159 f.). Parallelism and rhythm are rather less conspicuous in another elegy cited at the same place, viz. :

תמרים הניעו ראש | על צדיק כתמר

נשים לילות כימים | על משים לילית כימים

The palm-trees shook their head
  Over the righteous that was as a palm-tree (cp. Ps. xcii. 13).
(So) let us turn night into day (*i.e.* weep unremittingly)
  Over him who turned night into day (in the study of the law).

Yet another elegy cited in the same place contains the lines

אם בארוים נפלה שלהבת | מה יעשו אזובי קיר.

If on the cedars the flame fell,
  What can the hyssops on the wall do ?

Dr. Charles [1] finds a considerable element of poetry in the fragments of a Zadokite work of which the Hebrew text was first edited (with translation and introduction) by Dr. Schechter [2] in 1910. In the opinion of some this work is considerably later than IV. Esdras ; but Dr. Charles has strong reasons for concluding that it was written before A.D. 70. Be the date, however, what it may, except in quotations from the Old Testament, *parallelism* in this work is not at all conspicuous ; whether, therefore, the passages marked by Dr. Charles as possessing poetical form actually do so, turns on matters which have to be considered later. Happily, in this case the question can be considered, not through translations merely, but with the original text before us.

The Odes of Solomon, of which the Syriac text was first edited by Dr. Rendel Harris [3] in 1909, were scarcely written before A.D. 70, and they may belong to the second century A.D. ; in the

---

which recall, though the lines are longer, the ring of Ps. xi. 3. Two similar distichs follow. A further example occurs in *Ḥagigah* 15 b :—

אפילו שמר הפתח | לא עמר לפניך רבינו.

Even the keeper-of-the-door (of Gehenna)
Stood not his ground before thee, O our teacher.

As the sustained parallelism which is so characteristic of much of the Old Testament and Jewish literature to the second century A.D. appears to run back to origins in the popular poetry of the early Hebrews, so parallelism seems to have maintained an existence for some time in the occasional poetry of the later Jews, after it had ceased to be employed in more formal literature.

[1] *Fragments of a Zadokite work translated* . . . 1912.

[2] In *Documents of Jewish Sectaries*, vol. i.

[3] *The Odes and Psalms of Solomon published from the Syriac Version*, 1909 (ed. 2, 1911).

opinion of some they were written even later. The original language of these Odes is still undetermined.   But some of them (*e.g.* v., vi., vii.) are strongly parallelistic in character, though Dr. Harris refrained from distinguishing the parallel members in his translation.

It was long ago pointed out by Lowth that parallelism can be retained almost unimpaired in a translation ; easier still, therefore, was it for Jews to reproduce this feature in works written in the first instance in some other language than Hebrew ; and to some extent they did so.   The Book of Wisdom, which rests on no Hebrew original, but was written, as it survives, in Greek, is the best proof of this.   It is possible that the author of Wisdom attempted to imitate other features of ancient Hebrew poetry as well as its parallelism in his Greek work ; but these are questions that cannot be pursued now.

There is no other considerable book originally written in Greek which employs parallelism throughout ; but it has been held with differing degrees of conviction and consensus of opinion that Tobit's prayer (Tob. xiii.), the Prayer of Manasses, the Song of the Three Holy Children, and the latter part of Baruch were written in Greek, or at least, not in Hebrew ; and a Hebrew original for the Odes of Solomon was postulated neither by their first editor, nor by many who have followed him, though more recently Dr.

Abbott [1] has adduced some evidence which he thinks points to such an original.

The question of the original language of each of these works might, perhaps, with advantage, be reconsidered in connexion with the general question of the extent to which parallelism was adopted in Jewish writings not written in Hebrew. We have on the one hand the clear example of the use of parallelism in Wisdom, and on the other the exceedingly slight use of parallelism, for example, in the Sibylline oracles ; and we may recall again in this connexion the avoidance of parallelism in mediaeval Hebrew poetry. These avoidances or absences of parallelism are certainly worthy of attention in view of the ease with which this feature of Hebrew poetry could have been reproduced in Greek works, and even combined, if necessary, with the use of Greek metres like the hexameters of the Jewish Sibylline books. Was it merely due to the fact that the one was writing in Hebrew and the other in Greek, that the author of the Apocalypse of Baruch in his loftier passages employs the form of ancient Hebrew poetry, whereas his contemporary, St. Paul, even in such a passage as 1 Corinthians xiii.,[2] avoids it ? Or may we detect here the influences of different schools or literary traditions ?

[1] E. A. Abbott, *Light on the Gospel from an Ancient Poet.*
[2] See above, p. 26, *n.* 3.

D

CHAPTER II

PARALLELISM: A RESTATEMENT

CHAPTER II

THE literature of the Old Testament is divided into two classes by the presence or absence of what since Lowth has been known as *parallelismus membrorum*, or parallelism. The occurrence of parallelism characterises the books of Psalms, Job, Proverbs, Ecclesiastes (in part), Lamentations, Canticles, the larger part of the prophetical books, and certain songs and snatches that are cited and a few other passages that occur in the historical books. Absence of parallelism characterises the remainder of the Old Testament, *i.e.* the Pentateuch and the books of Joshua, Judges, Samuel, Kings and Chronicles (with slight exceptions in all these books as just indicated), Ezra, Nehemiah, Esther, Ruth, and part of the prophetical books, including most of Ezekiel, the biographical parts of Jeremiah, the book of Jonah (except the psalm in chapter ii.), and some passages in most of the remaining prophetical books. It had become customary to

distinguish these two divisions of Hebrew literature as poetry and prose respectively : parallelism
had come to be regarded as a mark of poetry, its
absence as a mark of prose ; and by the application
of the same test the non-canonical literature of
the Jews from the second century B.C. to the
second century A.D. was likewise coming to be
distinguished into its prose and poetical elements.

The validity of parallelism as a test to distinguish between prose and poetry in Hebrew
literature might be, and has been either actually
or virtually, challenged on two grounds : (1)
that parallelism actually occurs in prose ; and
(2) that parts of the Old Testament from which
parallelism is absent are metrical and, therefore,
poetical in form.

Parallelism is not a feature peculiar to Hebrew
literature : [1] it is characteristic of parts of Babylonian literature, such as the Epics of Creation

---

[1] Nor even to Semitic literature. Many interesting illustrations
from folk-songs and English literature are given by Dr. G. A. Smith in
The Early Poetry of Israel, pp. 14-16. Yet in most of these there is
more simple repetition without variation of terms than is common in
Hebrew, and an even more conspicuous difference is the much less sustained use of parallelism. In view of the great influence of the Old
Testament on English literature and the ease with which parallelism
can be used in any language (cp. p. 32 above), it is rather surprising
that parallelism, and even sustained parallelism, is not more conspicuous in English. But abundant illustrations of this sustained use may
be found in the Finnish epic, *The Kalevala*, if Mr. Crawford's translation keeps in this respect at all close to the original, with which I have
no acquaintance. Even here there are differences, as for example in
the absence of the tendency, so marked in Hebrew, for parallelism to
produce distichs. I cite a sufficiently long passage to illustrate what is
a frequent, though not a constant, characteristic of the style of *The
Kalevala* :—

(the *Enuma eliš* and others), the Gilgamesh epic
and the hymns to the gods.[1] It is as apparent
in translations from Babylonian as in the English
versions of the Psalms or the prophets ; as examples from Babylonian literature it may suffice to
cite the well-known opening lines of *Enuma eliš* [2]—

> When above the heaven was not named,
>   And beneath the earth bore no name,
> And the primeval Apsu, the begetter of them,
>   And Mummu and Tiâmat, the mother of them all—

> " Listen, bride, to what I tell thee :
> In thy home thou wert a jewel,
> Wert thy father's pride and pleasure,
> ' Moonlight,' did thy father call thee,
> And thy mother called thee ' Sunshine,'
> ' Sea-foam ' did thy brother call thee,
> And thy sister called thee ' Flower.'
> When thou leavest home and kindred,
> Goest to a second mother,
> Often she will give thee censure,
> Never treat thee as her daughter,
> Rarely will she give thee counsel,
> Never will she sound thy praises.
> ' Brush-wood,' will the father call thee,
> ' Sledge of Rags,' thy husband's brother,
> ' Flight of Stairs,' thy stranger brother,
> ' Scare-crow,' will the sister call thee,
> Sister of thy blacksmith husband ;
> Then wilt think of my good counsels,
> Then wilt wish in tears and murmurs,
> That as steam thou hadst ascended,
> That as smoke thy soul had risen,
> That as sparks thy life had vanished.
> As a bird thou canst not wander
> From thy nest to circle homeward,
> Canst not fall and die like leaflets,
> As the sparks thou canst not perish,
> Like the smoke thou canst not vanish."
>
>   J. M. CRAWFORD, *The Kalevala*, i. 341, 2.

[1] A convenient collection of all of these (transliterated text and translation) will be found in R. W. Rogers, *Cuneiform Parallels to the Old
Testament.*   [2] Cp. Rogers, pp. 3 ff.

and these lines from a hymn to the god Sin [1]—

When Thy word in heaven is proclaimed, the Igigi prostrate
themselves ;
When Thy word on earth is proclaimed, the Anunaki kiss
the ground.
When Thy word on high travels like a storm-wind, food and
drink abound ;
When Thy word on earth settles down, vegetation springs
up.
Thy word makes fat stall and stable, and multiplies living
creatures ;
Thy word causes truth and righteousness to arise, that
men may speak the truth.

Whether these passages are prose or poetry, and whether, if poetry, they are such primarily because of the presence of parallelism, turns on the same considerations as the corresponding questions with reference to parallelistic passages in Hebrew : and further discussion of these must be postponed.

But parallelism is characteristic not only of much in Babylonian and Hebrew literature : it is characteristic also of much in Arabic literature. And the use of parallelism in Arabic literature is such as to give some, at least apparent, justification to the claim that parallelism is no true *differentia* between prose and poetry ; for parallelism in Arabic accompanies *prose*—prose, it is true, of a particular kind, but at all events not poetry, according to the general opinion of Arabian grammarians and prosodists.   Not only is paral-

[1] Cp. Rogers, pp. 144, 145.

lelism present in much Arabic prose : it is
commonly absent from Arabic poetry, *i.e.* from
the rhymed and carefully regulated metrical
poetry of the Arabs. In illustration of this, two
passages may be cited from the *Maḳâmât* of
Ḥarîri. The translations here given are based
on Chenery's,[1] but I have modified them here
and there in order to bring out more clearly the
regularity of the parallelism in the original : for
the same reason I give the translation with line
divisions corresponding to the parallel members.
The first passage, which consists of part of the
opening address of Abu Zayd in the first Maḳâmah,
is from the prose fabric of Ḥarîri's work ; the
second is one of the many metrical poems which
are wrought into the prose fabric. The parallelism of the prose passage, as of innumerable other
passages which might equally well have served as
examples, is as regular and as sustained as that
of any passage in Hebrew or Babylonian literature, and indeed in some respects it is even more
monotonously regular : it is complex too, for at
times there is a double parallelism—a parallelism
between the longer periods, the lines of the translation, and also between the parts of each of
these (the half lines of the translation). This
prose passage is as follows [2] :—

---

[1] T. Chenery, *The Assemblies of Al Ḥarîri*, i. 109 f. and 192.

[2] In order that parallelism may be better studied I have hyphened
together word groups in English that correspond to a single word (combined in some cases with inseparable particles) in Arabic. But I have

O-thou-reckless in petulance, trailing the garment of vanity !
O-thou-headstrong in follies, turning-aside to idle-tales !
How long wilt-thou-persevere in thine error, and eat-sweetly-
of the pasture of thy wrong ?
And how far wilt-thou-be-extreme in thy pride, and not
abstain from thy wantonness ?
Thou provokest by-thy-rebellion the Master of thy forelock ;
And thou goest-boldly in-the-foulness of thy behaviour
against the knower of thy secret ;
And thou hidest-thyself from thy neighbour, but thou-art
in sight of thy watcher ;
And thou concealest-thyself from thy slave, but nothing
is-concealed from thy Ruler.
Thinkest thou that thy state will-profit-thee when thy
departure draweth-near ?
Or-that thy wealth will-deliver-thee, when thy deeds
destroy-thee ?
Or-that thy repentance will-suffice for thee when thy foot
slippeth ?
Or-that thy kindred will-lean to thee in-the-day-that thy
judgment-place gathereth-thee ?
How-is-it thou-hast-walked not in-the-high-road of thy
guidance, and hastened the treatment of thy disease ?
And blunted the edge of thine iniquity, and restrained
thyself—thy worst enemy.
Is-not death thy doom ?   What-then-is thy preparation ?
And is-not-grey-hair thy warning ?   What-then-is thy
excuse ?
And is-not-in the grave's-niche thy sleeping-place ?   What-
then-is thy speech ?
And is-not-to God thy going ?   Who-then-is thy defender ?
Oft the time hath-awakened-thee, but-thou-hast-set-thyself-
to-slumber :
And admonition hath-drawn-thee, but-thou-hast-strained-
against-it ;
And warnings have-been-manifested to thee, but-thou-hast-
made-thyself-blind ;

generally omitted to hyphen the frequently recurring article, " of "
(before a genitive), pronouns and the copulative particle (" and ") :
none of these form separate words in Arabic.

And truth hath-been-established to thee, but-thou-hast-
disputed-it ;
And death hath-bid-thee-remember, but-thou-hast-sought-
to-forget,
And it-hath-been-in-thy-power to impart, and thou-
imparted'st not.

The poem I select as an example is translated
by Chenery as follows :—

1 Say to him who riddles questions that I am the discloser
of the secret which he hides.
Know that the deceased, in whose case the law preferred
the brother of his spouse to the son of his father,
Was a man who, of his free consent, gave his son in marriage
to his own mother-in-law : nothing strange in it.
Then the son died, but she was already pregnant by him,
and gave birth to a son like him :
And he was the son's son without dispute, and brother of
the grandfather's spouse without equivocation.
6 But the son of the true-born son is nearer to the grandfather, and takes precedence in the inheritance over
the brother ;
And therefore when he died, the eighth of the inheritance
was adjudged to the wife for her to take possession ;
And the grandson, who was really her brother by her
mother, took the rest ;
And the full brother was left out of the inheritance, and
we say thou hast only to bewail him.
This is my decision which every judge who judges will
pattern by, every lawyer.

Nothing could be more prosaic than this last
passage : and the only approximation in it to
parallelism is line 5 ; nevertheless it is, so far as
form goes, a perfect poem in the original : the
rhymes are correct, and the well-known metrical
form called *khafîf* is maintained throughout.

So far, then, as Arabic literature is concerned, it is an unquestionable fact that sustained and regular parallelism is a frequent characteristic of prose, while the absence of parallelism is frequently characteristic of metrical poems. And yet this is not of course the whole truth even in regard to Arabic literature. Most literatures consist of poetry and prose : and what in them is not poetical in form is prose, and *vice versa*. But in Arabic there are *three* forms of composition : (1) *nathr* ; (2) *naẓm*, or *ši'r* ; (3) *saj'*. The usual English equivalents for these three Arabic terms are (1) prose, (2) poetry, (3) rhymed prose ; but " rhymed prose " is not, of course, a *translation* of *saj'* : that word signifies primarily a cooing noise such as is made by a pigeon ; and its transferred use of a form of literary composition does not, as the English equivalent suggests, represent this form as a subdivision of prose. We should perhaps do more justice to some Arabic discussions or descriptions of *saj'* by terming it in English " unmetrical poetry " ; [1] and in some respects this " rhymed prose " or " unmetrical poetry " is more sharply marked off from ordinary

---

[1] " The oldest form of poetical speech was the *saj'*. Even after this stage of poetical form had long been surpassed and the metrical schemes had already been fully developed, the *saj'* ranked as a kind of *poetical* expression. Otherwise his opponents would certainly never have called Mohammed *ša'ir* (poet), for he never recited metrical poems, but only spoke sentences of *saj'*. In a saying attributed to Mohammed in the Tradition, too, it is said : ' This poetry is saj'.' "—Goldziher, *Abhandlungen zur arabischen Philologie*, p. 59.

prose than from the metrical poetry between
which and itself the simplest form of metrical
verse, termed *rejez*,[1] may be regarded as a transi-
tional style.

To the Arabic *saj'*, as *rhymed* prose, Hebrew
literature has, indeed, little or nothing analogous
to show ; to *saj'* as *unmetrical* poetry possibly,
and certainly in the opinion of some writers it has
much. For example, if we disregard the rhyme,
such passages as that cited above from Ḥarîri
have, in respect of parallelism of terms and the
structure of the corresponding clauses, much that
is similar alike in Hebrew psalms and Hebrew
prophecy. And to some of these we may return.

At this point I raise this question with reference
to Hebrew, and a similar question might be raised
with reference to Babylonian literature : ought
we to recognise *three* forms of composition as in
Arabic, or two only as in most literatures ? Since
rhyme is so conspicuous in Arabic, and so incon-
spicuous in Hebrew, this may at first seem a
singularly ill-considered question : and yet it is
not ; for however prominent rhyme may be in
Arabic poetry, it is perfectly possible to think
the rhyme away without affecting the essential
form of Arabic poetry, or of the Hebrew mediaeval
poetry that was modelled on it. It would have
been as easy for an Arabic poet, had he wished

---

[1] " Fundamentally *rejez* is nothing but rhythmically disciplined
saj'." " Many Arabic prosodists do not admit that *rejez* possesses the
character of *ši'r*."—Goldziher, *ibid.* pp. 76, 78.

it, as it was for Milton, to dispense with rhyme :
his poetry would have remained sufficiently distinguished from prose by its rigid obedience to
metrical laws. So, again, it is possible to think
away rhyme from the rhymed prose without
reducing that form of composition to plain prose ;
the parallelism, and a certain balance of the
clauses, would still remain ; and as a matter of
fact much early Arabic parallelistic composition
existed from which regular rhyme was absent.[1]

Had then the ancient Hebrew three forms of
composition—metrical poetry and plain prose,
and an intermediate type differing from poetry
by the absence of metre, and from prose by obedience to certain laws governing the mutual relations
between its clauses—a type for which we might
as makeshifts employ the terms unmetrical poetry
or parallelistic prose ?

I am not going to answer that question immediately, nor, perhaps, at all directly. But it
seems to me worth formulating, even if no certain
answer to it can be obtained. It may help to
keep possibilities before us : and, perhaps, also
to prevent a fruitless conflict over terms. In the
present discussion it is not of the first importance
to determine whether it is an abuse of language

---

[1] Goldziher (*op. cit.* pp. 62 ff.) argues that rhyme first began to be
employed in the formal public discourses or sermons (*khutba*) from the
third century of the Hejira onwards. " The rhetorical character of
such discourses in old time was concerned only with the parallelism of
which use was made " (p. 64).

to apply the term poetry to any part of Hebrew literature that does not follow well-defined metrical laws simply on the ground that it is marked by parallelism ; what is of importance is to determine if possible whether any parts of the Old Testament are in the strictest sense of the term metrical, and, alike whether that can be determined or not, to recognise the real distinction between what is parallelistic and what is not, to determine so far as possible the laws of this parallelism, and to recognise all parts of the ancient Hebrew literature that are distinguished by parallelism as related to one another in respect of form.

It is because I approach the question thus that I treat of parallelism before metre : parallelism is unmistakable, metre in Hebrew literature is obscure : the laws of Hebrew metre have been and are matters of dispute, and at times the very existence of metre in the Old Testament has been questioned. But let us suppose that Sievers, to whose almost overwhelming contributions [1] to this subject we owe so much, whatever our final judgment as to some even of his main conclusions may be, is right in detecting metre not only in what have commonly been regarded as the poetical parts of the Old Testament, but also throughout such books as Samuel and Genesis ; [2]

[1] See below, pp. 143-154.
[2] Ed. Sievers, *Metrische Studien*, ii. " Die hebräische Genesis," and *Metrische Studien*, iii. " Samuel."

even then the importance and value of the
question formulated above remains. It is true
that some questions may require resetting : if
Samuel and Genesis are metrical throughout, if
even the genealogies in Genesis v. and xxxvi. are,
so far as form goes, no less certainly poems than
the very prosaic Arabic poem cited above, it will
become less a question whether the Old Testament contains metrical poems than whether it
contains any plain prose at all. But the distinction between what is parallelism and what is not
will remain as before : we shall still have to distinguish between parallelistic prose and prose
that is not parallelistic, or, if the entire Old Testament be metrical, between parallelistic and non-
parallelistic poetry.

The general description and the fundamental
analysis of parallelism as given by Lowth, and
adopted by innumerable subsequent writers, are
so well known that they need not be referred to
at length here : nor will it be necessary to give
illustrations of the familiar types of parallelism
known as synonymous and antithetic. But I
may recall Lowth's own general statement in the
Preliminary Dissertation (*Isaiah*, ed. 3, p. xiv) :
" The correspondence of one verse, or line, with
another, I call parallelism. When a proposition
is delivered, and a second is subjoined to it, or
drawn under it, equivalent, or contrasted with it,
in sense ; or similar to it in the form of gram-

matical construction ; these I call parallel lines, and the words or phrases, answering one to another in the corresponding lines, parallel terms. Parallel lines may be reduced to three sorts : parallels synonymous, parallels antithetic and parallels synthetic."

The vulnerable point in Lowth's exposition of parallelism as the law of Hebrew poetry lies in what he found it necessary to comprehend under the term synthetic parallelism : his examples include, indeed, many couplets to which the term parallelism can with complete propriety be applied ; in such couplets the second line *repeats* by means of one or more synonymous terms *part* of the sense of the first ; and by means of one or more other terms *adds* something fresh, to which nothing in the first line is parallel. In virtue of the presence of some parallel terms such lines may be called parallel, and in virtue of the presence of some non-parallel terms they may be called synthetic, or in full the lines may be termed *synthetic parallels*, and the relation between them *synthetic parallelism* ; but more convenient terms for such lines, which are of very frequent occurrence,[1] and for the relation between them, would be *incomplete parallels* and *incomplete parallelism*. In any case, term them as we will, such examples as these are in reality not distinct from, but mere subdivisions of synonymous or antithetic parallel-

---

[1] Many examples are cited below : see pp. 72-82.

ism as the case may be. On the other hand there
are other examples of what Lowth called synthetic parallelism in which no term in the second
line is parallel to any term in the first, but in
which the second line consists entirely of what is
fresh and additional to the first ; and in some of
these examples the two lines are not even parallel
to one another by the correspondence of similar
grammatical terms. Two such lines as these
may certainly be called synthetic, but they are
parallel to one another merely in the way that
the continuation of the same straight line is
parallel to its beginning ; whereas synonymous
and antithetic parallelisms, even of the incomplete
kind, do really correspond to two separate and,
strictly speaking, parallel lines. Now, if the
term parallelism, even though it be qualified by
prefixing the adjective synthetic, be applied to
lines which, though synthetically related to one
another, are connected by no parallelism of terms
or sense, as well as to lines which are connected
by parallelism of terms or sense, then this term,
(synthetic) parallelism, will really conceal an all-
important difference under a mere semblance of
similarity. And, indeed, Lowth himself seems
to have been at least half-conscious that he was
making the term synthetic parallelism cover too
much : for he admits that " the variety in the
form of this synthetic parallelism is very great, and
the degrees of resemblance almost infinite ; so that

sometimes the scheme of the parallelism is very
subtile and obscure " (*Lectures*, ii. 52) ; he very
fairly adds in illustration a really test couplet, viz.—

I also have anointed my king on Sion,
     The mountain of my sanctity (Psa. ii. 6).[1]

He perceives, though he does not dwell on the
point, that this couplet marks zero among " the
degrees of resemblance almost infinite " ;   for
when he says, " the general form and nature of
the Psalm requires that it should be divided into
two parts or versicles ; as if it were,

' I also have anointed my king ;
    I have anointed him in Sion, the mountain of my sanctity,' "

he supplies, by repeating the words, " I have
anointed," the one and only point of resemblance
that exists between the two lines in his own
reconstruction of a couplet which, in its true
original form, is really distinguished by the entire
absence of parallelism between its lines. As in
this instance, so often, the use of the term synthetic parallelism has served to conceal the fact
that couplets of lines entirely non-parallel may
occur in poems in which most of the couplets are
parallels, and in which the " general form and
nature " of the poem suggest a division of the
synthetic but non-parallel elements " into two
parts or versicles."

[1] The verse is so divided by Lowth ; for reasons which will appear
later it should rather be divided :

I also have anointed my king,
     On Sion, the mountain of my holiness.

Not only did Lowth thus experience some doubt whether parallelism as analysed by himself was the one law of Hebrew poetry, but he expressly concludes his discussion of these " subtile and obscure " examples of synthetic parallelism with a suggestion that behind and accompanying parallelism there may be some *metrical* principle, though he judged that principle undiscovered and probably undiscoverable.

In spite of the general soundness of Lowth's exposition of parallelism, then, there is, perhaps, sufficient reason for a restatement ; and that I shall now attempt.

The extreme simplicity of Hebrew narrative has often been pointed out : the principle of attaching clause to clause by means of the " waw conversive " construction allows the narrative to flow on often for long periods uninterrupted, and, so to speak, in one continuous straight line. Now and again, and in certain cases more often, the line of successive events is broken to admit of some circumstance being described ; but the same single line is quickly resumed. An excellent example of this is found in Genesis i. : with the exception of verse 2, which describes the conditions existing at the time of the creative act mentioned in verse 1, the narrative runs on in a single continuous line down to verse 26 ; thus—

1   2   3   26
___ ___ _____

The continuity of a single line of narrative is in parts of Genesis ii. nearly as conspicuous : as to other parts of Genesis ii. something will have to be said later.[1] But if we turn to certain other descriptions of creation elsewhere in the Old Testament, we immediately discern a difference. Thus we read in Psalm xxxiii. 6, 7, 9 :—

By the word of Yahweh the heavens were made,
   And by the breath of his mouth all their host.
He gathered as into a flask the waters of the sea,
   He put into treasure-houses the deeps.
For *he* spake and it came to pass,
   He commanded and it stood sure ;

and in Isaiah xlv. 12 the words of Yahweh run as follows :—

I made the earth,
   And man upon it I created ;
My hands stretched out the heavens,
   And all their host I commanded.

And again in Proverbs viii. 24-29 creation is described in a series of subordinate periods :—

When there were no depths . . .
   When there were no fountains abounding with water ;
Before the mountains were settled,
   Before the hills . . .
While as yet he had not made the earth, nor the fields,
   Nor the beginning of the dust of the world ;
When he established the heavens . . .
   When he set a circle upon the face of the deep ;
When he made firm the skies above,
   When the fountains of the deep became strong,
When he gave to the sea its bound,
   That the waters should not transgress his commandment,
   When he marked out the foundations of the earth.

---

[1] See pp. 221 f.

Now whether, as Sievers maintains, Genesis i. is as strictly metrical as Psalms, Proverbs or Isaiah xl.-lxvi., or whether, as has been commonly assumed, Genesis i. is plain, unadorned and unmetrical prose, between Genesis i. on the one hand and the passages just cited from Psalm xxxiii., Isaiah xlv. and Proverbs viii. there are these differences : (1) whereas Genesis i. is carried along a *single* line of narrative, the other passages are, in the main at least, carried forward along *two* lines, parallel to one another in respect of their meaning, and of the terms in which that meaning is expressed ; (2) whereas Genesis i. consists in the main of connected clauses so that the whole may be represented by a single line *rarely* broken, the other passages consist of a number of independent clauses or sentences, so that they must be represented by lines *constantly* broken, and at fairly *regular* intervals, thus—

════   ════   ════

Stated otherwise, as contrasted with the simpler style of Genesis i., these other passages are characterised by the *independence* of their successive *clauses* or short sentences, and the *repetition* of the same thought or statement *by means of corresponding terms* in successive short clauses or sections. Where repetition and what may be termed parallelism in its fullest and strictest sense occur, a constant breaking of the line of narrative or statement is the necessary consequence : a

thought is expressed, or a statement made, but
the writer, instead of proceeding at once to express the natural sequel to his thought or the next
statement, breaks off and harks back in order to
repeat in a different form the thought or statement which he has already expressed, and only
after this break and repetition pursues the line of
his thought or statement ; that is to say, one line
is, as it were, forsaken to pursue the parallel line
up to a corresponding point, and then after the
break the former line is resumed.   But the break
in the line and the independence of clauses may
occur even where there is no repetition of thought
or correspondence of terms ; just as breaks
necessarily occur *occasionally* in such simple
narratives as that of Genesis i.   The differences
between the two styles here shade off into one
another ; and everything ultimately depends on
the frequency and *regularity* with which the
breaks occur.   Where the breaks occur with as
much regularity as when the successive clauses
are parallel to one another, we may, even though
parallelisms of terms or thought between the
clauses are absent, term the style parallelistic,
as preserving one of the necessary consequences
of actual parallelism.

But not only is the question whether a passage
belongs to the one style or the other, so far as it
depends on the recurrence of breaks and the con-
sequent independence of the clauses, one of degree;

the question whether two such independent lines are correspondent or parallel to one another is also at times a question both of degree and of exact interpretation. To return to the passages already cited ; when the Psalmist writes :

> He gathered as into a flask the waters of the sea,

and then adds,

> He put into treasure houses the deeps,

it is clear that at the end of the first line he breaks the straight line of continuous statement : the second line adds nothing to the bare sense, and it carries the writer no further forward than the first ; the two sentences thus correspond strictly to two *equal* and parallel lines : where the first begins the second also begins, and where the first ends there also the second ends : each line records exactly the same fact and the same amount of fact by means of different but synonymous terms. And the same is true of the two lines,

> For he spake and it came to pass,
> He commanded and it stood sure.

We can without difficulty and with perfect propriety represent these two couplets thus—

═══   ═══

But what are we to say of,

> I made the earth,
> And man upon it I created ?

This is certainly not the simplest form of putting the thought to be expressed : the terms " made "

and " created " are synonymous, and the whole
thought could have been fully expressed in the
briefer form, " I made the earth, and man upon
it." But have we, even so, completely delimited
substance and form, the thought to be expressed
and the art used in its expression ? Probably
not ; the writer continues :

> My hands stretched out the heavens,
> And all their host I commanded.

Here we cannot simply drop a term as in the
previous lines and leave the sense unimpaired ;
but the correspondence of thought between the
two sets of statements may yield a clue to the
essential thought of the whole ; as the first two
lines mean no more than this : I created the earth
and its inhabitants ; so the second means simply
this : I created the heavens and their inhabitants.
But have we even yet determined the fundamental thought of the passage ? Did the writer
really mean to express two distinct thoughts in
each set of lines ? Was he thinking of the creation of man as something independent of the
creation of the earth ? Did he mean to refer
first to one creative act and then to a second and
independent creative act ? Or did he regard
the creation of man as part of the creation of
the earth, so that his lines are really *parallel* statements, a parallelism, to wit, of the part with the
whole, and not *successive* statements ? This
seems to me most probable ; his thought was :

Yahweh created the heavens and the earth ; but instead of expressing this in its simplest form by a sentence that would properly be represented by a single continuous line, he has artistically expressed it in a form that may once again, though with less complete propriety, perhaps, than in the case of the couplet from Psalm xxxiii., be expressed by two groups of parallel and broken lines :

If the thought of man and the host of heaven had a greater independence than this view recognises, we must still treat the statement (which is not, like Genesis i., the continuous statement of successive acts) not as a continuous line, but as a line broken at very regular intervals, thus—

though, if we wished diagrammatically to bring out the similarity in the verbal cast or grammatical build of the clauses rather than the independence of the thought, we might still adopt the form—

Before leaving this diagrammatic description I merely add, without illustrating the statement, that a poem rarely proceeds far along two parallel lines each broken at the same regular intervals, thus—

Either the two lines are broken at different points,

or one is for the time being followed to the neglect
of the other, thus—

══ ══ ══ ══ ── ── ══

I pass now by a different method to a more
detailed examination of parallel lines, and of the
degree and character of the correspondence
between them.   Irrespective of particles a line
or section to which another line or section approximately corresponds, consists of two, three,
four, five or six words, very seldom of more.
Complete parallelism may be said to exist when
every single term in one line is parallel to a term
in the other, or when at least every term or
group of terms in one line is paralleled by a corresponding term or group of terms in the other.
Incomplete parallelism exists when only some of
the terms in each of two corresponding lines are
parallel to one another, while the remaining
terms express something which is stated once
only in the two lines.   Incomplete parallelism
is far more frequent than complete parallelism.
Both complete parallelism and incomplete parallelism admit of many varieties ; and this great
variety and elasticity of parallelism may perhaps
best be studied by means of symbols, even though
it is difficult to reduce all the phenomena to
rigidly constant and unambiguous symbolic
formulæ.   I have already elsewhere [1] suggested
that the varieties of parallelism may be con-

[1] *Isaiah* (" International Critical Comm."), p. lxvi.

veniently described by denoting the terms in the first line by letters—a . b . c, etc.—and those in the second line by the differentiated letters— a′ . b′ . c′, where the terms, without being identical (in which case a . b . c would be used for the second line as well as for the first), correspond, or by fresh letters—d . e . f, where fresh terms corresponding to nothing in the first line occur.

The simplest form of complete parallelism is represented by   a . b

a′ . b′ :

here each line consists of two terms each of which corresponds to a term in the corresponding position in the other line. Examples are—

אחלקם ביעקב

ואפיצם בישראל

I-will-divide-them [1] in-Jacob,
And-I-will-scatter-them in-Israel.—Gen. xlix. 7c.d.

משגיח מן־החלנות

מציץ מן־החרכים

He-looketh-in at-the-windows,
He-glanceth through-the-lattice.
Cant. ii. 9 (the same chapter contains several other examples).

נעויתי משמע

נבהלתי מראות

I-am-bent-with-pain at-what-I-hear,
I-am-dismayed at-what-I-see.—Isa. xxi. 3.

---

[1] Where the suffix in one line corresponds to a noun in the other it may sometimes be convenient to represent the suffix by an independent symbol. If both suffixes were so represented here the scheme would be

a . b . c
a′ . b . c′.

כי רבו פשעיהם
עצמו משבותיהם

For their-transgressions are-many,
    Their-backturnings are-increased.—Jer. v. 6.
Hear Thy-servant,
    And-give-ear-to my-petition.—Apoc. Bar. xlviii. 12.

Complete parallelism between lines each containing three terms will be represented by

a . b . c
a' . b' . c'

Examples are—

חכלילי עינים מיין
ולבן שנים מחלב

Red-are his-eyes with-wine,
    And-white-are his-teeth with-milk.—Gen. xlix. 12.

מנשמת אלוה יאבדו
ומרוח אפו יכלו

By-the-breath of-God they-perish,
    And-by-the-blast of-his-anger are-they-consumed.—Job.
iv. 9.

כי-שמים כעשן נמלחו
והארץ כבגד תבלה

For the-heavens like-smoke shall-vanish-away (?),
    And-the-earth like-a-garment shall-wax-old.—Isa. li. 6.

More frequent than the fundamental scheme as given above and just illustrated are variations upon it, of which examples will be given below.

Complete parallelism of lines with four terms each, the terms being symmetrically arranged, will be represented by

a . b . c . d
a' . b' . c' . d'

An example is—

מענה רך ישיב חמה
ודבר עצב יעלה אף

A-soft answer turneth-away wrath,
But-a-grievous word stirreth-up anger.—Prov. xv. 1.

This scheme occurs not infrequently in antithetic proverbs, and Proverbs xv. contains several
other examples ; but it is rare elsewhere.   Variations on this scheme also will be given below.

Where the parallel sections consist of more
than four terms, and sometimes when they contain as few as four terms, each section tends to
break up into two of those independent clauses
which we have seen to be in part the necessary
consequence of parallelism, and in part a common,
even when not a necessary, accompaniment of
the style distinguished from simple narrative.
For example, Isaiah xlix. 2 is one of the nearest
approximations to the scheme,

a . b . c . d . e . f
a'. b'. c'. d'. e'. f'

but here the last two terms in each section stand
independent of the foregoing ; thus :

And-he-made my-mouth as-a-sharp sword :   in-the-shadow
of-his-hand he-hid-me ;
And-he-made-me[1] into-a-polished arrow :   in-his-quiver he-
concealed-me.

---

[1] The suffix *me* (b') is here parallel to the independent term *my
mouth* (b) ; and so is the suffix *his* in *his quiver* to the independent term
his hand : in this case, however, I have represented *shadow of his hand*
under the single symbol (e).

Such a combination of clauses is commonly
termed " alternate parallelism " and is said to
consist of four lines, of which the third is parallel
to the first and the fourth to the second. This
may be a convenient description : but the main
point is that, within the main independent
sections indicated by the parallelism, other
almost equally independent breaks giving rise
to subordinate independent clauses occur. This
fact is emphasised in many specimens of Arabic
" rhymed prose " ; in the passage already cited
on pp. 42 f. from Ḥarîri, almost all the parallel
sections fall into two independent clauses ; and
it is these independent, but, from the point of
view of the parallelism, subordinate, sections that
rhyme with one another ; that is to say, similarity
of rhyme connects, while emphasising their distinction, the shorter independent clauses which
are commonly not parallel to one another, and
change of rhyme marks off the well-defined longer
sections which are regularly parallel to one
another.   It is interesting to observe that in the
lines cited from Isaiah xlix. it is the entire parallel
periods and not the subsections that rhyme with
one another, though in view of the irregular use
of rhyme in Hebrew this may be a mere accident—

וישם פי כחרב חדה   בצל ידו החביאָנִי
וישימני לחץ ברור   באשפתו הסתירָנִי

In the illustrations of parallelism which have

been given so far not only has there been complete correspondence, term by term, between the parallel lines, but each corresponding term in the second line has occurred in the exactly corresponding position in the second line.   But in any considerable passage Hebrew writers introduce in various ways great variety of effect, a far greater variety, I believe, than was commonly sought or obtained by Arabic writers.   These varieties of parallelism can be readily and conveniently shown by a use such as I have suggested of symbols.   I proceed to classify and illustrate some of the chief classes of variations on the fundamental schemes which have been already described and illustrated.

I

Variety is attained by varying the position of the corresponding terms in the two lines.

In the simplest form of parallelism, which consists of lines containing two terms only, only one variation is possible from the scheme,

$$a \,.\, b$$
$$a' \,.\, b'$$

of which several illustrations have already been given.   This of course is

$$a \,.\, b$$
$$b' \,.\, a'$$

and this variation occurs very frequently, *e.g.*—

אם תבקשנה ככסף
וכמטמנים תחפשנה

If thou-seek-her as-silver,
And-as-for-hid-treasures search-for-her.—Prov. ii. 4.

אל־תצאי השדה
ובדרך אל־תלכי

Go-not-forth into-the-field,
And-by-the-way walk-not.—Jer. vi. 25.

Further examples will be found, for example, in Deuteronomy xxxii. 16, xxxiii. 9 d, e.

As the number of terms increases the greater becomes the possibility of variety and the number of actual variations; thus

$$a \ . \ b \ . \ c$$
$$a' \ . \ b' \ . \ c'$$

can alternate with

$$a \ . \ b \ . \ c$$
$$a' \ . \ c' \ . \ b'$$

or any of the other four possible permutations. Of the variation just given, Proverbs ii. 2 is an example—

להקשיב לחכמה אזנך
תטה לבך לתבונה

So-that-thou-incline unto-wisdom thine-ear,
(And-) apply thine-heart to-understanding.

The same variation of order, but with the repetition instead of a variation of the second term of

F

the first line at the end of the second line (*i.e.*
b instead of b'), occurs in Job xxxii. 17—

אענה אף־אני חלקי
אחוה דעי אף־אני

Will-answer I also my-part,
Will-declare my-knowledge I also.

An example may be found in Deuteronomy
xxxii. 30 a, b of

a . b . c
b' . a' . c'

איכה ירדף אחד אלף
ושנים יניסו רבבה

How should one pursue a-thousand,
Or-two put-to-flight ten-thousand.

The same poem also contains four examples
(Deuteronomy xxxii. 3, 18, 23, 38) of the scheme

a . b . c
c' . a' . b'

It may suffice to cite *v.* 18 (reading תשה for
תשי)—

צור ילדך תשה
ותשכח אל מחללך

The rock that-bare-thee thou-wast-unmindful-of,
And-forgattest the God that-gave-thee-birth.

Another example of this scheme may be found
in Proverbs v. 5.

The tendency in poetry to give the verb its
normal (prose) position at the beginning of the
first line, but, in order to gain variety, to throw

the verb to the end of the second line,[1] renders
the two remaining variations of the fundamental
scheme, viz.—

a . b . c

b′ . c′ . a′

and

a . b . c

c′ . b′ . a′

very frequent, though of course both of these
schemes may also arise from other causes.[2]
Examples of the former of the two schemes just
given are—

על־כן הכם אריה מיער

זאב ערבות ישדדם

Therefore shall-slay-them a-lion out-of-the-forest,
A-wolf of-the-steppes shall-spoil-them.—Jer. v. 6.

אל־תתהדר לפני מלד

ובמקום גדולׂים אל־תעמד

Glorify-not-thyself in-the-presence of-the-king,
And-in-the-place of-great-men stand-not.—Prov. xxv. 6.

Four further examples may be found in
Proverbs ii. 5, 8, 10, 20. See also *e.g.* Job iii.
6 b, c; Amos v. 23; Isaiah xi. 6 a, b, lx. 16 a, b;
Judith xvi. 10 (the last couplet in the passage
cited above, p. 25).

---

[1] The alternative of throwing the verb to the end of the first line,
and giving it the normal (prose) position in the second line, thus bringing
the two verbs together, is much less frequent. But a good example of
this is Deut. xxxii. 38 : see also *vv.* 3 and 18 in the same chapter.

[2] As *e.g.* in Job iv. 17.

Examples of

a . b . c

c′ . b′ . a′

are

מי־מדד בשעלו מים

ושמים בזרת תכן

Who hath-measured with-the-hollow-of-his-hand the waters,
Or-the-heavens with-a-span hath-regulated ?—Isa. xl. 12.

וימלאו אסמיך שבע

ותירוש יקביך יפרצו

That thy-barns may-be-filled-with plenty
And-that with-new-wine thy-vats may-overflow.

—Prov. iii. 10.

See also *e.g.* Isaiah xl. 26 c, d, 27 c, d ; Amos v. 7 ;
Psalm iii. 8 c, d.

The *possible* variations on

a . b . c . d

a′ . b′ . c′ . d′

are of course much more numerous ; the actual
examples are far fewer, partly because *complete*
parallelism over these longer periods is much
rarer, partly because these parallelisms in four
terms occur particularly in Proverbs, and proverbs,
being complete in themselves, do not call for the
variety which is naturally enough desired in a
long continuous passage.   It may suffice to refer
to one variation : when the first line begins with
a verb and its object, immediately following, is
expressed by an independent term, and the desire
for variety throws the corresponding clause to

the end of the second line, the scheme naturally produced is

a . b . c . d
c' . d' . a' . b'

as for example in

והכה ¹ ערץ בשבט פיו

וברוח שפתיו ימית רשע

And-he-shall-smite the-violent¹ with-the-rod of-his-mouth,
And-with-the-breath of-his-lips shall-he-slay the-wicked.
—Isa. xi. 4.

II

Another way of obtaining variety is to use in the second line two or more terms which, taken together, are parallel in sense to a corresponding number of terms in the first line, though the separate terms of the one combination are not parallel to the separate terms of the other combination. In its extreme form parallelism of this variety consists of two entire lines completely parallel in sense but with no two terms taken separately parallel to one another.² Denoting correspondence as before by a . a', etc., and the number of terms above one in which particular corresponding ideas are expressed by a figure attached to the letters, the kind of schemes that occur are—

a2 . b
a'2 . b'

¹ Reading עריץ for ארץ, *the earth.*
² See *e.g.* Gen. xlix. 15 c, d, 20 ; Ps. xxi. 6 ; Job iii. 10, 23, iv. 14.

For example—

עדה וצלה שמען קולי

נשי למך האזנה אמרתי

Adah and-Ṣillah, hear my-voice,
Ye-wives of-Lamech give-ear-to my-word.—Gen. iv. 23.

Here, too, further variety may be obtained by varying the position of the corresponding terms or groups of terms, so that such schemes as

$$a \ . \ b2$$
$$b'2 \ . \ a'$$

arise ; an example of this is Proverbs ii. 17,

העזבת אלוף נעוריה

ואת ברית אלהיה שכחה

Who-forsaketh the-friend of-her-youth,
And-the-covenant of-her-God forgetteth.

And another very effective variation arises when what is expressed by two terms in the first line is expressed by one in the second line, which in turn has two other terms corresponding to one in the first : one such variation is

$$a2 \ . \ b$$
$$a' \ . \ b'2$$

which is exemplified by Genesis xlix. 24,

ותשב באיתן קשתו

ויפזו זרעי ידיו

And-his-bow abode firm,
And-the-arms of-his-hands were-agile—

where the two words ותשב באיתן, *abode firm*, taken

together are parallel to וימזו, *were agile,* and the
single term קשתו, *his-bow,* to the two terms זרעי
ידיו, *the-arms of-his-hands,* taken together.

An example of

$$a \,.\, b \,.\, c2$$
$$a \,.\, c' \,.\, b'2$$

is afforded by Job iii. 17,

שם רשעם חדלו רגז

ושם ינוחו יגיעי כח

where ינוחו, *are-at-rest,* corresponds to חדלו רגז,
cease-from raging, and the single term *wicked* to
the phrase יגיעי כח, which is compound in Hebrew,
though it is represented by the single word *weary*
in E.V.

Once more in Deuteronomy xxxii. 11,

יפרש כנפיו יקחהו

ישאהו על־אברתו

He-spread-out his-wings, he-took-him,
He-lifted-him-up upon-his-pinions,

the single term על־אברתו, *upon-his-pinions,* at the
end of the second line is parallel to the two terms
יפרש כנפיו, *he-spread-out his-wings,* at the beginning
of the first line, taken together, and the scheme is

$$a2 \,.\, b$$
$$b' \,.\, a'$$

Further examples of some of these or similar
schemes will be found in Deuteronomy xxxii.
22 c, d, 35 c, d ; Psalms ii. 2 a, b, 9, lxviii. 10 ;

Proverbs xv. 9; Job iii. 25, iv. 4, xxxiii. 11;
Canticles ii. 3 c, d, 12.

Occasionally one or other of the compound
parallel phrases is interrupted by the insertion
of another parallel term in the midst of it; so,
for example, in Psalm vi. 6,

כי אין במות זכרך
בשאול מי יודה לך

For there-is in-death no-remembrance-of-thee;
In-Sheol who shall-praise thee?

death and *Sheol* are parallel terms, and the phrase
there is no remembrance of thee to the interrogative
phrase, which is equivalent to a negative statement, *who shall praise thee?* But in the first
line the parallel term is inserted between the two
parts of the parallel phrase.

III

The third main method of introducing variety
into parallelism and avoiding the monotonous
repetition of the same scheme consists in the adop-
tion of various forms of incomplete parallelism.

The variety of effect rendered possible by this
method is immense, except in the shortest
parallels consisting of two terms only: with
these the fundamental variations are reduced
to two, viz.—

a . b
b' . c

and

a . b

a' . c

Examples of these are—

מדוע קדמוני ברכים

ומה שדים כי־אינק

Wherefore did-the-knees receive-me,
    And-why the-breasts that I-should-suck (Job iii. 12),

and

צרה החזקתני

חיל כיולדה

Anguish hath-seized-me,
    Pangs as-of-a-woman-in-travail (Jer. vi. 24),

unless we prefer to treat the former of these examples on the ground of the differentiation of the interrogative particles as an example of

a . b . c

a' . c' . d

and the latter example as

a . b

a'2

The latter kind of ambiguity frequently arises.

Further variety is obtained when variations corresponding to those illustrated under I. and II. are combined with incomplete parallelism : this frequently happens, especially when one at least of the parallel members contains more than two terms. But before giving illustrations of such variations it will be convenient to point out that incomplete parallelisms fall into two broad classes which may be distinguished as *incomplete parallelism with compensation* and *incomplete parallelism without compensation*. If one line contains a given number of terms and another line a smaller number of terms, the parallelism is generally [1] incomplete ; such incomplete parallelism may be termed incomplete parallelism without compensation ; but if the two lines contain the same number of terms, though only some of the terms in the two lines are parallel, the lines may be said to constitute incomplete parallelism with compensation.   Thus such schemes as

$$a \cdot b \cdot c$$
$$a' \cdot b'$$

or

$$a \cdot b \cdot c$$
$$a'2$$

are incomplete without compensation ; whereas such schemes as

$$a \cdot b \cdot c$$
$$a' \cdot d \cdot c'$$

or

$$a \cdot b \cdot c$$
$$a'2 \cdot b'$$

are incomplete parallelism with compensation.

[1] Not invariably ; for such schemes as

$$a2 \cdot b$$
$$a' \cdot b'$$

give to the two lines an unequal number of terms, and yet the parallelism may be said to be complete.   See *e.g.* Lam. ii. 11, cited below, p. 97.

I now give illustrations of different schemes of both types.

A

Incomplete parallelism without compensation.

ואשיבה שפטיך כבראשנה
ויעציך כבתחלה

I-will-restore thy-judges as-at-the-first,
  And-thy-counsellors as-at-the-beginning (Isa. i. 26),

is an example of

a . b . c
b′ . c′

and so are Proverbs ii. 18; Canticles ii. 1, 14; Numbers xxiii. 19 c, d, 24 a, b, xxiv. 5 a, b; Psalm vi. 2; Deuteronomy xxxii. 7 c, d, 21 a, b, 34.[1]

רכב בשמים בעזרך
ובגאותו שחקים

Who-rideth through-the-heavens as-thy-help,
  And-in-his-dignity through-the-skies (Deut. xxxiii. 26),

---

[1] A further example of this scheme occurs in the present text of Hos. vii. 1—

ונגלה עון אפרים | ורעות שמרון,

Revealed are the iniquity of Ephraim
And the wickedness of Samaria.

On the second of these lines Harper ("International Crit. Comm.") remarks : " Here a word is needed to complete the parallelism as well as the metre." But this is incorrectly put, unless it can be shown that incomplete parallelism is impossible, or improbable in this connexion ; and this cannot be done in view of another case of incomplete parallelism (a . b . c | a′ . c′) in v. 3, which Harper retains. Since the line quoted above and v. 3 are *possibly* not metrically identical (v. 3 being perhaps 3 : 3), a *metrical* consideration in favour of supplying a word in v. 1 *may* survive ; but the argument from parallelism is invalid.

is an example of

a . b . c
c′ . b′

and so is Isaiah xlii. 23 a, b.

איש הרגתי לפצעי
וילד לחברתי

A man have I slain for wounding me,
    And a youth for bruising me (Gen. iv. 23),

is an example of

a . b . c
a′ .   c′

and so is Hosea vii. 3.

כי מגפן סדם גפנם
ומשדמת עמרה

For of the vine of Sodom is their vine,
    And of the fields of Gomorrah (Deut. xxxii. 32),

is an example of

a . b . c
a′ . b′

B

Incomplete parallelism with compensation.

יהוה בצאתך משעיר
בצעדך משדה אדם

Yahweh, when-thou-wentest-forth out-of-Seir,
    When-thou-marchedst out-of-the-field of-Edom (Jud. v. 4),

is an example of

a . b . c
b′ . c′2

and other examples are Deuteronomy xxxii.
13 c, d, xxxiii. 23; Job iii. 11; Isaiah xli. 26 a, b,
lx. 3.

וישכן ישראל בטח
בדד עין יעקב

And-so-dwelt Israel securely,
  By-itself the-fountain of-Jacob (Deut. xxxiii. 28),

is an example of

a . b . c
c' . b'2

and other examples are Amos v. 24; Proverbs ii.
1, 7; Job iii. 20; while Isaiah xliii. 3 c, d ex-
emplifies the scheme

a . b . c
c'2 . b'

In Judges v. 26,

ידה ליתד תשלחנה
וימינה להלמות עמלים

Her-hand to-the-tent-peg she-stretched-forth,
  And-her-right-hand to-the-workmen's mallet,

will be found an example of

a ..b . c
a' . b'2

and another example of the same scheme in
Psalm xxi. 11.

Examples of compensation by means of a
fresh term or terms are—

יהוה מסיני בא
וזרח משעיר למו

Yahweh from-Sinai came,
  And-beamed-forth from-Seir unto-them (Deut. xxxiii. 2),

which is an example of

a . b . c
c′ . b′ . d

and

ישימו ליהוה כבוד
ותהלתו באיים יגידו

Let-them-ascribe unto-Yahweh glory,
And-his-praise in-the-isles let-them-declare (Isa. xlii. 12),

which is an example of

a . b . c
c′ . d . a′

Examples of distichs in which each line has but one parallel term and two terms non-parallel are given below (p. 94), and instances of compensation by a fresh term in lines containing two terms only have already been given above (p. 73).

I will conclude the present discussion with two illustrations of the value of a minuter analysis of parallelism than has hitherto been considered necessary, and of some such method as I have been suggesting of measuring or classifying the various types of parallelism.

An effective scheme of parallelism that occasionally occurs consists of two lines each containing three terms but held together by a single parallel term in each line, these parallel terms standing one at the end of the first line, and the other at the beginning of the second. The scheme is—

a . b . c
c′ . d . e

Now, if the articulation of the parallelism is not observed, couplets of this type are reduced to ordinary prose, or even to nonsense, or at best feeble repetition ; but if it is properly articulated, the couplet is an effective form of " synthetic parallelism " as Lowth would have called it, of incomplete parallelism with compensation as I should term it.   Examples of this type occurring in Genesis xlix. 9 (cf. Num. xxiv. 9) and Deuteronomy xxxiii. 11 are correctly articulated in the Revised Version :

> He-stooped-down, he-couched as-a-lion,
> And-as-a-lioness : who shall-rouse-him-up ?
>
> Smite-through the-loins of-them-that-rise-up-against-him,
> And-of-them-that-hate-him, that they-rise-not-again.

But if the parallelism is not correctly perceived, and the words otherwise articulated, how unsatisfactory does the former of these couplets become !   " He stooped down, he couched as a lion and as a lioness : who shall rouse him up ? " This suggests a comparison with two different beasts, whereas the parallelism really expresses comparison with the lion-class, which it denotes by the use of two synonymous terms.   Yet this very mistaken articulation is found in Numbers xxiii. 23, both in the Revised Version and, I regret to say, in my commentary on Numbers. If we articulate

> Now shall it be said of Jacob and Israel,
> What hath God wrought !

the natural suggestion is that Jacob and Israel
are different entities, which they are not ; Jacob
and Israel are here, as elsewhere in these poems
(Num. xxiii. 7, 10, 21, 23 ; xxiv. 5, 17, 18 f.),
synonymous terms belonging to different members
of the parallelism. The proper articulation of
the passage is,

> Now shall it be said of Jacob,
> And of Israel, What hath God wrought !

and it is interesting to observe that this not very
common type of parallelism occurs twice (see
also xxiv. 9) in the oracles of Balaam.

The strongly marked pause in the middle, and
the marked independence of the last part, of the
second line are characteristic of all the distichs
just cited. If from these observations we turn
immediately to Hosea iv. 13 c, d, we shall probably conclude that the difficulties which have
been felt with regard to these lines are unreal,
that the emendations which have been proposed [1]
wholly unnecessary, and that, in respect of
parallelism and structure, the lines closely resemble Numbers xxiii. 23, xxiv. 9, and Deuteronomy xxxiii. 11 ; in this case the correct articulation is,

תחת אלון ולבנה
ואלה כי־טוב צלה

> Under oak and poplar,
> And terebinth : for good is the shade thereof.

---

[1] See *e.g.* W. R. Harper, *Commentary on Amos and Hosea* (" International Critical Commentary "), pp. 260, 261.

My second illustration of the advantages of some method that enables similarities and dis-similarities of parallelism to be easily detected and presented is of a different character, and shows the bearing of these studies on textual criticism.

Psalm cxiv. consists of eight couplets, each of which, in the present text at all events, shows one form or another of incomplete parallelism, for the most part with compensation. The char-acteristic incompleteness of the parallelism rings through even a translation :

> 1 When Israel went forth out of Egypt,
>   The house of Jacob from a barbaric people,
> 2 Judah became his sanctuary,
>   Israel his dominion.
>
> 3 The sea saw it and fled,
>   Jordan turned backward,
> 4 The mountains skipped like rams,
>   The hills like young sheep.
>
> 5 What aileth thee, O thou sea, that thou fleest,
>   Thou Jordan, that thou turnest back ?
> 6 Ye mountains that ye skip like rams,
>   Ye hills like young sheep ?
>
> 7 At the presence of the Lord tremble, O earth,
>   At the presence of the God of Jacob,
> 8 Which turned the rock into a pool of water,
>   The flint into a fountain of water.

The scheme in the Hebrew is as follows :

$$1\ a\ .\ b\ .\ c \qquad\qquad 2\ a\ .\ b\ .\ c$$
$$b'2\ .\ c'2 \qquad\qquad\qquad b'\ .\ c'$$

G

```
3 a . b . c            6 a . b . c
    a'    c'2              a'    c'2
4 a . b . c            7 a . b . c . d
    a'    c'2              a . b'2
5 a . b . c            8 a . b . c2
    b' . c'2               b' . c'2
```

There seems to me strong ground for holding that this consistent use of incomplete parallelism was intentional, or, at any rate, if not intentional, it is at least an unconscious expression of the writer's general preference—in a word, it is a stylistic characteristic; as such it ought not without good reason to be obliterated. For this reason Dr. Briggs's reconstruction of this Psalm in the "International Critical Commentary" is open to grave objection. The emendations proposed by Dr. Briggs and the effect of them on the parallelism is as follows : (1) he strikes out as glosses verses 2 and 8, though both verses show the characteristic incomplete parallelism ; (2) in verse 7 he deletes חולי, *tremble*; then אדון becomes construct before ארץ, and the expression " Lord of the earth " becomes parallel to " God of Jacob," and the verse as a whole an example of complete parallelism,

```
a . b . c
a . b' . c'
```

(3) in verses 4 b and 6 b he inserts הלְיׁ (of which חולי in verse 7 is supposed to be a misplaced cor-

ruption), thus again turning incomplete into regular complete parallelism,

$$a \cdot b \cdot c$$
$$a' \cdot b' \cdot c'$$

Thus merely by a study of the parallelism this reconstruction is rendered improbable quite apart from the question whether metre requires any such changes, or whether Dr. Briggs's is not a much more prosaic poem than that of the Hebrew text.

In the LXX Psalm cxiv. is united with Psalm cxv. This union has been very generally regarded as not representing the original text : in addition to the reasons commonly given for holding that the division between the two Psalms in the Hebrew text is correct, we may now add the difference in the type of parallelism. In cxv. 5-7 we find three successive examples of complete parallelism, and although elsewhere in the Psalm there are examples of incomplete parallelism, these are mostly incomplete parallelisms of a different kind from those which occur in Psalm cxiv.

CHAPTER III

PARALLELISM AND RHYTHM IN THE BOOK OF LAMENTATIONS

CHAPTER III

PARALLELISM AND RHYTHM IN THE BOOK OF LAMENTATIONS

THE Book of Lamentations has played a conspicuous part in the constantly renewed discussions of the subject of Hebrew rhythm. Apart from any analysis of its cause, and without any exceptional degree of attention, the reader of the Hebrew text, or even indeed of the English version, of the Lamentations, perceives something in the rhythm or cast of the sentences that is common to practically the whole of the first four chapters of the book. This same something that brings these four poems into a common class, sharply marks them off from the fifth chapter or poem, and at the same time, too, from the greater quantity of the poetry of the Old Testament, though careful examination has discovered not a little in various books of the Old Testament that resembles the first four chapters of Lamentations in the peculiarity in question.

But though this striking peculiarity is common

to the four poems constituting the first four
chapters of Lamentations, there are other features
that distinguish them one from another—the
differing alphabetic sequences that are followed
by the initial letters of successive divisions of the
poems (פ preceding ע in ii., iii., and iv., following
it in i.), the differing lengths of the divisions,
the differing degrees of passion, spontaneity and
vividness with which the subject, common to
them all, is handled. These differences have
attracted and received attention ; but, so far as
I am aware, the differences in the use of parallelism as between the four poems have not yet
been analysed : and, yet, such differences exist.
Owing to uncertainties of text and interpretation, it does not seem to me easy or even practic-
able to give exact statistics of these differences ;
yet, by the help of a more accurate measurement
of parallelism, such as I have suggested in the
previous chapter, it will, I hope, be possible to
make manifest the existence and general character of the differences ; and, in any case, by an
examination of these chapters, I hope to carry
further my line of approach to rhythmical questions through parallelism.

Though I cannot undertake any comprehensive survey of the history of the study of
rhythm in Lamentations, it will be worth while
to refer to two discussions of the subject—that
of Lowth, who was the first to point out and to

attempt to analyse the rhythmical peculiarity of Lamentations i.-iv., and that of Budde, who, by a series of contributions to this subject, beginning with his fundamental article in the *Zeitschrift für die alttestamentliche Wissenschaft* for 1882, has profoundly influenced subsequent investigation and terminology.

Lowth devoted his 22nd and 23rd lectures to the Hebrew elegy, and he returned to some of the points then discussed in the preliminary dissertation to his *Isaiah* (vol. i. pp. xxxiv-xliii, ed. 3). The genius and origin of the Hebrew elegy, of the *ḳinah* or *nehi* as the Hebrews called it themselves, he traces to their manner of celebrating the funeral rites ; and in particular to the employment of professional mourners who sang dirges. The natural language of grief, he remarks, " consists of a plaintive, intermitted, concise form of expression " : and as in other arts, so in that of the Hebrew elegy, " perfection consisted in the exact imitation of nature. The funereal dirges were, therefore, composed in general upon the model of those complaints which flow naturally and spontaneously from the afflicted heart : the sentences were abrupt, mournful, pathetic, simple and unembellished. . . . They consisted of verse and were chanted to music." [1]

Lowth then points out the peculiarity of the

_____
[1] *Lectures* . . . (ed. Lond. 1787), ii. 123, 127.

first four poems in Lamentations, and remarks :
" We are not to suppose this peculiar form of
versification utterly without design or importance :
on the contrary, I am persuaded, that the prophet
adopted this kind of theme as being more diffuse,
more copious, more tender, in all respects better
adapted to melancholy subjects. I must add,
that in all probability the funeral dirges, which
were sung by mourners, were commonly composed in this kind of verse : for whenever, in the
prophets, any funereal lamentations occur or any
passages formed upon that plan, the versification
is, if I am not mistaken, of this protracted kind.
. . . However, the same kind of metre is sometimes, though rarely, employed upon other occasions. . . . There are, moreover, some poems
manifestly of the elegiac kind, which are composed in the usual metre, and not in unconnected
stanzas, according to the form of a funeral dirge." [1]

The peculiarities of this elegiac versification
are best summarised in the *Isaiah*, as follows :
" The closing pause of each line is generally very
full and strong : and in each line commonly,
towards the end, at least beyond the middle of
it, there is a small rest, or interval, depending on
the sense and grammatical construction, which
I would call a half-pause. . . . The conjunction
ו . . . seems to be frequently and studiously
omitted at the half-pause : the remaining clause

[1] *Lectures*, ii. pp. 136, 137.

being added, to use a grammatical term, by apposition to some word preceding ; or coming in as an adjunct, or circumstance depending on the former part, and completing the sentence." [1]

The parallelism accompanying the versification of this kind is, according to Lowth, for the most part of the constructive order,[2] which is, as we have previously seen, Lowth's way of saying that strict parallelism is at best incomplete, and is more often entirely absent.

There is in the passages just cited or summarised a surprising amount of correct and acute observation or fruitful suggestion. Some subsequent scholars neglected this important part of Lowth's inquiries, and, in consequence, Ewald, for example, never clearly saw, as Lowth had seen, the sharp distinction between Lamentations i.-iv. and v.

For our present purpose it will suffice to refer much more briefly to Budde's important discussions. In the main his advance on Lowth consisted in the detailed working out of two important points : (1) the nature of the unequal division of the rhythmical periods ; and (2) the extent to which the rhythm characteristic of Lamentations i.-iv. occurs elsewhere in the Old Testament. As to the division of the rhythmical periods, Budde's position may be stated thus :—(1) the *kinah* rhythm rests on the division of the rhythmical

---

[1] *Isaiah*, ed. 3, p. xxxix.   [2] *Ibid.* p. xxxv.

period into two unequal parts of which the longer part precedes the shorter part; (2) the normal length of the longer part is three words, of the shorter two words; (3) but by legitimate variations a longer part consisting of four words may be followed by a shorter consisting of (a) three, or (b) two, words; (4) the period is never equally divided; [1] if, as sometimes happens, each part consists of two words, the two words of the first part are heavier and weightier than the two words of the second part; (5) between the two parts of the verse, there is no strict and constant rhythmical relation beyond the fundamental fact of inequality of length.

To some of these metrical questions I shall return : meantime I proceed to examine the parallelism of the poems, and I will begin with the isolated fifth chapter which happens to be an excellent storehouse of examples of the types of parallelism occurring in poetry that is free from the well-marked peculiarities of Lamentations i.-iv. By comparison with the more ordinary parallelism of Lamentations v., any peculiarities in the parallelism of Lamentations i.-iv. may be the better discerned.

The majority of the twenty-two verses of Lamentations v. may be treated as containing six terms *equally* divided among the two stichoi that compose each verse, *i.e.* each stichos normally

---

[1] *Zeitschr. für die alttest. Wissenschaft*, 1882, pp. 4 f.

contains three terms. Seventeen of these distichs show strict parallelism between at least one term in each stichos ; of the remaining five distichs, one (*v.* 5) is too uncertain to classify, and two (*vv.* 8, 16) are best regarded as lacking strict parallelism. In the two verses or distichs that still remain (*vv.* 9 and 10) the stichoi are certainly not parallel to one another : but these two verses in their entirety seem to be (incompletely) parallel to one another : for disregarding the first half of *v.* 10, which may be corrupt, we may represent the parallelism between the two verses thus :

$$a . b . c . d . e . f$$
$$. \quad . \quad . \quad d' . e' . f'$$

If this parallelism of the last parts of these verses was intentional, it is likely enough that such naturally parallel terms as נפשנו, *our soul* (R.V. *lives*), עורנו, *our skin*, which occur in the first parts of the verses, were originally more really parallel than they now are.

Of the twenty-two distichs, then, contained in Lamentations v., seventeen at least show parallelism between the stichoi. In five, or, on one interpretation of *v.* 12, in six, of these the parallelism is complete :[1] in the remaining twelve (or eleven) incomplete. The several examples may be classified thus :—

---

[1] For the meaning of the terms complete and incomplete parallelism see above, pp. 59, 74.

I. Examples of Complete Parallelism

Form.	Number of Occurrences.	Verses.
a . b . c a'. b'. c'	3	4, 13, (17)
a . b . c b'. a'. c'	(1)	12 (on one interpretation)
a . b2 a'2 . b'	1	15
a . b b'. c'	1	22

II. Examples of Incomplete Parallelism

(1) With compensation.

a . b . c a'2 . b'	4	1, 11, 12 (on one interpretation), 20

or similar types

a . b . c a'. d . e	2	6, 7

(2) Without compensation.

a . b . c a'. b'	4	2, 3, 14, 18

or similar types

a . b . c . d a' c'2	1	19
a . b . c . d a'2 e	1	21

The occurrence in this poem of incomplete parallelisms without compensation raises questions that must be considered later.

In turning now to consider Lamentations i.-iv. we are faced with a difficulty of terminology. Lamentations iii., as is well known, consists of sixty-six Massoretic verses distinguished from one another by the occurrence, at the beginning of each, of the letter of the alphabet appropriate to the alphabetic scheme, so that each of the first three verses begins with א, each of the next three with ב, and so forth. Chapters i. and ii., though they number each but twenty-two Massoretic verses, contained [1] each of them sixty-six sections of the same length as the Massoretic verse in iii., and these sections are still easily distinguishable, though the letters of the alphabetic scheme occur at the beginning of every fourth section only. Chapter iv. consists of forty-four similar sections. What is the proper term to apply to these sections : are they lines or couplets, stichoi or distichs ? Are they, as compared with the stichoi of chapter v., " protracted lines," as Lowth described them, or, as compared with the distichs of chapter v., truncated couplets or distichs, as Budde considers them ? These ques-

[1] In the present text, owing to what is generally recognised as textual expansion (in i. 7, ii. 19), the number of sections is sixty-seven both in chaps. i. and ii. The R.V. for the most part distinguishes the sections correctly, but occasionally so divides the verses (e.g. i. 1, ii. 2, and even iv. 22) as to give them the appearance of consisting of four sections.

tions can best be considered later : I will, for the
time being, use the neutral term section, meaning
by that a Massoretic verse in chapter iii. and the
equivalent sections of the remaining chapters, *i.e.*
the third of a Massoretic verse in i. and ii., and
the half of such a verse in iv. Similarly, for the
two parts of these sections, the longer first and
the shorter second part, I will use the term subsection.

As the normal number of terms in a verse of
chapter v. is six, so the normal number of terms
in each section of chapters i. and iv. is five. It
follows from this at once that in chapters i.-iv.
the common form of complete parallelism

$$a \cdot b \cdot c$$
$$a' \cdot b' \cdot c'$$

will not readily [1] occur in a normal section, and,
as a matter of fact, it does not, I think, occur at
all in any section, whether normal or abnormal.
This, however, is not equivalent to saying that
complete parallelism between the subsections is
either impossible or actually non-existent in
these poems ; on the other hand complete parallelism actually occurs, though relatively with
much less frequency than in chapter v. An
example is ii. 11 :—

---

[1] The force of this qualifying adverb will become clear later. As a
matter of fact, though $\frac{a \cdot b \cdot c}{a' \cdot b' \cdot c'}$ does not occur, a corresponding type
of incomplete parallelism with compensation does occur : see iv. 11.

כלו בדמעות עיני | חמרמרו מעי

Consumed with tears are mine eyes, | in a ferment are my
bowels.

The scheme is a2 . b | a′ . b′ ; and it is prefer-
able to regard iii. 4,

He hath worn out my flesh and my skin, | he hath broken
my bones,

as an example of a . b2 | a′ . b′ rather than of the
scheme a . b . c | a′ . b′.

Other examples of complete parallelism in
chapters i.-iv. occurring in sections that are not
perhaps strictly normal are

על-ההרים דלקנו | במדבר ארבו לנו

Upon the mountains they chased us, | in the wilderness they
lay in wait for us.

השביעני במרורים | הרוני לענה

He hath filled me with bitterness, | he hath sated me with
wormwood.

These will be found in iv. 19 and iii. 15 ; they
are both examples of a . b | a′ . b′, or, if we
prefer to regard the pronominal suffixes as in-
dependent terms, of a . b . c | a′ . b′ . c ; another
example occurs in iv. 13, and there are perhaps
a few others : but in the 242 sections of chapters
i.-iv. there are but few, if any, more examples
of complete parallelism than in the twenty-two
distichs of chapter v. ; or, in other words, complete parallelism is, relatively, about eleven times
as frequent in chapter v. as in chapters i.-iv.

H

If, however, the section of chapters i.-iv. be a " protracted line," we might expect to find complete parallelism occurring as between the sections rather than as between the subsections. As a matter of fact, incomplete parallelism between the sections is not uncommon in chapters i.-iv. ; it is less common, indeed, than parallelism between the stichoi in chapter v. ; it is, on the other hand, much commoner than parallelism between whole verses, of which we noted but one example, in chapter v.   And yet *complete* parallelism between sections is exceedingly rare, and in fact, I think, does not once occur.   Probably the nearest approach to complete parallelism between sections is where four of the five terms correspond, as in ii. 2 a, b, where the scheme is

$$a . b . c . d . e$$
$$a' . \quad c' . d' . e'2$$

בלע אדני ולא־חמל את־כל־נאות יעקב
הרס בעברתו מבצרי בת־יהודה

The-Lord hath-swallowed-up unpityingly all the-homesteads of-Jacob,
He-hath-thrown-down in-his-wrath the-strongholds of-the-daughter of-Judah.

A much greater relative amount of those forms of what Lowth called synthetic or constructive parallelism, in which there is a complete absence of strict parallelism, is another feature of Lamentations i.-iv. which sharply distinguishes these poems (with one exception) from Lamentations v.

Other differences exist as between one or more
of these poems and chapter v. ; and these will
appear when we turn, as we must now, to a closer
examination of the parallelism in chapters i.-iv.,
and of the differences in this respect to be discerned as between these chapters considered
severally.

Budde quotes with approval a remark of De
Wette's that in Lamentations " merely rhythmical parallelism," another term for Lowth's constructive or synthetic parallelism, is most prominent, and that parallelism of thought, when it
occurs, occurs mostly as between the subsections,
i.e. between the clauses or sentences which consist alternately of (as a rule) three and two terms,
not between the sections, which consist, as a rule,
of five terms ; put otherwise, this amounts to
the assertion that parallelism in these poems is
chiefly of the general type

$$a \cdot b \cdot c$$
$$a' \cdot b'$$

not of the type

$$a \cdot b \cdot c \cdot d \cdot e$$
$$a' \cdot b' \cdot c' \cdot d' \cdot e'$$

Budde's only criticism of this is that De Wette
considerably underrates the extent of this
parallelism between the subsections, which we
may briefly term subsectional parallelism. But
neither De Wette nor Budde carried the analysis

of this feature sufficiently far ; had they done so they would have seen that a general statement such as they make cannot be rightly made with reference to all the poems indiscriminately. I hope to show that the statement that " merely rhythmical parallelism " is most prominent is substantially true of chapters i. and iii. and very misleading in reference to chapter ii., and in a less degree in reference to chapter iv. ; and also that the statement that parallelism, when it occurs, occurs mostly between the subsections is the very opposite of the truth with regard to chapter ii., though substantially correct with regard to chapter iv.

I will examine chapter iii. first. In a certain sense the whole of the first eighteen verses or sections might be said to consist of eighteen parallel statements of the fact that Yahweh is chastening the speaker ; the first person singular pronoun appears in each separate verse, and gives a certain degree of parallelism to them all ; and similarly throughout the poem large groups of sections express, mainly by a succession of figurative statements, the same thought : but beyond this general repetition of thought there is seldom any real parallelism of individual terms or even of groups of terms. Moreover, there is a feature of this poem that suggests that some even of the apparent examples of parallel sections are due more to accident than design ; I refer to the fact that the clearest apparent examples of sectional parallelism occur between the last section beginning with one letter of the alphabet and the first section beginning with the next letter ; [1] thus, there are throughout the poem no sections more parallel to one another than, and few as much so as, the following (*vv.* 12, 13 ; 48, 49 ; 60, 61).

He hath bent his bow and set me as a target for his arrow ;
He hath caused to enter into my kidneys the shafts of his
quiver.

In streams of water my eye runs down for the destruction
of my people ;
My eye hath poured down unceasingly, because there are no
respites.

Thou hast seen all the vengeance they took, all their devices
against me ;
Thou hast heard all their reproaches (of me), O Yahweh, all
their devices against me.

The first of these couplets consists of the last line beginning with ד and the first with ה, the second of the last line with פ and the first with ע, the third of the last with ר and the first with ש.

There are not more than about a dozen [2] couplets of contiguous sections that are as

---

[1] The significance of this does not seem to me to be affected by the fact that in Ps. cxi., cxii. the alphabetic scheme distinguishes each stichos, not each distich, by successive letters of the alphabet, and therefore *regularly* and necessarily gives to parallel stichoi different initial letters.

[2] The sections that may most reasonably be regarded as more parallel (though whether always by the intention of the writer is doubtful) to one another than is almost any section of the poem to any other are : *12, 13* ; 19 (pointing זְכָר), 20 ; 28, 29, 30 (?) ; 34, 35, 36 (?) ; 40, 41 ; *48, 49* ; *60, 61* ; 64, 65. The italicised numbers are cited above.

parallel to one another as the foregoing, or indeed that are strictly parallel to one another at all.

In about one-third of the entire number of sections parallelism more or less clear and conspicuous between subsections [1] occurs ; examples are *vv.* 10 (a . b . c2 | a′ . b′) and 14 (a . b . c | b′ . d) :—

דב ארב הוא לי | אריה במסתרים

As a bear lying in wait is he unto me, | a lion in secret places.

הייתי שחק לכל־עמים | נגינתם כל־היום

I am become a derision to all peoples, | their song all the day.

Clearly, then, since subsectional parallelism occurs in considerably less than half, and probably in not more than a third, of the sixty-six sections of the poem, and sectional parallelism, which might have occurred thirty-three times, actually occurs scarcely a dozen times at most, " merely rhythmical parallelism " is more conspicuous here than real parallelism of thought and terms ; whether subsectional is much or any more relatively frequent than sectional parallelism depends on the view taken as to the reality of parallelism in the couplets specified on p. 101 and as to the character of the more doubtful examples of subsectional parallelism given below.[1]

---

[1] The clearest examples of subsectional parallelism occur in the following fifteen verses : 4, 9, 10, 14, 15, 17, 18, 22, 23, 25, 33, 47, 58, 60, 61. The text of some even of these (*e.g.* 22, 23, 33) is open to question : but probably parallelism existed in the original text. More doubtful examples may be found in *vv.* 5, 7, 11, 16, 19, 30, 39, 43, 53, 56, 65.

Chapter ii. differs greatly from chapter iii. The repetition in chapter iii. of the initial letter before each of the three sections belonging to it corresponds to a real independence, as a general rule,[1] of the sections in that poem. On the other hand, the three sections which belong to each letter of the alphabet in chapter ii., but of which the first section only is distinguished by beginning with that letter, are closely connected with one another ; and this connexion is formally marked by the frequency with which *the entire sections* within the several alphabetic divisions *are parallel to one another*. The exact number of these sectional parallelisms depends on interpretation, and in some cases on textual questions : but I believe it may be safely asserted that in a large majority at all events of the twenty-two alphabetic divisions two at least of the three sections are parallel to one another, and in several all three sections are so. I should myself put the number of parallelisms between two, if not all three, sections as high as eighteen, if not higher.[2]

Over against this frequency of sectional parallelism we have to set the relative infrequency of subsectional parallelism : this latter kind of parallelism, which might have occurred sixty-six

---

[1] *Vv.* 34-36 form an exception.

[2] Absence of parallelism or a near approach to it will be found in *vv.* 4, 17, 18, 22, but even this may be partly due to textual corruption. In most of the remaining verses parallelism is obvious, in all it was probably intended.

times, actually occurs only a dozen[1] times, more
or less, according to the view taken of two or
three doubtful cases.

Thus it is not true of chapter ii. that " merely
rhythmical parallelism " is more frequent than
real parallelism of thought and term, nor is it
true that parallelism occurs mainly between the
subsections ; quite the reverse : we must, to be
accurate, put the case thus : In chapter ii. real
(though incomplete) parallelism is very frequent ;
the *fundamental* parallelism is between the sections ; but this is *occasionally* reinforced by an
additional and *secondary* parallelism between the
subsections, much in the same way that the
fundamental rhymes at the close of the (alternate)
lines of a quatrain are in some English poems
occasionally reinforced by an additional rhyme
in the middle of one or more lines, as often in
Coleridge's *Ancient Mariner, e.g.*—

> The sun came up upon the left,
>   Out of the sea came he !
> And he shone bright, and on the right
>   Went down into the sea.

The fact is, parallelism in Lamentations ii. is
singularly intricate and skilfully varied. It is
rarely complete either as between sections or subsections, but it is generally clear enough and
sufficient to constitute a real formal connexion

---

[1] See *vv.* 4 a (?), 5 b, 6 a (?), 7 a, 9 a (read שָׁבְרוּ for אבר ושבר), 10 b, 11 a,
(*not* 13 a : A.V.), 15 c (present text), 17 a, c, 18 c, 20 b, 21 c.

between the three sections of the several alphabetic divisions, or at least between two of them,
the remaining section being sometimes not parallel,
as is frequently one stichos of a tristich in other
poems. Since the nature of the parallelism in
chapter ii. and, consequently, an important formal
difference between chapters ii. and iv. have
hitherto not been clearly observed, I give a few
verses of this poem with a translation and notes
on the parallelism :—

1 איכה ¹ יעיב באפו אדני | את בת ציון
השליך משמים ארץ | תפארת ישראל
ולא זכר הדום רגליו | ביום אפו

1 How hath the Lord beclouded¹ in his anger | the daughter
of Sion !
He hath cast down from heaven to earth | the ornament of
Israel ;
And he hath not remembered his footstool | in the day of
his anger.

Here all three sections are parallel : observe
the daughter of Sion (d 2) ‖ *the ornament of Israel*
(d′ 2) ‖ *his footstool* (d″ 2), and *beclouded* (a) ‖
cast down from heaven to earth (a′ 3) ‖ *hath not
remembered* (a″). Moreover, the unity of the entire
alphabetic division is emphasised by the additional parallelism *in his anger* (b) ‖ *in the day of
his anger* (b′ 2) in the first and last sections ; a
similar effect is obtained in *v.* 12 which opens with
לאמתם, *to their mothers*, and closes with אמתם, *their
mothers*. Variety is obtained not only by varying

¹ *Hath . . . beclouded* : read היעיב for יעיב, *beclouds.*

the number of terms by means of which corresponding ideas are expressed, but also very effectively by bringing the object of the verb much
nearer to the beginning in the third section than
in the two that precede : a somewhat similar
effect is obtained in *v.* 8 (cp. also i. 1).

There. is no subsectional parallelism in any of
these three sections.

2 בלע אדני ולא חמל | את כל נאות יעקב

הרס בעברתו | מבצרי בת יהודה

הגיע לארץ חלל | ממלכה ושריה

2 The Lord hath destroyed unsparingly | all the homesteads
of Jacob ;
He hath pulled down in his wrath | the strongholds of
Judah ;
He hath brought to the ground, hath profaned | the realm
and its princes.

Here, again, all three sections are parallel, but
in none is there parallelism between the subsections. This time all the object-clauses stand
at the end of their respective sections and, as in
v. 1, the parallel verbs or verbal clauses הגיע לארץ
חלל (*he hath brought to the ground, hath profaned*),
הרס (*he hath pulled down*), בלע (*hath destroyed*) at
the beginning. The additional parallelism of
terms is not as in *v.* 1 between the first and
third, but between the first and second sections
(*unsparingly* ǁ *in his wrath*), unless, indeed, with
Löhr, we emend by transposing the clauses *He
hath brought to the ground* and *in his wrath* ; then,

as before, the fuller parallelism will be between the first and third sections.

10 ישבו לארץ ידמו | זקני בת ציון

העלו עפר על ראשם | חגרו שקים

הורידו לארץ ראשן | בתולת ירושלם

10 They sat on the ground dumb— | the elders of Sion ;
   Lifted up dust on their head, | were girded with sack-
                                        cloth ;
   They lowered to the ground their head— | the virgins of
                                        Jerusalem.

Here in the second section we find subsectional parallelism ; each clause in it mentions one sign of mourning and grief ; parallel to each of these clauses and to one another are the first clauses of the first and third sections, but these sections contain no subsectional parallelism : on the other hand, the second parts of the first and third sections are very strictly parallel to one another (*the elders of Sion* || *the virgins of Jerusalem*). But there is still further and in part rather subtle verbal parallelism between the *sections* : note לארץ (*on* (*to*) *the ground*) in the first and third sections ; ראשם and ראשן (*their head*) in the second and third respectively ; and the antithesis העלו (*lifted up*) and הורידו (*lowered*) which is emphasised by the parallelism in a way which it is impossible to represent adequately in translation : what they lift up is dust, what they cast down is their heads ! Very clearly, then, *sectional* parallelism is again primary ; but here it is reinforced by subsectional parallelism in *one* of the three sections.

A correct appreciation of the main and secondary parallelism in this poem may set some questions of textual interpretation in a new light. Verse 3 reads,

גדע בחרי אף | כל קרן ישראל
השיב אחור ימינו | מפני אויב
ויבער ביעקב כאש להבה | אכלה סביב

He hewed off in fierce anger | all the horn of Israel;
He turned backward his right hand | from the face of the foe;
And he kindled in Jacob a flaming fire | which devoured round about.

Whose is the right hand here referred to, Israel's or Yahweh's ? It is commonly taken to be Yahweh's, and there is certainly much to be said for this view. But the parallelism of the sections, which certainly exists in any case, would become still clearer and more complete if the right hand be Israel's. Then, for the use of the pronoun only in the middle section corresponding to the two parallel proper names for the nation in the first and third sections, there are two exact parallels in this poem : see *vv.* 5 and 10.

In both 4 a and 15 c it is generally admitted that a word or more has intruded. But which word or words should we omit ? If subsectional parallelism was primary, and as frequent as it is in Lamentations iv. and Isaiah xiv., parallelism would furnish a strong argument for those who retain כצר, *as a foe* (parallel to *as an enemy*), in *v.* 4, and both the clauses *perfection of beauty*

and *joy of the whole earth* in *v.* 15. But, since
subsectional parallelism is merely secondary and
not very frequent in this poem, such an argument
has little if any weight : and it may certainly be
doubted whether it is nearly strong enough to
justify those who omit שיאמרו, with the characteristic ש in *v.* 15, in order to retain both the
parallel clauses at the end of the verse without
at the same time keeping a section so long as the
existing text presents.

Verse 8 is also interesting. Had subsectional
parallelism been primary, the author would
naturally have written—

Rampart and wall lament ; | together they languish ;

but to gain a closer parallelism with the two preceding *sections*, each of which begins with a verb
of which Yahweh is the subject, he avoided what
would have been a more perfect subsectional
parallelism and wrote instead—

He caused to lament rampart and wall ; | together they
languish.

By many who refrain from postulating unity
of authorship for the Book of Lamentations,
chapters ii. and iv. at least are attributed to the
same writer. Be this as it may, there is an
appreciable difference, though it has hitherto
been overlooked, in the use of parallelism in the
two poems, just as there is a difference in the
length of the alphabetic divisions. In chapter ii.

sectional parallelism is fundamental and frequent, subsectional parallelism secondary and relatively rare : in chapter iv. subsectional parallelism is relatively more frequent, perhaps even considerably more frequent than sectional parallelism, though neither type is quite so unmistakably primary or quite so persistent as the sectional parallelism in chapter ii. Subsectional parallelism occurs in nearly, if not quite, or even more than, a half [1] of the sections in chapter iv. as compared with a bare fifth in chapter ii. ; on the other hand, less than half, perhaps scarcely a third, of the sections are parallel to one another,[2]

---

[1] The sections in Lamentations iv. number 44, of which two (v. 15) are through corruption very uncertain. Subsectional parallelism is clearest in these 17 sections : 1 a (see below), 2 a, b, 3 a, b, 7 a, b, 8 a, b, 11 a, b, 12 a, 13 a, 16 b, 18 b, 19 b, 21 a. To these should be added the two similarly constructed sections, 6 a, 9 a, perhaps also 5 a, b (antithetical parallels), 6 b, 14 a, 15 a, 21 b, 22 a, b. Subsectional parallelism is at all events sufficiently frequent to raise the question whether the text of v. 1 is correct ; subsectional parallelism would indeed be perfect even in the present text if we ventured to divide the section equally (cp. R.V.) : but rhythm, as we shall see later, forbids this, and if the text is sound Dr. Smith (*Jerusalem*, ii. 279) rightly arranges as follows :

> How bedimmed is the gold, how changed
> The best of the gold.

I suspect, however, that either (1) ישנא is a gloss (Aramaic ?) on יעם, or (2) that הטוב should be omitted, leaving כתם parallel to זהב as in Job xxxi. 24. Then we have either

> How bedimmed is the gold,
> Even the best fine gold,

or

> How bedimmed is the gold,
> Changed the fine gold.

[2] The most conspicuous sectional parallelisms will be found in vv. 4, 5, 8, 17, 22 : see also vv. 1, 7, 19, but in these latter verses, as also in the antithetical sections of v. 3, the sectional parallelism is much less conspicuous than the synonymous subsectional parallelism in one or, in most of the verses, in both sections.

and there is little or nothing of that subtle linking of the sections which occurs in chapter ii.

In Lamentations i., in spite of the sustained and well varied parallelism of the first three sections, strict parallelism is decidedly less frequent than in either chapter ii. or chapter iv., or even than in chapter iii. Subsectional parallelism is perhaps rather more frequent [1] than in chapter ii., where it is infrequent and secondary : but sectional parallelism is very decidedly *less* frequent [2] than in chapter ii. : the result is that it is difficult to select either type of parallelism as primary ; and the more important fact is that the form of the greater part of this poem is independent of strict parallelism.

It is not surprising that the Book of Lamentations has driven even unwilling scholars to the consideration or reconsideration of the question of metre or rhythm in Hebrew poetry. Budde, who, like many others, had in 1874, after an examination of existing theories in regard to Hebrew metre, rejected them all and expressed the most thoroughgoing scepticism with regard to any new theories that might arise, found himself eight years later, after a study of Lamentations, venturing, to quote his own phrase, " on

---

[1] See *vv.* 1 (three antithetical parallels), 2 a, c, 3 a, b, 4 b, c, 5 a, 7 c, d, 13 c, 16 a, b, 18 b, 20 a, c ; possibly also *vv.* 8 a (omit על־כן ?), b (omit כי ?), c, 9 c, 13 a, 22 a.

[2] See *vv.* 1, 10 a, b, 11 a, b, 12 b, c, 15, 20 a, b: perhaps also 2 b, c, 4 a, b, 5 a, c, 8.

the dangerous slippery ice " ; and it has generally
been admitted that he skated with considerable
skill over the corner of the ice to which he confined
himself.

The challenge lies here : there is a common
and well-marked peculiarity in the 242 sections
that make up the first four chapters of Lamentations ; it is a rhythmical peculiarity, and yet a
rhythmical peculiarity that cannot be explained
by the parallelism. In putting it thus, I recognise, as I think we well may, that parallelism
might create rhythm, and may even, as a matter
of fact, in the remote past have created the
dominant Semitic and Hebrew type of rhythm
in particular : a habit of expressing a thought
in a given number of terms, and then repeating
it by corresponding terms, would necessarily produce a certain rhythmical effect : thus, for
example, the habit of expressing thought in the
mould symbolised by

$$a \cdot b \cdot c$$
$$a' \cdot b' \cdot c'$$

would produce a *rhythm* which may be expressed
by 3 : 3 ; and thought expressed in a mould
symbolised by

$$a \cdot b \cdot c$$
$$a' \cdot b'$$

would produce a rhythm that may be expressed
by 3 : 2.

But as soon as parallelism becomes incomplete,

and still more when it becomes merely synthetic, *i.e.*, strictly speaking, disappears, and yet the lines retain the same number of words or terms, obviously the rhythmical relation between the lines is no longer, even if it was originally, merely secondary : thus rhythm is no longer a mere result of parallelism, but an independent desire for rhythm is at least a contributory cause, if with

$$a \; . \; b \; . \; c$$
$$a' . \; b' . \; c'$$

such schemes as

$$a \; . \; b \; . \; c$$
$$a'2 \quad . \; c'$$

or

$$a \; . \; b \; . \; c$$
$$a' . \; d \; . \; e$$

or

$$a \; . \; b \; . \; c$$
$$d \; . \; e \; . \; f$$

constantly alternate, but schemes such as

$$a \quad . \; b \; . \; c$$
$$a'2 . \; b' . \; c'$$

or

$$a \; . \; b \; . \; c$$
$$a' . \; b' . \; c' . \; d$$

rarely or never ; or, again, if with schemes such as

$$a \; . \; b \; . \; c \; . \; d \; . \; e$$
$$a' . \; b' . \; c' . \; d' . \; e'$$

there alternate schemes such as

a . b . c . d . e
a' . b'2 . d' . e'

but not such as

a . b . c . d . e
a' . b'2 . c' . d' . e'

or with schemes

a . b . c
a' . b'

schemes such as

a . b . c
a'2

or

a . b . c
a' . d

but not such as

a . b . c
a'2 . b'

Now, if my analysis is even approximately correct, what, stated in general terms, are the facts of the Book of Lamentations, and the questions, which, once the facts are analysed and classified, almost necessarily arise?   Lamentations iii. contains sixty-six sections unmistakably marked off from one another by the alphabetic scheme : there is no *complete* parallelism between any two successive sections : there is incomplete parallelism between perhaps fifteen groups of two sections : there is none at all between the rest.   Why are

these sections nevertheless of equal length, or at
least even in the present text so closely approxim-
ated to equality of length ?   Again, these sections
fall into subsections : in some twenty sections the
two subsections are parallel to one another, though
often only incompletely parallel ; why alike in
these twenty sections and in the remaining forty
odd sections in which there is no parallelism
between the subsections does the longer subsection precede the shorter : why is the ratio
between the two subsections so constant ?

Again, why are the twenty-two alphabetic
divisions of Lamentations ii. each divided into
three equal divisions marked off from one another
by a strongly marked division of sense, each
section again into subsections by a less strong but
still clearly marked pause ?   Why do the sections
so constantly consist of five terms, the subsections
of three terms and two terms respectively, the
shorter regularly following the longer ?   Why all
this, though, while many of the sections are
parallel to one another, *complete* parallelism
between sections scarcely, if ever, occurs, and
though in only about a dozen out of the sixty-six
sections does even incomplete parallelism occur
between the subsections ?

The answer to all these questions and the
similar questions which Lamentations i. (with a
difference) and Lamentations iv. provoke has
been increasingly found by admitting the play

of a rhythmical principle ; and what is called the *ḳinah* rhythm has accordingly gained recognition amongst many who still remain sceptical of other Hebrew rhythms.

What, then, is really meant by the *ḳinah* rhythm ?   A certain ambiguity seems to lurk in the usage of the term.   Does it mean five terms forming a complete sentence with a well-marked pause after the third ?   or a *succession* of such sentences ?   If the first sentence of Genesis— בראשית ברא אלהים | את־הארץ ואת־השמים—occurred in any of the first four chapters of Lamentations, every one would accept it as a rhythmically normal line.   Is, then, the first sentence in Genesis an example of *ḳinah* rhythm occurring sporadically in prose, as hexameters occur sporadically in the Authorised Version ?   Scarcely, for it is probable that those who define *ḳinah* rhythm as verse unequally divided by a pause, and normally in the ratio 3 : 2, tacitly mean by *ḳinah* rhythm a *succession* of such verses.   And certainly it was the frequent repetition of such verses in Lamentations i.-iv. that first drew attention to the peculiarity of their style or rhythm.

Five words with a pause after the third is, even in Hebrew prose, too frequently occurring and too easily arising a phenomenon to possess by itself anything distinctive.   An hexameter is a noteworthy phenomenon wherever it occurs ; five words with a pause after the third are not ;

on the other hand, a dozen or twenty repetitions of five words with a pause after the third do constitute something as noteworthy as an hexameter.

Not the sporadic occurrence, but the regular recurrence of a particular type of word-combination is apart from, or in addition to, any parallelism that may accompany it, the peculiarity of Lamentations i.-iv. And yet, as soon as we frame the conclusion thus, it is necessary, if all the facts, especially of chapter i., are to be recognised, to add that the particular type of word-combination in question falls into two sub-types ; and as soon as we define the sub-types as consisting respectively of combinations of five words with a pause occurring after the third, and combinations of four words equally divided by a pause, we may at first appear to destroy the whole theory of a *ḳinah* rhythm which we were attempting to formulate. The actual fact is not quite so serious as this, for while the normal section of five accented words, unequally divided, may contract to four words equally divided, it probably does not expand to six words equally divided.

However, whether the facts seriously weaken the theory or not, the main question at present is this : is Budde correct in denying that the sections in Lamentations were ever (in the original text) equally divided ? And is his attempt to maintain the appearance of inequality by calling

two words " heavy " as against two others that
are to be called " light," any better than the
attempt to cover up the absence of parallelism
between two lines by speaking of them as synthetic
parallels ?

To this question we shall return. Meantime,
I will only say that the theory of light and heavy
groups of words seems to me to suffer shipwreck
on the very first verse of the book : for it is very
difficult to believe that if רבתי בגוים at the end of
the second section is light, שרתי במדינות at the
beginning of the third is heavy. The truth is
rather that Lamentations i. 1 b, c are both lines
of four words equally divided : and Sievers is
probably not far wrong in finding a full half of
the entire number of lines in Lamentations i. to
be of the same nature.[1]   In any case, Lamenta-

[1] The sections treated by Sievers as containing four accented words
and as being equally divided by the caesura are 1 b, c, 2 b, 4 c, 5 b, c, 6 a,
c, 7 a (to ומרוריה), c, 8 b, c, 9 b, 10 a, b, 11 a, 12 c, 13 a, b, c, 14 b, c, 15 a, b,
17 c, 18 b, c, 19 a, b, c, 22 b, c ; marked as less certain sections of the same
kind are 2 c, 3 b, c, 4 b, 15 c.   Sections of this kind are far less frequent
in the remaining poems ; those treated as such by Sievers are : ii.
12 (a, b) c, 14 a, b, c, (19 d) ; iii. 6, 10, 13, 15, 23, 24, 50 (58, 59, 60) ; iv.
3 b, 5 a, b, 6 b, 13 a, b, 14 (a) b, (15 a, b), 18 a (b), 20 (a) b, 21 (a) b. References
to uncertain examples are enclosed in brackets.   It is interesting and
instructive to compare with this classification the examples given by
Budde (Zeitschr. für die alttestamentliche Wissenschaft, 1882 : cp. his
commentary on Lamentations in the Kurzer Handkommentar, 1898)
of the verses in which the first part contains only two words—these
being, on his theory, " long " or " heavy."   Budde cites i. 1 b, c, 4 c,
9 b, 13 c, 14 b, 17 c, 18 c, 19 a, b ; ii. 12 b, c ; iii. 15 ; iv. 5 a, 13 b, 17 b. The
large number of sections treated by Sievers as evenly divided, but not
treated by Budde as containing two words only in their first parts,
consists of lines in which Budde either allows a full word-value to
prepositions or other particles (e.g. i. 8 c, 10 b, 11 a), or emends the text
(e.g. in i. 5 b he inserts הוא after יהוה).

tions i. is of crucial importance in the study of
the *ḳinah* rhythm : any one who has sufficient
ingenuity to discover an unequal division in all
its sections need have little fear of being able to
do the same for the three succeeding chapters or
any other passages where the occurrence of some
unequally divided lines suggests to him the
" *ḳinah* " rhythm. If, on the other hand, the
occurrence in the present text of Lamentations i.
of equally divided lines of four terms is too
frequent to admit of doubt that *some* such lines
occurred in the original text, then we may suspect
that the same variations also occurred or may
have occurred in other *ḳinah* poems.

And as a matter of fact the variation is probably to be found in one of the earliest *ḳinahs* that
survive.   In Amos v. 2 the prophet's *ḳinah* over
the house of Israel is given : it consists of two distichs, or long lines as we may here by preference call
them :

נפלה לא־תוסף קום | בתולת ישראל
נטשה על־אדמתה | אין מקימה

Fallen to rise no more | is the daughter of Israel,
 Stretched out upon the ground | with none to raise her.

The parallelism resembles the dominant parallelism in Lamentations ii. : it is between the
long lines, not between the parts of these, the
scheme being

$$a \quad . \, b2 \mid c2$$
$$a'2 \qquad \mid b'2$$

The first of these two long lines is quite unambiguously divided into two unequal parts : rhythmically it is 3 : 2 ; but the second can only be forced
into the same scheme by giving to the preposition
a full stress.   If, however, we find other examples
of periods in *kinahs* that cannot be anything but
2 : 2, we shall certainly do better so to regard the
second period here and to give על־אדמתה but one
word-accent.

CHAPTER IV

THE ELEMENTS OF HEBREW RHYTHM

CHAPTER IV

THE ELEMENTS OF HEBREW RHYTHM

THE study of parallelism must lead, if I have so far observed and interpreted correctly, to the conclusion that parallelism is but one law or form of Hebrew poetry, and that it leaves much to be explained by some other law or form. Complete and exact correspondence of all the terms in two parallel lines necessarily produces the effect of exact or approximate rhythmical balance. But such complete parallelism is relatively rare in Hebrew poetry; the parallelism is more often incomplete; and, moreover, along with lines completely parallel and lines incompletely parallel there frequently occur also lines unconnected by the presence in them of any parallel terms. And yet, alike in the incompletely parallel, and in the non-parallel couplets, there will often be found, consistently maintained, the same kind of rhythm as in those that are completely parallel. We are thus driven back behind parallelism in search of an independent rhythmi-

123

cal principle in Hebrew poetry which will account for the presence of balance, or other rhythmical relation, as between two lines in which the parallelism is not such as necessarily to involve this balance or other rhythmical relation.

Some such rhythmical principle, whether or not its nature can ever be exactly and fully explained, seems to govern much of the present text of the Old Testament, sometimes for long consecutive passages, as for example in Lamentations and many parts of Job and Isaiah xl.-lv., sometimes for a few lines only, and then to be rudely interrupted by what neither accommodates itself to any rhythmical principle that can be easily seized, nor produces any rhythmical impression that can be readily or gratefully received.

The difficulties in the way of discovering and giving any clear and full account of this principle are considerable. In the first place, as was pointed out in the first chapter, no clear tradition or account of the rhythmical or other laws of Hebrew poetry has descended to us from the age when that poetry was still being written. The remarks of Josephus are interesting, but in themselves anything but illuminating. Then we are faced with serious textual uncertainties in all the so-called poetical books and in the prophetical books, and in the ancient poems, such as the song of Deborah, and the blessing of Jacob, embodied in some of the narrative books. Feeling, as in my opinion we ought to do, that much of the poetical contents of the Old Testament has suffered serious textual corruption, we might well view with suspicion any metrical theory that found all parts of the existing text equally metrical ; for though a textual corruption may accidentally at times have the same metrical value as the original reading, this is the kind of accident that cannot happen regularly. On the other hand, a metrical theory which finds innumerable passages corrupt, though they show, metre apart, no sign of corruption, has this disadvantage : given the right to make an equal number of emendations purely in the interests of his theory, another theoriser might produce an equally attractive theory ; and we should be left with the uncertainty of choice between two alternatives both of which could not be right, but both of which might be wrong. A sound metrical theory, then, must neither entirely fit, nor too indiscriminately refuse to fit, the present text of the Old Testament. A third serious difficulty lies in our imperfect knowledge of the vowels with which the texts were originally intended to be read. This last difficulty may, perhaps, always leave a considerable degree of detail ambiguous, even if the broader principles of rhythm become clear.

In spite of these difficulties, how far is it possible in the first instance to determine the exact *rhythmical* relations between, let us say, the several examples or types of two sections, sentences, lines, call them what we will, that are associated with one another by some degree of parallelism of terms or at least by some similarity of structure, by being, if not parallel, yet parallelistic ?   Parallelism both associates and dissociates ; it associates two lines by the correspondence of ideas which it implies ; it dissociates them by the differentiation of the terms by means of which the corresponding ideas are expressed as well as by the fact that the one parallel line is fundamentally a repetition of the other. The effect of dissociation is a constant occurrence of breaks or pauses, or rather a constant recurrence of two different types of breaks or pauses : (1) the break between the two parallel and corresponding lines ; and (2) the greater break at the end of the second line before the thought is resumed and carried forward in another combination of parallel lines. And even when strict parallelism disappears, the regular recurrence of these two types of pauses is maintained. Thus there are in Hebrew parallelistic poetry no long flowing verse-paragraphs as in Shakespearian or Miltonic blank verse, but a succession of short clearly defined periods as in much English rhymed verse and in most pre-Shakespearian blank verse. Rhyme in English and parallelism in Hebrew alike serve to define the rhythmical periods ; but the relation between rhyme and sense is much less

close than between parallelism and sense, and
consequently rhyme in English has nothing like
the same power as parallelism in Hebrew to produce coincidence between the rhythmical periods
and the sense-divisions ; accordingly, though
rhyme very naturally goes with " stopped-line "
verse, as it is called, it is also compatible with
non-stop lines ; so that non-stop lines and verse-
paragraphs that disregard the line divisions almost
as freely as Shakespearian or Miltonic blank verse
are by no means unknown in English rhymed
poetry. On the other hand, parallelism is,
broadly speaking, incompatible with anything
but " stopped-line " poetry. Whether or not
there may be in Hebrew a non-parallelistic poetry
in which rhythmical and sense divisions do not
coincide is not, for the moment, the question ;
it is rather this : parallelism, even incomplete
parallelism in its various types, offers a very
large number of couplets in which we can be
perfectly certain of the limits of the constituent
lines ; how strict, how constant, of what precise
nature is the rhythmical relation between these
lines which are thus so clearly defined ? If we
can determine this question satisfactorily, we
may obtain a measure to determine whether the
same rhythmical periods occur elsewhere without
coinciding with sense-divisions.

I have referred to two types of English verse ;
but the closest analogy in English to Hebrew

poetry is probably to be found neither in blank
verse nor in rhymed verse, but in the old Anglo-
Saxon poetry, and its revival (with a difference)
in Chaucer's contemporary, the author of *Piers
Ploughman*. That poetry has one feature which
is no regular, nor even a particularly common,
feature of Hebrew poetry, viz. alliteration ; but
that feature, though a most convenient indication
of the rhythm, is absolutely unessential to it.
Apart from the references to this alliteration, how
admirably does Professor Saintsbury's description of this type of English poetry correspond,
mutatis mutandis, to the *rhythmical* impressions
left by many pages of Hebrew psalms or prophecy.
" The staple line of this verse consists of two halves
or sections, each containing two ' long,' ' strong,'
' stressed,' ' accented ' syllables, these same syllables being, to the extent of three out of four,
alliterated. At the first casting of the eye on a
page of Anglo-Saxon poetry no common *resemblances* except these seem to emerge. But we see
on some pages an altogether extraordinary *difference* in the lengths of the lines, or, in other words,
of the number of ' short,' ' weak,' ' unstressed,'
' unaccented ' syllables which are allowed to
group themselves round the pivots or posts of
the rhythm. Yet attempts have been made, not
without fair success, to divide the sections or half-
lines into groups or types of rhythm, more or less
capable of being represented by the ordinary

marks of metrical scansion. . . . A sort of mono-
tone or hum . . . will indeed disengage itself
for the attentive reader . . . but nothing more
. . . the sharp and uncompromising section, the
accents, the alliteration—these are all that the
poet has to trust to in the way of rules *sine queis
non*. But before long the said careful reader
becomes aware that there is a ' lucky license,'
which is as a rule, and much more also ; and that
this license . . . concerns the allowance of unaccented and unalliterated syllables. The range
of it is so great that at a single page-opening,
taken at random, you might find the lines varying
from nine to fifteen syllables, and, seeking a little
further, come to a variation between eight and
twenty-one." [1] In *Piers Ploughman* the verse still
consists of " a pair of sharply-separated halves
which never on any consideration run syllabically
into each other, and are much more often than
not divided by an actual stop, if only a brief one,
of sense " ; [2] but there is a greater approximation,
though only an approximation, to regularity in
the length of the lines : and the first hemistich
(measured of course syllabically, not by its stressed
syllables, which are always equal in number) is
generally longer than the second. [3]

As between Anglo-Saxon poetry or *Piers*

---

[1] G. Saintsbury, *A History of English Prosody*, i. 13 f.
[2] *Ibid*. i. 182.
[3] Cp. *ibid*. i. 184. Professor Saintsbury gives the well-known opening lines of the poem as an illustration. A briefer specimen from else-

K

Ploughman and Hebrew parallelistic poetry these resemblances are certain : (1) the isolated verse in Anglo-Saxon corresponds to the parallel distich in Hebrew ; (2) the strong internal pause in Anglo-Saxon to the end of the first parallel period of the Hebrew distich ; (3) there is a correspondingly great irregularity in the number of the syllables in successive lines of Anglo-Saxon, and in successive distichs of Hebrew. Yet whether the two poetical materials, the Anglo-Saxon and the Hebrew, agree in what is after all most fundamental in Anglo-Saxon, viz. the constant quantity of stressed syllables in a verse, and the constant ratio of the stressed syllables in the two parts of a verse to one another remains

---

where (ed. Wright, i. 6442-6457) may serve for the comparison with Hebrew poetry made above.

> On Good Friday I fynde · a felon was y-saved,
> That hadde lyved al his life · with lesynges and with thefte ;
> And for he beknede to the cros, · and to Christ shrof him,
> He was sonner y-saved · than seint Johan the Baptist ;
> And or Adam or Ysaye, · or any of the prophetes,
> That hadde y-leyen with Lucifer · many longe yeres,
> A robbere was y-raunsoned · rather than thei alle,
> Withouten any penaunce of purgatorie, · to perpetuel blisse.

The most famous example in later English literature of rhythm resting on equality in the number of accented syllables accompanied by great inequality in the total number of the syllables is Coleridge's *Christabel*. The accented syllables in the lines are always four ; the total number of syllables commonly varies, as Coleridge himself puts it, from seven to twelve, and in the third line of the poem drops down to four. For reference I cite the five opening lines—

> 'Tis the middle of night by the castle clock,
> And the owls have awakened the crowing cock ;
> Tu-whit !—Tu-whoo !
> And hark, again ! the crowing cock,
> How drowsily it crew.

for consideration ; the answer is not immediately obvious, for Hebrew does not so unambiguously and conveniently indicate what are the stressed syllables in a line as does Anglo-Saxon by its alliterative system. In many Hebrew lines we cannot immediately see for certain either which, or how many, are the stressed syllables : what means exist for ultimately determining these uncertainties in part or entirely I will consider later. But first I return to a point already reached in the last chapter.

Even parallelism suggests a division of Hebrew distichs into two broad types of rhythm : in one of these two types the two parallel lines balance one another, whereas in the other the second comes short of and echoes the first. No great attention is required in reading Lamentations v., or Job xxviii., or many other passages in Job or the Deutero-Isaiah, or many Psalms, such as, *e.g.*, li., in order to become aware of the dominance and, in some cases, of the almost uninterrupted recurrence of balance between the successive couplets of mostly parallel lines ; nor, again, in reading Lamentations ii., iii., iv. to become aware of the different rhythm produced when a shorter line constantly succeeds to a longer one. So far we can get without any theory as to the correct method, if there be one, whereby these rhythms should be more accurately measured or described, or as to the best nomenclature wherewith to distinguish these differences when we wish to refer to them. But if we get thus far, it further becomes clear that, if we admit the prevalence in Lamentations iv. of a clearly defined rhythm fit to receive a name of its own, whether or not the name *ḳinah* by which this rhythm commonly goes be the best term to define it, then Lamentations v. and Job xxviii. also have, though a different, yet a no less clearly defined rhythm whether we give it a name or not ; and of course, if we wish to discuss the subject, we must find some convenient way of referring to this rhythm no less than to the other.

To distinguish these two broad classes of clearly distinguished types of rhythm I have suggested the terms *balancing rhythm* and *echoing rhythm*.[1] This terminology seems to me free from some of the objections which attach to the term *ḳinah* as a term for the echoing rhythm, even if we could discover a good companion term to *ḳinah* to describe the other type. As I pointed out in the last chapter, *ḳinah* rhythm is really a rather ambiguous term, meaning either the total rhythmical effect of a poem in which a particular echoing rhythm is prevalent, or that particular echoing rhythm even though it be confined to a single line or period. And one serious disadvantage of the term *ḳinah* rhythm lies in the ease with which it obscures the fact

[1] *Isaiah* ("International Critical Commentary"), i. p. lxiii.

that within the same elegy (*ḳinah*) or other rhythmically similar poem more than one type of rhythm as a matter of fact occurs.

But whether even *echoing rhythm* and *balancing rhythm* be a satisfactory terminology for the two broad classes of Hebrew rhythm under which sub-classes may be found, this broad fundamental distinction itself is nevertheless worth keeping clear ; it forms a comfortable piece of solid ground from which to set out and to which to return from excursions into the shaking bog or into the treacherous quagmire that certainly needs to be traversed before the innermost secrets of Hebrew metre can be wrested and laid bare.

In Lamentations v. a balancing rhythm, in Lamentations iv. an echoing rhythm prevails ; a rapid reading of the two chapters will suffice to verify this general statement. But, if the reader will re-read the chapters with closer attention to details, he will probably feel that Lamentations v. 2—

נחלתנו נהפכה לזרים
בתינו לנכרים

Our inheritance is turned unto strangers,
Our houses unto aliens,

differs not only in respect of its parallelism but also of its rhythm from most of the other verses in the same chapter, and also that, while it is rhythmically unlike most of chap. v., it is

rhythmically like most of Lamentations iv.;
it is, for example, rhythmically unlike Lamentations v. 13—

בחורים טחון נשאו
ונערים בעץ כשלו

Young men bare the mill,
And youths stumbled under the wood;

it is, on the other hand, rhythmically like, *e.g.*,
Lamentations iv. 8—

זכו נזיריה משלג
צחו מחלב

Her nobles were purer than snow,
Whiter than milk.

One or two other verses in Lamentations v. may
at first seem ambiguous : are verses 3 and 14,
for example, in balancing or echoing rhythm ?

Again, in Lamentations iv., where the echoing rhythm clearly and greatly prevails, a few
verses disengage themselves as exceptions; *e.g.*
verse 13—

מחטאות נביאיה
עונות כהניה

For the sins of her prophets,
The iniquities of her priests,

gives the impression of balance rather than echo,
though the entire rhythmical impression is not
quite that which is left by the balancing rhythm
of Lamentations v.

Thus, without any more detailed examination
or exacter measurement of lines, we reach the
important conclusion, which a close study of

Lamentations i. abundantly confirms, that the same poem may contain distichs of different metrical character.

But within what limits may or do these and other differences occur within the same poem? If that question is to be answered we must discover some principle of measurement which will enable us to determine in less simple cases than those just cited when the rhythm remains constant and when it changes, and how.

Is balance, then, due to (1) equality in the *number* of syllables in the two lines, and echo to inequality in the number of syllables? If this be so, then Lamentations v. 3,

יתומים היינו אין אב

אמותינו כאלמנות

Orphans were we, without father,
(And) our mothers (were) as widows,

is in balancing rhythm, the number of syllables in each line being eight.

Or (2) is balance due to the sum of the metrical values of all syllables in each line being the same, even though the number of the syllables differs? The number of syllables in a Latin hexameter varies; but the sum of the metrical values of the syllables must always be equivalent to six spondees. If this were the true account of Hebrew rhythm, it would become necessary to determine what syllables are metrically long, what short.

Or (3) is balance due to equality in the number of stressed or accented words or syllables in the two lines, echo to the presence of a greater number of stressed syllables in the first line, and a smaller number in the second ?   If so, is there *no* limit to the number of unstressed syllables that each stressed syllable can carry with it ?   If there is a limit, what is it ?   Is it no wider than in *Christabel* ? or is it as wide as, or wider than, in Anglo-Saxon poetry ?

Of these three possibilities, the first two seem to me to have been ruled out in the course of discussion and investigation concerning Hebrew metre. I confine myself to some discussion of the third.

It is just possible that some of the ancients had analysed the laws of Hebrew poetry sufficiently to detect the essential character of the stressed syllables. The interesting suggestion has been thrown out [1] that the author of Wisdom, who certainly attempted to naturalise parallelism in Greek, also attempted a new Greek rhythm on the model of the Hebrew by making the parallel periods in Greek contain the same number of accented syllables. Then, again, in the opinion of some the difficult passage in Origen which refers to the subject of Hebrew metre implies an appreciation of the stressed syllables.[2]

[1] *Encyclopaedia Biblica*, col. 5344.
[2] Origen's scholion has already been cited above, p. 12 *n*. The subject of the scholion is Psalm cxix. 1—

Be this as it may, there has certainly been an increasing agreement among modern students of this subject, particularly under the influence of Ley,[1] to find in the stressed words or syllables the " pivots or posts," to use Professor Saintsbury's phrase, of the Hebrew rhythm.

But allowing this, what is the limit—for there surely must be some limit—to the number of unstressed syllables that may accompany each or any of the stressed syllables ? Again, is there any law governing the position of the stressed syllable in relation to the unstressed syllables that go with it ?

Taking the first of these two questions first :— Does a single word extending beyond a certain given number of syllables *necessarily* contain more than one stress ? or is such a word ambiguous, capable of receiving two, but capable also of receiving only one stress ? And is the actual number of unstressed syllables that may accom-

---

אשרי תמי דרך

ההלכים בתורת יהוה

which contains six fully stressed words and is rendered in the LXX—

Μακάριοι οἱ ἄμωμοι ἐν ὁδῷ,

οἱ πορευόμενοι ἐν νόμῳ κυρίου,

which contains six accents. Ley (*Zeitschr. für die AT. Wissenschaft*, 1892, pp. 212 ff.) argues that one of the things which Origen is struggling to express is that in this particular verse we find the unusual phenomenon of text and translation containing the same number of stressed words and consequently the same rhythm.

[1] Julius Ley, *Die metrischen Formen der hebräischen Poesie*, 1866 ; *Grundzüge der Rhythmus, des Vers- und Strophenbaues in der hebräischen Poesie*, 1875 ; *Leitfaden der Metrik der hebräischen Poesie*, 1887.

pany a stressed syllable neither less nor more than the number of syllables in the longest Hebrew word with inseparable attachments such as a preposition at the beginning and a suffix at the close ? In other words, is the general rule : one word, one stress, to which words of more than a certain number of syllables, say four, so far form an exception that they *may* receive a second stress ? Or, to put it otherwise, in such longer words may the counter-tone as well as the tone count as a full stress ? I incline to the opinion that by the rule that words of a certain length may, but do not necessarily, receive a double stress, we at least approximate closely to an actual law of Hebrew rhythm. But there is a second question : docs every single word receive a stress, or, as in several lines of *Christabel*, may we in Hebrew poetry have not only several syllables but also more words than one to each stress ?

We obtain some light on both these questions from certain characteristics of the Massoretic punctuation, and on the second of them from Assyrian analogy also. The effect of *makkeph* in the Massoretic system is to render unaccented any word which is thus joined to a succeeding word. We may believe that the principle of the Massoretic *makkeph* corresponds to a principle in the ancient language without accepting every particular use of *makkeph* in the Massoretic text as corresponding to the intention of the original writers. Nothing is more probable than that the negative particle לֹא, conjunctions like כִּי, and other particles were frequently toneless : but were they so regularly ? If not, and if also we cannot unquestioningly follow the Massoretic punctuation, then an element of uncertainty arises as to the number of stressed syllables in a given line; for example, do the two lines in Isaiah i. 3,

ישראל לא ידע
עמי לא התבונן

Israel doth not know,
My people doth not perceive,

contain each three stresses (as in MT), or each but two ? We cannot determine this off-hand. If, indeed, we lay down the principle that two stressed syllables must not immediately follow one another, then the two לֹא's must be makkephed, for in each line the syllable that precedes לֹא is stressed; but it is decidedly dangerous to lay this down as a rigid principle, in spite of the strong tendency in MT to use *makkeph* in order to avoid such concurrences. Modern Palestinian popular songs, which have much that is analogous to Hebrew poetry, according to the express testimony of Dalman,[1] admit the concurrence of two tone-syllables. And the import-

---

[1] " Zuweilen stossen auch zwei betonte Silben unmittelbar auf einander," *Palästinischer Diwân*, p. xxiii.

ance of לֹא (*not*) in the two lines above cited
(for the antitheses to the two lines that precede
depend on it) rather strongly indicates that it
there received the stress in each line.

But there are other combinations of words
that are frequently makkephed in the Massoretic
text; for example, constructs and genitives.
Again the question arises : were such combinations regularly read with a single stress ? if not,
has the MT always preserved a correct tradition
of the intention of the original writer ？ We are
thus faced with another group of uncertainties.
These can perhaps be reduced by observing that
in MT there is a far greater tendency to makkeph
construct and genitive if the construct case is
free from prefixed inseparable particles such as
prepositions or the copula ; so, *e.g.*, in Lamentations iv. 9 we find חללי־חרב with, but מחללי הרב
without *makkeph*.

The Massoretic punctuation rests partly on
an ancient tradition, partly on an exegetical
theory, partly on an accommodation of the text
to a recent mode of reading it. It is valuable,
therefore, to have such principles as that the
negative particles are normally, and construct
cases often, toneless, supported by Assyrian
analogy.

In the *Zeitschrift für Assyriologie* for 1895
(pp. 11 ff.) Zimmern published an interesting
Assyrian inscription, a poem as it appeared to be,

though since, as Dr. Langdon informs me, neither Zimmern himself nor any one else has yet succeeded in making a consecutive translation, it may be in reality a succession of disconnected verses written out in illustration of scansion. In any case the important point is that here we seem to have visualised a mode of scansion that throws light on the composition of the feet or rhythmical units in Assyrian, for these verses are divided by longitudinal lines into four sections, and by latitudinal lines into groups of eleven. The longitudinal lines mark off into separate compartments the four stressed syllables or words with their accompanying unstressed syllables, which here, as in most Assyrian and Babylonian poetry, compose the line.

I will briefly summarise the statements made by Zimmern at the time, based on his first examination of this document ; these were amplified in a later article, to which reference will be made below. According to Zimmern, then, the following metrical facts are attested by these scansion tablets :—

(1) Normally there is to one word, one stress ; but (2) the relative pronoun (monosyllabic in Assyrian), the copula, prepositions, the negative particles *la* and *ul*, and the optative particle *lu* receive no stress, but go with the following word to form a single-stress group of syllables ; so also (3) the status constructus and the genitive

generally receive but one stress — on the other hand, if the second substantive has a pronominal suffix they receive two ; (4) two particles and a word, or one particle and a word with a pronominal suffix, form single-stress groups ; (5) two words expressing closely related ideas form a single-stress group—*e.g. abi u banti* ; (6) a vocative may be inserted without being reckoned in any of the four stress-groups that compose the line.

Though we make the most of the suggestions from both sources, the Massoretic punctuation of the Hebrew text and the scansion of the Assyrian tablets, we shall still be left with a fair range of uncertainty, and many lines of Hebrew poetry will occur in which, judged by themselves, the number of stresses will remain ambiguous. And that ambiguity will be still further increased when we attempt to determine what single words, if any, may receive two stresses ; here again some light is cast on the possibility of such double stress by the Massoretic punctuation ; for as the effect of *makkeph* is to bring two or more words under one tone, so the effect of *metheg* is to indicate the presence in the same word of two tones, of a counter-tone in addition to the main tone. But there is no probability that all the counter-tones marked by *metheg*, such, for example, as the first syllable in forms like קְטָלִי, really received a stress ; and for this theory of double-stressed words we receive, I think, no very helpful analogy from Assyrian.

The question, then, arises : Can we discover a more accurate method of determining the limits of what may accompany a stressed syllable ? It is the attempt to answer this question that occupies in the main the attention of recent theorisers on Hebrew metre, and it is in the attempt to answer it that they diverge from one another.

The popularity which for a time was enjoyed by Bickell's [1] system has waned in favour of that of Sievers, which has the advantage of being very much more elaborately and systematically worked out. I propose very briefly to summarise some of the chief points in Sievers' system, premising at the outset that if it could be held to be established it would (1) greatly reduce, though not entirely eliminate, lines of ambiguous measurement ; and (2) give for every line, regarded by itself independently of its association with any other line, a clear rhythmical definition.

In connexion with the present discussion the two fundamental laws of Sievers' system can, perhaps, best be stated thus : (1) the number of unstressed syllables that may accompany a

---

[1] Gustav Bickell, *Metrices biblicae regulae exemplis illustratae* (1879) ; *Carmina Veteris Testamenti metrice* (1882); *Die Dichtung der Hebräer* (1882). The English reader will find a useful summary of Bickell's system in W. H. Cobb, *A Criticism of Systems of Hebrew Metre*, pp. 111-128.

stressed syllable must never exceed four, and only in a particular type of cases may it exceed three. Corollary : every word containing more than five syllables must have two stresses. (2) The stressed syllable regularly *follows* the unstressed syllables that accompany it ; and more than a single unstressed syllable may never follow the stressed syllable that it accompanies.

Using the term anapaest not of course of a combination of two short followed by a long syllable, but of two unstressed syllables followed by one that is stressed, Sievers claims that the Hebrew rhythm rests on an anapaestic basis, and that the normal foot is

$$\times \times \acute{-}$$

examples of such feet being דְּרָכִים, יִקְטְלוּ, עַל־בְּנֵי. Possible variations of the normal foot are—

(1) $\times \times \times \acute{-}$
(2) $\times \acute{-}$, and even
(3) $\acute{-}$

Moreover, since the stress may fall on a syllable which with an additional and secondary short syllable corresponds to an original single syllable, as in the segholates, further variations are $\times \times \breve{\,} \times$, $\times \times \times \breve{\,} \times$, etc., an example of such feet being לִפְנֵי־הַמֶּלֶךְ.[1]

---

[1] After Sievers had indicated his theory in outline, Zimmern (*Zeitschrift für Assyriologie*, xii. 382-392) returned to the examination of the scansion tablets referred to above (p. 140 f.), and found that between

If this theory be entirely sound, or even if it closely approximate to the truth, it will considerably diminish the range of uncertainty that must remain so long as we leave entirely undetermined the limits of the unstressed syllables that may accompany a stressed syllable. This may be illustrated by an example : how many stressed syllables are there in each of these lines in Psalm i. 1,

ובדרך חטאים לא עמד

ובמושב לצים לא ישב ?

The question turns on the treatment of לא ; was it stressed or unstressed ? The Massoretic punctuation leaves the negative in each line disunited from the verb and therefore capable at least of being stressed ; and Dr. Briggs [1] in calling the lines tetrameters certainly allows a stress to each לא. I think it may be urged against this

---

two stressed syllables at least one, generally two, and not rarely three unstressed syllables occurred, but never or quite rarely more than three.

It may be worth while adding here that Dalman (*Palästinischer Diwân*, p. xxiii, with footnote) has found that, in the modern Palestinian (Arabic) poems that follow not a quantitative but an accentual system, one to three, and occasionally four, unstressed syllables occur between the stressed syllables. The value of these Palestinian analogies lies in the fact that we are dealing not with speculations as to how a written poem was or could be pronounced, but with the manner in which hitherto unwritten poems were actually read to the editor who committed them to writing.

[1] It so happens that I have mainly referred to details in Dr. Briggs' work with which I disagree ; the more reason, therefore, that I should recall the fact that in the subject with which I am now dealing Dr. Briggs was a true pioneer, and that he was one of the first writers in English to insist on the fundamental importance in Hebrew prosody of the stressed syllable.

L

that לֹא has nothing like the need of emphasis and stress here that it has in the lines previously cited from Isaiah i. 3, where לֹא יָדַע is antithetic to יָדַע in the previous distich. I should therefore think it most probable that the lines were three-stressed and not four-stressed; but apart from the bearing of the rest of the Psalm on the question we cannot determine the point unless we are justified in calling in such a theory as that of Sievers. Now it is perfectly true that even on that system monosyllabic feet are possible, and that לֹא in particular at times, as in Isaiah i. 3, stands by itself as a foot; but if the anapaest is the basis of the rhythm, we cannot naturally divide each of the two perfectly normal anapaests לֹא־יָדַע and לֹא־יָשׁב into a monosyllabic and a dissyllabic foot; on Sievers' theory the only natural way of reading the two lines is with three stresses; they are, to use Dr. Briggs' terminology, trimeters, not tetrameters.

Sievers' theory, then, if established, would reduce the number of lines which, measured with exclusive reference to the stressed words or syllables only, are ambiguous. Is the theory, then, as a matter of fact, so firmly established on perfectly certain data that it does actually diminish the number of uncertainties that are left when we attempt to count stressed syllables simply without very closely defining either the position which such stressed syllables must

occupy, or the number of unstressed syllables
which may accompany them ? I doubt it. I
cannot here undertake any examination or criticism of Sievers' long and exhaustive exposition
of his theory ; nor can I examine the arguments,
worthy as most of them are of the closest attention, by which he supports certain theories of
vocalisation on which his metrical system rests.
But these theories, however much may be said
for some of them, are not all of them as yet so
certainly established as to allow the metrical
system, which in part suggests them, but which
also certainly rests upon them, to furnish a
sufficiently sure instrument for eliminating the
uncertainties that arise when we measure a
Hebrew text by the stressed syllables only. The
degree of uncertainty which the theory would
remove is largely counterbalanced by the insecurity of the basis on which it rests.

In illustration of what I have just said it must
suffice to refer to a few classes of the conjectural
vocalisation adopted by Sievers, all of which are
more or less essential to the smooth working out
of his system.

(1) Partly on general phonetic grounds, partly
from actual features of the Massoretic vocalisation, such as the alternative forms of the type
לִמְּלָכִים and לִמְלָכִים, and the complete abandon-
ment of the reduplication and also of the following
syllable in such inflexions as זִכְרוֹ from זֵכֶר, שְׁבִינוֹת

from שִׁבָּיוֹן, Sievers infers that *regularly* when, owing to inflexion, the full vowel after a reduplicated consonant is lost, the reduplication and also the vowel that followed it were entirely lost also; and that, for example, לְמַלָּכִים was always pronounced *lamlachim* in three syllables, never *lammᵉlachim* in four, and וִיהִי always *waihi* in two syllables (cp. מִידֵי not מִידֵי), and never *wayᵉhi* in three syllables.

(2) Again, the consonantal text of the Old Testament distinguishes two forms of the second person perfect alike in the masculine and the feminine. The second person masculine is generally of the form קָטַלְת, more rarely of the form קָטַלְתָה, and again the feminine is generally קָטַלְת, and more rarely קָטַלְתִי. According to the received vocalisation, the masculine, however spelt, was pronounced *ḳaṭalta*, and the feminine *ḳaṭalt*. Sievers, however, treats *both* the rarer forms קָטַלְתָה and קָטַלְתִי as trisyllabic, pronouncing them *ḳaṭalta* and *ḳaṭalti* respectively; and he treats the more frequent form קָטַלְת, alike whether masculine or feminine, as dissyllabic, pronouncing it *ḳaṭalt*.

(3) Certain pronominal forms were originally pronounced with a syllable less than in MT; thus MT יָדְךָ, pausal יָדֶךָ, has replaced יָדְךָ; cp. such forms in Origen's *Hexapla* as ηχαλαχ = הֵיכָלֵךְ, βαχ = בָּךְ, and in Jerome *goolathach* = גְּאֻלָּתֵךְ. And it is also argued that the endings הָ, הָ were once monosyllabic.

It will be seen from the foregoing examples that the tendency of Sievers' vocalisation is to reduce the number of syllables below the number produced by the received system. Consequently what I stated as the first fundamental law of his metrical system, viz. that not more than *four* unstressed syllables may under any circumstances accompany one stressed syllable, often means not more than *five* stressed syllables counted according to the received system.

One other of Sievers' theories with regard to the pronunciation of Hebrew poetry must also be noted ; it works in an opposite direction, and is designed to supply unstressed syllables when their absence would be too keenly felt. Sievers admits monosyllabic feet, but he abhors the concurrence of two stressed syllables ; he calls to his aid the analogy of singing : as in singing a single syllable is sung to more than one note by virtually repeating the vowel sound, so Sievers postulates that when tone-syllables appear to follow one another immediately the long tone-syllable was broken up into two in pronunciation ; *e.g.* in such circumstances לא was pronounced not *lō*, but *lŏ-ō*, and קול not *kōl*, but *kŏ-ōl*, and the metrical foot is in each case not ◡́ but × ◡́.

Two things seem to me to gain probability from Sievers' exhaustive discussion, even though the elaborated system rests on too much that is still uncertain or insecure : (1) the natural basis of Hebrew rhythm is anapaestic rather than dactylic ; this is really an obvious corollary from the regularity with which the Hebrew accent falls on the last syllable of words, and the infrequency of detached monosyllables, and earlier metrists also have for the most part detected a prevalence of anapaestic or iambic rhythm in Hebrew ; (2) in the union of two or more words under one stress, and in the distribution of long words among two stress groups we should be guided by the principle that the stress groups within the same period are likely to be not too dissimilar in size and character ; and in general it is safer to proceed on the assumption that particles like כִּי, עַל, etc., rarely receive the stress unless for some reason an actual sense-emphasis falls upon them.

The sum of the whole matter is that we are left with an instrument for the measurement of rhythm capable of doing some service, but much less delicately accurate, or much less clearly read, than we could wish. With this instrument we must work at the difficult question, which I have so far merely indicated, but which I shall examine more closely in the next chapter : What limits, if any, are set to the number of different rhythms that may be introduced into the same poem ?

In concluding the present chapter I will consider one further possible, and even probable, service which it appears to me that parallelism may render in reducing the element of uncertainty in determining the rhythm of particular lines. In Anglo-Saxon, alliteration clearly distinguishes three of the stressed syllables in a line, leaving only the fourth outwardly undistinguished; Hebrew has no such outward indication of this all-important element in the rhythm; in particular all particles, all construct cases, and some other types of words are rhythmically ambiguous; in any given line they may be stressed or they may not. What I suggest is that parallel terms tended at least to receive the same treatment in respect of stress or non-stress. I will give one or two illustrations of the value of this law if its probability be admitted. If we take by itself the line (Isa. i. 10),

שמעו דבר יהוה קציני סדם

Hear the word of Yahweh, ye judges of Sodom,

we may certainly be in doubt whether דבר יהוה received one stress or two, and whether the whole line was read with four stresses or five. Sievers gives it but four, and thereby in its context, as I believe, treats it wrongly. I suggest that דבר (*word*) ought to receive the same metrical value as its parallel term תורת (*law*) in the completely and symmetrically parallel line or period that

follows, and that we should read both periods
alike with five stresses—

שמעו דבר יהוה קציני סדם
האזינו תורת אלהינו עם עמרה

Heár the-wórd of-Yahwéh, júdges of-Sódom,
Give-eár-to the-láw of-our-Gód, peóple of-Gomórrah.

A more troublesome example is Isaiah i. 4—

הוי גוי חוטא
עם כבד עון

Ah ! sinful nation,
People laden with iniquity.

This Sievers reads thus—

הוי גוי־חוטא
עם־כבד עון

and so far observes the rule which I am suggesting
that he leaves both the parallel terms גוי and עם
unstressed ; on the other hand, חוטא and its
parallel כבד עון do not receive the same treatment, though they are quite capable of so doing.
A more probable reading of the lines will be
either

הוי־גוי חוטא
עם כבד־עון

or

הוי | גוי חוטא
עם כבד־עון

I take as a last example an *apparent* exception
to the law. Lamentations i. 1 reads—

איכה ישבה בדד | העיר רבתי עם
היתה כאלמנה | רבתי בגוים
שרתי במדינות | היתה למס

How doth she sit solitary, | —the city (once) great in popula-
tion !
She is become like a widow, | she that was great among the
nations :
She that was mistress over provinces, | she hath been (set)
to forced labour.

Budde suspected העיר, *the city*, in the first
line on the ground that at present the second
half of the first line contains three stresses,
whereas it should only contain two. Sievers
removes the ground for suspicion by treating
רבתי-עם, *great in population*, together as a single
stress. At first this seems, by making רבתי,
great, unstressed, to give a term in the first
line a metrically different character from that
of corresponding terms, רבתי and שרתי, *mistress*,
in the second and third lines. But the parallelism
of רבתי in the first line with רבתי in the second
and שרתי in the third is, as a matter of fact, not
complete ; the real parallel in the first line to
רבתי, *great*, in the second line and שרתי, *mistress*,
in the third is not רבתי by itself but רבתי עם, *great
in population*, i.e. *populous*, which, so taken
together, is also an antithetic parallel to the
single-stressed word בדד, *solitary*, in the first half
of the line ; it is only when taken together
that the words רבתי עם express the idea in the
mind of the writer, viz. the populousness of the

city, whereas רבתי in the second and שרתי in the
third line sufficiently express by themselves the
ideas of the " great lady " (in antithesis to " the
widow ") and " the princess " ; בגוים, *among the
nations,* and במדינות, *over provinces,* respectively
serve merely to amplify the two ideas. The
distinction between רבתי עם and רבתי בגוים is
shown grammatically by the difference in construction ; and the writer probably allowed himself to repeat the same word רבתי in the two lines
instead of using two different and synonymous
terms on the same kind of principle as that of
the well-known law of Arabic poetry that the
same word may be repeated in the course of a
poem as the rhyme word, provided that the word
is used on the two occasions with some difference
of meaning.

Thus, perhaps, a close examination of Lamentations i. 1 confirms, rather than reveals an exception to, the law which I have suggested, and
incidentally shows that העיר is not merely metrically possible, which Budde had denied and which
is all that Sievers claimed, but metrically required.

CHAPTER V

VARIETES OF RHYTHM: THE STROPHE

CHAPTER V

HEBREW rhythms fall into two broad classes according as the second line of the successive distichs is equal in rhythmical quantity to, and therefore balances, the first line, or is less in quantity than, and so forms a kind of rhythmical echo of, the first line. Distichs in which a shorter first line is followed by a longer second line are relatively speaking so rare [1] that in a first broad division they may well be neglected; and we may classify the great majority of rhythms not merely as distichs consisting of equal or unequal lines, but, so as to bring out the regular and more striking difference between them, as balancing and echoing rhythms respectively.

But before we can discuss the question of the extent to which, or the sense in which, strophe may be said to be either a regular or an occasional form of Hebrew poetry, it becomes necessary to subdivide these two broad classes of rhythms

---

[1] Examples are given below, pp. 176–182.

157

which have hitherto mainly engaged our attention,
and then to consider to what extent different
rhythms may enter into one and the same poem.
This subdivision must be carried through by
applying a measure which, as I have pointed
out in the previous chapter (p. 150), is less
accurate than we could desire, and leaves us with
corresponding uncertainties which must not be
forgotten. Even when we may be certain of the
general class into which a particular distich may
fall we may remain uncertain of its exact measurement ; for example

ישראל לא ידע
עמי לא התבונן

a distich which occurs in Isaiah i. 3, is certainly
a distich of equal lines (balancing rhythm): but
whether each line contains three or only two
stressed words is, as we have already seen (p. 139),
in some measure uncertain.

Whether the unit in Hebrew poetry is the line
or the distich has been much discussed ; regarded
from the standpoint of parallelism, it is obviously
the distich that is the unit ; the single line in this
case is nothing ; it is incapable of revealing its
character as a parallelism. On the other hand,
it is rhythmically just as easy to measure a single
line as to measure a distich ; and at times it is
necessary so to do : for, as there alternate with
distichs that consist of parallel lines distichs that

contain no parallelism, so occasionally there alternate with these distichs single lines or mono-stichs, and also tristichs in which one of the three lines may or may not be parallel to the other two. For these non-parallel isolated stichoi, or the third stichoi of tristichs, measurement of the line becomes necessary.

At the same time, unless an anapaestic rhythm such as Sievers claims to discover, or other rhythm equally well defined, can be shown to prevail within the lines, these isolated stichoi owe their rhythmical character, so far at least as we can discern or measure it, to the fact that they contain the same number of stressed syllables as the halves of the distichs among which they occur.

Thus in any case the distich remains so char-acteristic of Hebrew poetry that it is better, so far as possible, even in a rhythmical classifica-tion, to measure and classify by distich rather than stichos : though the stichos when isolated will of course call for measurement too.

Distichs consist of (i.) those in which the lines are equal ; and (ii.) those in which one line (generally the second) is shorter than the other.

The first class of distichs subdivides into (*a*) distichs with two stresses in each line, for which we may use the formula 2 : 2 ; (*b*) distichs with three stresses in each line (3 : 3) ; and (*c*) distichs with four stresses in each line (4 : 4).

Of these three types of balancing rhythm the first
and third are intimately connected : for four-
stress lines are commonly divided into two equal
parts by a caesura, and the pause at the caesura
is often strong enough to justify, regard being
had to rhythmical grounds alone, treating each
period of four stresses as a distich of two-stress
lines.   Any isolated group of two periods of four
stresses is best classified as a single distich of
four-stress lines, or two distichs of two-stress
lines, according as parallelism occurs between the
clauses or sentences of two stresses or of four
stresses.   But in view of this intimate connexion
it is not surprising that combinations of two
two-stress clauses or sentences, and combinations
of two four-stress sentences, occur in the same
poem.   Such a mixture of rhythms, if in such
case we are right in speaking of a mixture of
rhythms at all, exactly corresponds to the fact
that, in the same *ḳinah* or elegy, parallelism
sometimes occurs between the two unequal
sections of three and two stresses respectively,
and sometimes does not ; in the latter case we
may, if we will, speak of a line of five stresses, and
in the former of a distich in which a two-stress
line follows a three-stress line ; but the line in
the one case and the distich in the other are
rhythmically identical, since each contains five
stresses ; there is no real change in the rhythm,
though the change in the parallelism introduces

a markedly different effect[1] which it is well to render as manifest as possible.

If, at least where parallelism commonly takes place between sections of three and two stresses respectively, we more properly speak of a *distich* of unequal lines than of a *line* of five stresses, then clear examples of distichs of two-stress lines are those which interchange with the 3 : 2 distichs in Lamentations i., iii., iv. : as, for example, iii. 15—

השביעני במרורים
הרוני לענה

He hath filled me with bitterness,
He hath sated me with wormwood.

However we choose to term them, combinations of parallel clauses of two stresses do, as a matter of fact, interchange within the same poem with distichs of four-stress parallel lines : so, for example, in 2 Samuel i. 22—

מדם חללים
מחלב גברים
קשת יהונתן לא־נשוג אחור
וחרב שאול לא־תשוב ריקם

From the blóod of the sláin,
From the fát of the míghty,
The bów of Jonathán túrned not báck,
And the swórd of Sául retúrned not émpty.

For are we not forced by the parallelism to place a much greater pause between the first two sets

[1] Cp. *e.g.* Isaiah i. 10 f., 18-20, 21-26, and see *Isaiah* ("International Critical Commentary"), p. lxvi (Introduction, § 54) ; see also *ibid.* pp. 4 f., 26, 31.

M

of two words than between the next two sets, at
the end of the first of these four lines than in the
middle of the third or fourth line ?   And are not
the two short parallel periods really separated
by almost as strong a pause as the two longer
ones that follow ?   If we call the two longer ones
a distich of four-stress lines, why not the two
shorter ones a distich of two-stress lines ?   Does
not the passage really consist of two distichs
rather than of a single tristich (cp. R.V.) of three
four-stress lines ?

For another example of this combination we
may turn to Isaiah xxi. 3—[1]

עַל־כֵּן מָלְאוּ מָתְנַי חַלְחָלָה
צִירִים אֲחָזוּנִי כְּצִירֵי יוֹלֵדָה
נַעֲוֵיתִי מִשְּׁמֹעַ
נִבְהַלְתִּי מֵרְאוֹת

Thérefore fílled are my lóins with wríthing,
    Pángs have séized me as of a wóman in trávail.
I am bént (with pain) at what I héar,
    I am dismáyed at what I sée.

Here the first two periods must be regarded as a
distich of four-stress lines : the lines cannot be
subdivided into distichs of two-stress lines as
which so much of the rest of the poem may be,
and, indeed, is best read.[2]

[1] Cp. *Isaiah*, pp. 348 f. ; also my article, "The Strophic Division of
Isaiah xxi. 1-10, and xi. 1-8," in the *Zeitschr. für die AT. Wissenschaft*,
1912, pp. 190 ff.

[2] The existence of two-stress lines in Isa. xxi. 1-10 is, indeed, denied
by Lohmann. In the *Zeitschr. für die AT. Wissenschaft*, 1912, pp.
49-55, he had urged, and in reply to my criticism (contained in the
article mentioned in the previous footnote) he maintains (in the same

Which is the best way to divide the Hebrew text, or even an English translation, though this at least should as far as possible be divided according to the parallelism, often becomes a delicate question. For example, does

המו גוים מטו ממלכות

נתן בקולו תמוג ארץ (Ps. xlvi. 7)

consist of one distich of four-stress lines incompletely parallel to one another (so R.V., *v.* 6) ? or of two distichs of two-stress lines, the lines in the first distich being completely parallel, the lines in the second not parallel at all ? Thus—

> Nations were in tumult,
> Kingdoms were moved ;
> He uttered his voice,
> The earth melted.

If Psalm xlvi. 7 be treated as a single distich, then the first line of the distich is marked by an internal and secondary parallelism ; and it is

journal, 1913, pp. 262-264), that the whole of this poem except *vv.* 8 and 9 originally consisted of four-stress periods, and that *vv.* 8 and 9 consisted of five six-stress periods, each equally divided by a double caesura into three two-stress sections. But this theory rests on textual emendations that appear to me to lack support independent of the theory itself. I should not very confidently maintain that *v.* 10 must be in its original form ; but it is surely very precarious criticism to argue that because the words הצפה צפה are absent from the LXX in *v.* 5, therefore two other words in the same verse, viz. אכול שתוה, were absent from the original text, and that the words absent from the LXX were present in the original text. Nor again can the words " eating, drinking " be dismissed as " trivial." It is distinctly more probable that the princes were bidden to rise after the banquet had begun rather than while the tables were still being laid. But while in this detail I differ from Lohmann, I repeat what I said in my article, that his discussion is in the main a valuable criticism of Duhm's mistaken treatment of Isa. xxi. 1-10.

to be observed generally that the well-defined
caesura which regularly occurs in four-stress
periods renders it particularly easy for the halves
to receive such secondary parallelism, and so to
assume, when isolated, an appearance of greater
independence. Whatever view we take of particular examples, whether we break them up
into distichs of two-stress lines or distichs of
four-stress lines, the rhythm remains essentially
the same, and our only problem is how best to
do justice to other formal elements in the poem
which differentiate what are, in the last resort,
rhythmically identical periods. There is nothing
that is peculiar to Hebrew poetry in this particular
kind of uncertainty which is produced when,
within a rhythm that remains constant, another
poetical form is irregularly followed. A popular
metre with English poets in the sixteenth century
was the " poulter's " measure, in which lines
of twelve syllables alternate with lines of a
" poulter's " dozen, *i.e.* of fourteen syllables ;
these long but unequal lines rhymed.[1] Divide
the twelve-syllable line of the poulter's measure
in half, and the fourteen-syllable line into lines
of eight and six syllables respectively, supply the
four short lines thus produced with two sets of

[1] Four lines of Grimald in *Tottel's Miscellany* (ed. Arber, p. 110)
may serve as an example :
Of all the heavenly gifts that mortal men commend,
    What trusty treasure in the world can countervail a friend ?
Our helth is soon decayed ; goods, casual, light and vain ;
    Broke have we seen the force of power, and honour suffer pain.

rhymes instead of one so that they rhyme alternately, and the form of the typical short metre
of our hymn-books is the result. But in some
cases the origin of short metre asserts itself, and
within the same hymn the first and third lines
sometimes rhyme and sometimes do not ; as,
for example, in these two consecutive verses of
Wesley's translation of Gerhardt's hymn—

> Give to the winds thy fears,
>   Hope and be undismayed ;
> God hears thy sighs, and counts thy tears,
>   God shall lift up thy head.
>
> Through waves and clouds and storms
>   He gently clears thy way :
> Wait thou His time ; so shall that night
>   Soon end in joyous day—

and so throughout the hymn, though in no
regular alternation, we may observe rhymed and
unrhymed first and third lines. Rhythmically
the two long lines of the old poulter's measure
and the four short lines of modern short metre
are identical : where rhymes regularly mark off
the shorter periods, it is obviously convenient
to make this prominent by dividing into four
lines ; but where the first and third sections
only occasionally rhyme, either course might be
adopted : and so with a Hebrew poem in which
parallelism sometimes, but not invariably or
even predominantly, exists between the halves
of successive periods of four stresses.

Yet, clearly allied as 2 : 2 and 4 : 4 are, at

times it makes some difference whether we treat
the passage as in the one form or the other;
the main difference lies here, that in ambiguous
cases we shall naturally give to the separate lines
of what we regard as a distich of two-stress lines
a greater independence than if we were to regard
these two-stress clauses as merely parts of a
single four-stress line. I take as an example
Psalm xlviii. There are in this Psalm, as is
well known, some difficult phrases and some
doubtful text, but the presence of several short
parallel clauses, enough, I think, to be characteristic of the poem, is certain : on the other
hand, in the present text there is no single clear
case of parallelism between four-stress periods.
This being so, verse 4 (R.V., *v.* 3) ought, I believe,
to be taken not as a single four-stress line (R.V.),
but as a distich 2 : 2 ; it consists of two independent parallel lines—

אלהים בארמנותיה
גודע למשגב

God is in her palaces;
  He hath made himself known as a high retreat.[1]

---

[1] If—and it surely is—it is a good thing to preserve, when this can
be done without detriment to the sense or to English idiom, as much
as may be of the swing and rhythm of the original, the Prayer-Book
version of Psalm xlviii. is not happy, and A.V. ruins the first verse
by omitting a comma. On the other hand, R.V. in *vv.* 1, 2 (Hebrew
2, 3) is very happy, and only goes astray with the crucial verse 3 (Hebrew
4). Its rendering, which does not differ here essentially from P.B.V.
and A.V., might pass if the rhythm of the original were 4 : 4, but is
improbable if the rhythm in the previous verses is, as taken, and
correctly taken, as I believe, by R.V. to be, 2 : 2. Dr. Briggs, on the
other hand, by the help of some emendations, reduces the whole of
verses 1-3 (2-4) to 4 : 4 and renders as follows :—

The latter part of verse 3 (2) of the same Psalm offers, if the text is correct, an example of a tristich of two-stress lines. Clearer examples of the way in which the rhythm produced by a succession of two-stress parallel lines or clauses may expand not only into four-stress periods with a caesura, but also at times into six-stress periods with a double caesura, may be found in Isaiah iv. and xxi. 1-10 : I have already cited two-stress and four-stress distichs from the latter passage ; the six-stress passage occurs in verse 8—

על־מצפה אדני | אנכי עמד | תמיד יומם
ועל משמרתי | אנכי נצב | כל הלילות

Upon a watch tower, O Lord, | am I standing | continually
by day,
And upon my guard-post | am I stationed | all the nights.

Great and highly to be praised in the city is our God.
His Holy Mount is beautiful in elevation, the joy of the whole earth.
Mount Zion on the northern ridge is a royal city.
Yahweh doth strive in her citadels, is known for a high tower.

Apart from the validity of the emendations presupposed, this treatment of the passage seems to me to have against it the fact that it gives an aesthetically inferior result. Some corruption of the text there may be, and in particular the tristich in verse 3 is questionable, but substantially we may, I think, reproduce the sense and rhythm of the original as follows :—

Great is Yahweh,
And highly to be praised,
In the city of our God,
The mountain of his holiness.
Fair in elevation,
The joy of the whole earth,
Is the mountain of Sion,
The recesses of the North,
The City of the Great King.
God is in her palaces ;
He hath made Himself known as a high retreat.

The importance of this expansion of 2 : 2 into 4 : 4 or 6 : 6, as the case may be, will appear later.

Of the balanced rhythm, produced by the union of three-stress lines (3 : 3), it is unnecessary to say much at the present point. These lines *may*, but rarely do, admit a caesura ; [1] and this may occur after the first or the second stress : it may be somewhat strongly marked, as in

וכלביא | מי יקימנו

And as a lioness—who shall rouse him up ?

(Num. xxiv. 9)

or slighter as in both lines of Psalm li. 9—

תחטאני באזוב | ואטהר
תכבסני | ומשלג אלבין

Unsin me with hyssop, | and I shall be clean ;
Wash me, | and I shall be whiter than snow.

While, therefore, 3 : 3 differs from 2 : 2 owing to its greater fullness, it differs from 4 : 4 not only

---

[1] If Vetter's theory of caesura, as propounded in his *Metrik des Buches Job* (1897), were correct, caesura in 3 : 3 would, indeed, be common enough. For 3 : 3 is common in the Book of Job, and Vetter argues that every line of that poem contains a caesura, and thereby differs from Lam. i.-iv. where the longer line (of the 3 : 2 distichs) alone contains a caesura, the shorter being without one. But, according to Vetter's own primary statistical analysis, in only 577 lines out of a total of over 2000 is the caesura immediately obvious ; and of these 577 lines not a few are four-stress lines. In many of the three-stress lines among the 577 there is certainly a caesura, though perhaps not actually in all ; and Vetter's attempt to prove that there is a real caesura in the 1500 odd lines in which it is not immediately obvious, breaks down : see especially König's careful criticism in his *Stylistik*, pp. 323-330. Incidentally Vetter's book contains a large amount of carefully classified and valuable observation.

owing to its less fullness, but also owing to this general absence of caesura, which is almost constantly present in 4 : 4 ; or, if caesura is present in 3 : 3, this rhythm still differs markedly from 4 : 4 owing to the fact that in the one case the caesura necessarily creates an unequal division of the line, whereas in the other it regularly creates an equal division of the line. In either case the difference between 3 : 3 and 4 : 4 is more than a mere difference of fullness, and the effect is strikingly dissimilar.

We come now to consider distichs of which the two lines are not of equal length, or, as we may prefer to regard some of the examples, lines of which the two parts separated by a caesura are not of equal length. With reference to what is in any case the normal echoing rhythm, viz. 3 : 2, it is unnecessary to add anything to what has been already said above. But, as legitimate variations of 3 : 2, Budde, as we have seen (p. 92), admitted in addition to 2 : 2, which by his theory of heavy words he endeavoured to equate with 3 : 2, distichs of the type 4 : 2 and 4 : 3. Whether either 4 : 2 or 4 : 3 ever really produces the echo that is characteristic of 3 : 2 is doubtful; for in most cases at all events the longer line of 4 : 2 and 4 : 3 is itself divided into two equal parts by a caesura ; so that 4 : 2, so far from producing the echo which this arithmetical symbol might suggest, often closely approximates in *rhythmical*

character to a tristich of two-stress lines (2 : 2 : 2),
i.e. to a *balancing* rhythm ; and in the same way
4 : 3 tends to approximate to 2 : 2 : 3, where
also the effect of echo may be and sometimes
certainly is lost.   Be this, however, as it may,
neither 4 : 2 nor 4 : 3 is, as a matter of fact, at
all a frequent variation of 3 : 2, though, unless
we correct the existing text simply in order to
eliminate them, it cannot be denied that such
variations do occasionally occur in poems where
the dominant rhythm is unmistakably 3 : 2.
Such a poem is Isaiah xiv. 4-21, and the present
text contains two 4 : 2 distichs—in *v.* 5 [1] and
v. 16 c, d.   These read—

שבר יהוה | מטה רשעים ‖ שבט משלים

Yahwéh hath bróken | the stáff of the wícked,
  The ród of the rúlers ;

and

הזה האיש | מרגיז הארץ ‖ מרעיש ממלכות

Is thís the mán | who made the eárth trémble,
  Who made kíngdoms quáke ?

In both these examples the caesura dividing
the longer line into two equal halves is obvious ;
and the effect produced is an approximation of
the whole of each complete period to a tristich
in balanced measure (2 : 2 : 2).   True, in these
particular examples owing to the shorter line

---

[1] Sievers' attempt to read this verse (which, to be sure, he pronounces
to be a " sehr fragliche Vers ") even in the present text as 3 : 2 by treating
מטה־רשעים as one stress, and its parallel שבט משלים as two, violates the
law discussed at the end of the last chapter.

being exactly and completely parallel to the
latter half of the longer line, there is a *sense*
echo, which we may represent in symbols thus—
a . b . c . d | c′ d′. But if we wish to reduce the
lines to 3 : 2, so as to obtain the characteristic
rhythmical echo, we must omit יהוה in the one
case and האיש in the other : this leaves admir-
able distichs—

> Bróken is the stáff of the wícked,
>> The ród of the rulers;

and

>> Is thís who made eárth trémble,
>> Who made kíngdoms quáke ?

but for these omissions the only really strong
reason would be the theory, the validity of which
is in question, that 4 : 2 may never occur in a
poem mainly consisting of 3 : 2.

Even apparent examples of 4 : 2 in Lamentations i.-iv. are very few. Perhaps the only [1] actual
example is iv. 20—

רוח אפנו | משיח יהוה ‖ נלכד בשחיתותם

> The bréath of our nóstril, the anóinted of Yahwéh,
>> Is táken in their píts.

But this is an actual example, for it could not be
satisfactorily reduced to 3 : 2 by makkephing one

---

[1] It is very improbable that iv. 18 b was really another, as it appears
to be in the existing text—

קרב קצנו מלאו ימינו כי־בא קצנו

The first קצנו is almost certainly incorrect, and perhaps, as has
been suggested, the two words קרב קצנו stand where there was originally
the one word קצרו. Budde cites also, as examples of 4 : 2 in Lam. i.-iv.,
ii. 13 a and iii. 56; but ii. 13 a can be read, as in MT, as 3 : 2, and in
iii. 56 the text is doubtful.

and one only of the two pairs of words that constitute the first line.　Here again the caesura in the longer line is obvious ; and in this instance there is no sense echo even ; the real parallelism is between the two halves of the longer line ; the parallel scheme is a . b | a′. b′ | c . d, and the approximation to a balanced tristich 2 : 2 : 2 strikingly close.

Whether either 4 : 2 or 4 : 3 ever acquired the same independence as 2 : 2, 3 : 3, 4 : 4, or 3 : 2 is doubtful ; neither ever seems to constitute the dominant rhythm of a poem of any length, still less to prevail throughout such a poem. But neither 4 : 2 nor 4 : 3 is a mere variant of 3 : 2 ; as such the occurrence of these rhythms is at most very infrequent.　On the other hand, the existence certainly of 4 : 2, and probably of 4 : 3, apart from poems in which the dominant rhythm is 3 : 2, is well established.　Sievers was, I believe, the first to claim clearly that 4 : 3 was, so to speak, a rhythm in its own right, that, at all events, it was not only a mere variant of 3 : 2 ; he thereby made it possible to regard certain poems as more regular than they had previously appeared to be.　In his earlier work [1]

---

[1] *Metrische Studien*, i. 102, 117, 569-571. In his *Text-proben* he found, in addition to many examples in Ps. ix., x. discussed above, several doubtful examples of 4 : 3 in Ps. iv., and six or seven examples in Mal. i. 10-13.　A few other examples selected from his *Text-proben* or his collection in the appendix (570 f.) are : Judg. v. 4 c, d ; Ps. i. 5, 6, xii. 4 ; Job iii. 6 (to שׁוה), iv. 10, 11 ; Prov. i. 5, 8 ; Isa. xl. 12 c, d. An example not cited by Sievers may be found in the present text

Sievers himself regarded this rhythm as rare, though in an appendix he briefly stated, what he has since endeavoured to work out, that, though rare in those parts of the Old Testament which have commonly been understood to be poetry, it was the regular rhythm of those Hebrew narratives which, though they have commonly been regarded as prose, are in reality metrical. The one poem among those first studied by Sievers in which 4 : 3 seemed to him to be frequent, was Psalms ix. and x. In some respects this is obviously a bad specimen to be obliged to work from, for the destruction in parts of it of the alphabetic scheme gives us a fair warning that the text is corrupt.[1] Still, making all allowance for this, Sievers seems to me to make out a tolerably safe case for 4 : 3 as an independent rhythm, though, unless he is right in finding it prevalent in narratives commonly regarded as prose, it was nothing like so frequent as 2 : 2, 3 : 3, 4 : 4, and 3 : 2.

Some years ago, before I had familiarised myself with Sievers' work, and, I think, before I had ever even looked into his book, I attempted a reconstruction of Psalms ix., x.[2] In so doing

---

of Hos. viii. 4 ; but this may originally have been 3 : 3, for הם may well be a mere dittograph of the first two letters of the following word הכליכו. See also Job i. 21.

[1] See below, Chapter VIII.

[2] In an article in the *Expositor* (Sept. 1906, pp. 233-253): this now appears as Chapter VIII. of the present work.

I remarked : " The lines throughout the poem are of equal or approximately equal length, the normal length being three or four accented words. Of the eighty-three lines into which the Revised Version divides the two Psalms, fifteen are abnormally long or short, *i.e.* they contain more than four or less than three accented words." But as I then proceeded to show, these fifteen exceptionally long or short lines in the Revised Version mostly vanish when even the present Hebrew text is correctly divided and punctuated. The poem, then, consisted almost, if not quite, entirely of *lines* of three or four accents. This conclusion was, of course, consistent with some or all of the *distichs* being 4 : 3 ; but Dr. Cheyne, who had a short time before devoted a careful study[1] to the metre as well as to other aspects of the poem, excluded this possibility, for he found in the fact that the poem was partly trimeters, partly tetrameters, an indication either of the imperfect skill of the Psalmist in the management of his metre, or of the interference of a second writer with the original. Dr. Briggs's view[2] seems to be similar. But if it was the *intention* of the writer to use some 4 : 3 *distichs*, it is that intention and neither lack of skill nor subsequent

[1] In the *Book of Psalms* (1904), i. 27 f.

[2] In the " International Critical Commentary," p. 70, and the notes, pp. 72 and 74, on the ז and נ strophes : he rejects these strophes in their entirety because they appear to him to consist of four-stress lines, and according to his theory the poem was originally exclusively 3 : 3.

alteration of the poem that is the real reason why the poem contains both trimeter and tetrameter *lines*. Dr. Cheyne's criticism is tantamount to a denial of the existence of a rhythm 4 : 3, just as it would be tantamount to a denial of 3 : 2 to complain that Lamentations i.-iv. consists partly of trimeters and partly of dimeters.

Of the forty distichs measured by Sievers in Psalms ix., x. he regards twelve [1] as clear examples and twenty-two others as probable examples of 4 : 3 ; the latter and larger group depend on assuming some textual corruption, and a few, or perhaps even most, of the smaller group are in some degree ambiguous ; but, even if we had no other evidence than that of Psalms ix., x., it would seem to me unsafe to deny the probability of the actual existence of 4 : 3 distichs. We shall have to examine some interesting examples of these in the next chapter (p. 234); meantime, I give two of the clearest examples in Psalms ix., x., viz. x. 16 and ix. 9 :

יהוה מלך עולם ועד [2]
אבדו גוים מארצו

Yahweh [2] hath become king for ever and ever,
Perished are the nations out of his land.

---

[1] Viz. ix. 9, 10, 12, 13, 20; x. 1, 2 (to חשבו), 13, 14 a, b and c, d, 15, 16.

[2] Briggs reduces this to 3 : 3 by omitting יהוה: he is then compelled to treat יהוה as a vocative and to render,

O King, for ever and ever.

¹ והוא ישפט תבל בצדק
ידין לאמים במישרים

And 'tis He¹ will judge the world in righteousness,
He will pass sentence on the peoples in equity.

Before we pass to a further consideration of
4 : 2 rhythm it will be convenient to refer briefly
to what might in the abstract appear to be
natural variations of 4 : 3 and 3 : 2, viz. 3 : 4 and
2 : 3 ; as a matter of fact both these last-named
rhythms are exceedingly rare.   Nor is this difficult to understand, if the desire that was satisfied
by 4 : 3 and 3 : 2 was a desire for an echoing
effect : for 3 : 2 produces a rhythmical echo,
2 : 3 does not ; whether 4 : 3 commonly produced
such an echo is more doubtful, and certainly the
proportion of apparent examples of 3 : 4 to
4 : 3 distichs is much greater than that of 2 : 3
to 3 : 2.   The unambiguous examples of 2 : 3 are
so few that some scholars, even where nothing
but rhythmical considerations suggest it, would
simply convert 2 : 3 into 3 : 2 by transposing the
longer and shorter lines.   As good an example
of 2 : 3 as any may be found in the first of the
two following long and incompletely parallel lines
from Isaiah xxxvii. 26 :

הלא שמעת | למרחוק אותה עשיתי
מימי קדם ויצרתיה | עתה הבאתיה

Hast thou not heard ? | Long ago I wrought it ;
In days of old I formed it ; | now I have brought it to pass.

---

¹ In order to reduce this to 3 : 3 Briggs omits הוא.

The position of the caesura in the first line here is unmistakable ; and equally unmistakable is the greater length of the second than of the first part of the line. But unless rhythm demands it, there is no ground for transposing the two parts, though sense would clearly *admit* of such transposition.[1]

Another clear case of the shorter preceding the longer section is Isaiah i. 23 (from יתום) if, as the dominant rhythm suggests, this is a five-stress rather than a six-stress period.[2] Again

---

[1] The transposition was suggested by Haupt and adopted by Cheyne in his critical Hebrew text in Haupt's edition of *The Sacred Books of the Old Testament* ("The Polychrome Bible "). Stade in his edition of the Books of Kings for the same work, which was published later, declined to admit the transposition ; but Haupt still maintained his opinion, and remarked that, if the transposition were made, the first hemistich of the first line became parallel to the first hemistich of the second line. This remark is correct, but if it is intended as an argument, it is precarious : the parallelism between the two lines in the existing text may be represented thus—

$$a \quad . b \mid c . d2$$
$$c'2 . d' \mid e . f$$

Adopting the transposition, it becomes

$$a \quad . b2 \mid c . d$$
$$a'2 . b' \mid e . f$$

But in view of what has been said in Chapter II., and especially on pp. 64 ff., the former of these schemes cannot be regarded as abnormal, though it is of a less frequent type than the second. As a matter of fact Lam. i. 11 a, b, 20 a, b present two schemes similar to that of the existing text of Isa. xxxvii. 26. The transposition was suggested afresh by Sievers (*Metrische Studien*, i. p. 441) : some considerations against it are offered by Stade (*op. cit.* p. 280).

[2] Sievers treats the line as 2 : 2 : 2, for which (or rather for 2 : 4) in another connexion there would be much to be said. Should we perchance read יֵרְבוּ for יבוא אליהם ? The LXX does not clearly correspond to the present Hebrew text. If we read יֵרְבוּ the line is unmistakably 2 : 3—unless we transpose its parts.

N

Lam. iii. 27 is clearly a five-stress period, and seems most naturally read as 2 : 3 ; and so with ii. 8 b—

נטה קו | לא־השיב ידו מבלע

He stretched out the line, | he withdrew not his hand from destroying.

But is it so certain, as it might seem to be at first sight, that in the following four cases the main pause was meant to be placed after the second and not after the third word ?

(a) זכור תזכר ותשיח עלי נפשי

Surely remembereth and is bowed down upon me my soul.

(Lam. iii. 20.)

(b) אלה אזכרה ואשפכה עלי נפשי

These I remember and pour out upon me my soul.

(Ps. xlii. 5.)

(c) אז איתם ונקיתי מפשע רב

Then shall I be perfect and innocent from the great transgression.—(Ps. xix. 14.)

(d) מאז שכבת לא־יעלה הכרת עלינו

Since thou hast lain down, the feller cometh not up against us.

(Isa. xiv. 8.)

It is worth while to consider these in the light of seven consecutive lines of five stresses which occur in Isaiah xli. 11-13—

הן יבשו ויכלמו כל־הנחרים בך

יהיו כאין ויאבדו אנשי ריבך

תבקשם ולא תמצאם אנשי מצתך

יהיו כאין וכאפס אנשי מלחמתך

כי־אני יהוה אלהיך מחזיק ימינך

האמר לך אל־תירא אני עזרתיך

אל־תיראי תולעת יעקב מתי ישראל

which may be translated thus, so as to preserve
the order of the Hebrew clauses—

Behold, they shall be ashamed and confounded—all that
                              were enraged at thee;
They shall become nought and perish—the men who con-
                              tended with thee;
Thou shalt seek them and not find them—the men who
                              strove with thee;
They shall become nought and nothing—the men who
                              warred with thee;
For I am Yahweh, thy God, who holdeth fast thy right hand;
Who saith to thee, Fear not; I have helped thee;
Fear not, thou worm Jacob, ye men of Israel.

The last three lines are very obvious examples
of the rhythm 3 : 2 ; and that the four previous
lines are to be read in the same way is scarcely
less certain ; the last clauses in each of these
four lines consist of two words, and they are
parallel to one another ; in the third line the
last clause is in apposition to, or a detached
expansion of, the object (ם . .) of the sentence
which forms the longer half of the line—" them—
the men who strove with thee " ; in the remaining
three lines the last clauses *could* be regarded as
the subjects of the verbs in the longer parts of
the lines, though the normal position for them in
this case would be immediately after the (first)
verb, viz. יבשו in the first, יהיו in the second,
and יהיו in the fourth line ; in view of the
parallelism of these clauses in the first, second,
and fourth lines with the *necessarily* detached
clause at the end of the third line, it is more

probable that they were treated by the writer as
detached amplifications of the subject implicit
in the verbal forms יבשו ויכלמו, ויאבדו . . יהיו and יהיו
respectively; in other words, if we would preserve
in translation the structure of the sentences intended by the writer, we must translate as above
and not as the sentences are translated, for
example, in the Revised Version.

If now we return to the four examples given on
p. 178, we may feel that in (*a*) the writer intended
the nominative clause עלי נפשי to be preceded
by a pause, the two verbs with the common
subject being taken rapidly together; in any
case the sentence is constructed with some
artifice, for the normal position of נפשי would
be after the first clause. Example (*b*) but for
the reminiscence of (*a*) certainly looks like a
genuine 2 : 3, for עלי נפשי in its entirety belongs
to ואשפכה and not at all to אזכרה. But in (*c*)
is מפשע רב intended to be taken with the second
verb only? Finally, in (*d*) are not the contrasted verbs to be closely associated, יעלה
sufficiently completing the sentence for the
moment and then being reinforced by the
nominative sentence which follows, but which
was intended to be pronounced after a pause?
If this view be correct we may translate, not
as above, but—

> Since thou hast lain down, there cometh not up
> The feller against us.

Though several apparent instances [1] of 2 : 3 are found on examination to be open to suspicion, it is probable that this rhythm was actually used though with extreme infrequency. Instances, at least apparent instances, of 3 : 4 are actually rather more numerous than those of 2 : 3, and consequently the proportion of 3 : 4 to 4 : 3, itself a rare rhythm, is much greater than that of 2 : 3 to 3 : 2.   One or two illustrations may suffice here : in Exodus xv. 14 we have

שמעו עמים ירגזון | חיל אחז ישבי פלשת [2]

The peoples heard, they trembled ;
Pangs took hold on the inhabitants of Philistia.

Another example may be found in Psalm iv. 8—

נתתה שמחה בלבי | מעת דגנם ותירושם רבו

Thou hast put gladness in my heart
Greater than when their corn and new wine increase.

In addition to seven [3] examples of 3 : 4 which he regards, whether rightly or wrongly, as incontestable, Sievers (pp. 113 f.) examines thirty-one possible examples, including Numbers xxiv. 3,

---

[1] In addition to those given above Sievers (p. 111) gives as possible, but not all of them probable, examples, Isa. i. 19, v. 1 (to לכרמו), Ps. v. 11 (to ממעצותיהם), all of which might perhaps be 2 : 2 ; Jonah ii. 5, Jer. ii. 28 (from כי־מספר) ; Isa. xl. 4 (but ? read וכל־הר ישפל and so obtain a distich 2 : 2). The two consecutive examples of 2 : 3 at the end of Jonah i. 7 occur in a passage commonly treated as prose, but by Sievers as poetry.

[2] But if חיל אחז (‖ to ירגזון) be makkephed, even this example becomes 3 : 3.

[3] Jer. ii. 20 (to אעבור), 24 (to רוח), Ezek. ii. 1, xv. 7 (to תאכלם), Hos. ii. 4, 7 (from נאני), Prov. iii. 7.

Judges v. 2, 2 Samuel xxiii. 1, Isaiah v. 5, 17, 25, Psalm iv. 8, Job iv. 12, 20, but he finds these almost all open to doubt : either the text [1] is doubtful, or it is not clear that the periods in question must be read as 3 : 4.

The rare occurrence of 4 : 2 as a variant of 3 : 2 has already been considered (pp. 169-172) : there remains for consideration the use of this rhythm in other connexions. A full period of six stresses admits of several modes of division, and these actually occur, (1) 2 : 2 : 2, which, if the sections are marked by parallelism, or are other-wise strikingly independent, may be termed a tristich of two-stress lines ; (2) 3 : 3, the com-monest of all divisions of the six-stress period ; [2] and finally (3) 4 : 2 and 2 : 4. In these last there may be, and commonly is, a slight pause in the longer part of the period, but it is so much less strong than the pause that divides the entire six-stress period into the two unequal divisions that

[1] The influence of textual corruption in the production of apparent examples of 3 : 4 can be observed by comparing the two texts of Ps. xviii.=2 Sam. xxii. The text of the Psalm presents three fairly clear examples of this rhythm : see vv. 7 (from יִשְׁמָע), 29, 35 ; but in the text of 2 Sam. the line in v. 7 is 3 : 2 (it was, perhaps, originally 3 : 3), and v. 29 is 3 : 3. The Hebrew text of v. 35 is rhythmically identical in the Psalm and 2 Sam., but the Lucianic text of the LXX suggests a text which is 3 : 3.

[2] Six-stress periods divided now into two equal parts (3 : 3) by a single caesura, now into three equal parts (2 : 2 : 2) by a double caesura, may occur in the same poem (e.g. Isa. xxvi.) ; Sievers has compared the alternation of hexameters with a single and a double caesura as in the first two lines of the *Iliad*—

Μῆνιν ἄειδε, θεά, ‖ Πηληιάδεω ᾿Αχιλῆος
οὐλομένην ‖ ἣ μυρί᾿ ᾿Αχαιοῖς ‖ ἄλγε᾿ ἔθηκεν.

the difference between 4 : 2 and 2 : 4 on the one hand and 2 : 2 : 2 on the other is clear. The rhythms 4 : 2 and 2 : 4 occur, mainly at all events, as alternatives to 3 : 3. Thus the long poem in Isaiah ix. 7–x. 4, in which 3 : 3 clearly predominates, opens with a 4 : 2 distich—

דבר שלח אדני ביעקב
ונפל בישראל

> The Lord hath sent a word against Jacob,
> And it shall fall upon Israel.

And we may probably find an example of 2 : 4 preceding 3 : 3 in Psalm i. 1—

אשרי האיש
אשר לא־הלך בעצת רשעים
ובדרך חטאים לא־עמד
ובמושב לצים לא־ישב

> Happy is the man
> Who hath not walked in the counsel of the wicked;
> Nor stood in the way of sinners,
> Nor sat in the company of scorners.

The interest of these rhythms, 4 : 2 and 2 : 4, is considerable; though, rhythmically, a distich appears to be the union of two lines, so that the line rather than the distich might be regarded as the rhythmical unit, the practice, which is not, to be sure, very frequent, of equating two periods of six stresses, though in one the two sections produced by the caesura are equal, in the other unequal, indicates that the unity of the six-stress period was strongly felt—a fact which is further

indicated by the occasional parallelism of complete periods of six stresses.[1] Moreover, if we
can trust [2] the text in Psalm cxii. 6—

כִּי־לְעוֹלָם לֹא־יִמּוֹט
לְזֵכֶר עוֹלָם יִהְיֶה צַדִּיק

> For never can he be moved,
> An everlasting remembrance shall the righteous be—

we have, as Sievers has pointed out, yet another
indication that the division of a six-stress period
into two unequal sections was considered as
legitimate as the division into two (or three)
equal sections, and the two unequal parts in
the one case were regarded as each possessing
the same degree of independence and completeness as each of the equal parts in other cases ;
for Psalm cxii. is an alphabetic psalm in which
the alphabetic scheme marks off not successive
six-stress periods, but sections of such periods.

I have now indicated, and given a few typical
or more secure examples of, certain kinds of
differences that may occur within the same
poem. I will now briefly resume two or three
of the more important points : (1) The typical
echoing rhythm is 3 : 2 ; with this 2 : 2 alternates,
sometimes occasionally, sometimes, as in Lamentations i., frequently ; other distichs of unequal
lines, 4 : 3 or 4 : 2, are at best much rarer alterna-

---

[1] *E.g.* in Lam. v. 9, 10 : see above, p. 93.

[2] But it is obviously not improbable that צדיק has shifted down
from the first into the second line.

tives. (2) Of the fundamental balancing rhythms 2 : 2 and 4 : 4 are closely allied and interchange, and by expansion a further natural and occasional variant is 2 : 2 : 2. (3) But this last-mentioned alternative to 2 : 2 or 4 : 4 constitutes a link with the third fundamental balanced rhythm, viz. 3 : 3 ; for 3 : 3 and 2 : 2 : 2 are but different ways of dividing the same higher unity, viz. the six-stress period, which may yet again divide into 4 : 2 or 2 : 4. But (4) in respect of these possible variants poems differ much : some poems contain almost or quite exclusively 3 : 2 distichs, not even admitting the variant 2 : 2, and similarly 3 : 3 is maintained without any break through entire poems or long passages in the book of Job ; in other poems, the alternatives, clear or ambiguous, are so numerous that even what is the basal or dominant rhythm remains doubtful.[1]

[1] In many of these cases where parallelism or other features indicate that we have to do with a poem, but the metrical irregularity or ambiguity is so great that we cannot even determine what is the dominant rhythm, the question of interpolation almost necessarily arises, unless indeed we assume that a Hebrew poet mingled not only distichs of different types, but with these also entirely unrhythmical periods. For this we should find an analogy in Babylonian, if we may accept a recent assertion of Dr. Langdon's that " Babylonian poets felt themselves at liberty to insert prose lines at any juncture " in a poem. This assertion occurs in a note (*Proceedings of the Society of Biblical Archaeology*, xxxiv. (1912), p. 77, *n*. 32) on a transcription and translation of a recently published Assyrian text in which some lines are divided into hemistichs by a space in the middle of the line, and others are not. The tablet certainly seems to contain lines that fit with difficulty into the rhythm 2 : 2 (or 4 : 4) ; but some of the lines without a space in the middle seem as clearly rhythmical as those which have the space. Thus of lines 6 and 7—

I am perhaps leaving too much insecure for it to be wise to advance further ; but the question of the strophe towards which I have been working in this chapter I will briefly discuss—briefly, because what can be safely said here does not require many words to state it, and what has been both unsafely and erroneously asserted has already received, perhaps, sufficient refutation from other writers.

Variations in rhythm would be very readily explained if it could be shown that the poems in which they are found fall into sections in which the same variations recur regularly and in the same manner. But even the alleged evidence of this is slight. Sievers (pp. 121 f.) suggests that originally in Lamentations i. each alphabetic section consisted of one five-stress line (or 3 : 2 distich) followed by two four-stress lines (or 2 : 2 distichs) ; and that the same rhythmical variation 5 : 4 : 4 was thus repeated originally twenty-two times. Unfortunately, this rhythmical scheme can only be imposed upon the poem by much

---

Šâru la tâbu it-ta-bak u-ri-e-a
me-ḫu-û dannu   kakkadi ut-ti-ik,

the former lacks and the latter shows the space; but the former is as clearly a four-stress line as the latter, and they are closely parallel to one another, as we may see from Dr. Langdon's translation—

An evil wind is blown upon my roof,
A mighty deluge passes over my head.

The use of the space to mark the hemistich is not of course peculiar to this tablet; it is found in some of the texts of the Creation Epic (see Zimmern in Gunkel's *Schöpfung u. Chaos*, p. 401 *n.*; King, *Seven Tablets of Creation*, i.).

quite arbitrary textual emendation. Again, in
Canticles i. 4 Sievers finds two strophes each
containing two distichs 3 : 3 followed by a
two-stress monostich. But at best such cases
seem too rare to point to any strophic system
in Hebrew based on this principle.

There are, however, one or two obvious
features of certain Hebrew poems that have
frequently been admitted to prove the existence
of strophes in Hebrew poetry ; and rightly, if
we use the term strophe in no too restricted
sense. The first of these features is the alphabetic
scheme in certain poems. It does not seem to
me a sound criticism of the argument from that
feature to say that the alphabetic scheme cannot
point to a strophic division because in Psalms
cxi., cxii. it marks off single stichoi. All that
follows is that in this instance the units of which
the succession is marked by their initial letters
being the successive letters of the alphabet is
the stichos ; and so in Nahum i. and Psalm xxv.
it is the distich. It is perfectly possible that,
when the alphabetic sections are more than a
distich long, these sections may have something
more characteristic of them than that they
consist of so many distichs or lines. And as a
matter of fact in Lamentations i., ii., and iv., and
very conspicuously in ii., the groups of 3 : 2
(or 2 : 2) distichs form real verse - paragraphs,
for which we may conveniently use the term

strophe ; the clear but slight sense-pause within the distich, and the greater sense-pause at the end of each distich, are matched by a regularly recurring still greater sense-division at the end of every third distich in Lamentations i. and ii., of every second in Lamentations iv. ; and for this reason a single use of the alphabetic letter at the beginning of each *group* of distichs suffices, for the sense holds the group together and gives it a unity. On the other hand, in Lamentations iii., and, I think, the same may be said of Psalm cxix., the distichs united under the same letter have no regular close sense-connexion with one another, or sense-separation from the distichs united under the neighbouring letters of the alphabet ; and indeed in Lamentations iii., it will be remembered, the best examples of distichs parallel to one another, and, therefore, closely related to one another in sense, are distichs belonging to *different* alphabetic groups.[1] Now it is remarkable that precisely in this poem, where the successive distichs of an alphabetic section are not welded together by sense-connexion and so form no organic unity, their union is secured by the purely external device of repeating the same initial letter at the beginning of each distich of the alphabetic section ; and so in Psalm cxix. Lamentations i., ii., and iv. each consists of twenty-two equal verse-paragraphs

[1] See above, p. 141.

which coincide with the alphabetic sections of the poems ; Lamentations iii. consists of sixty-six distichs, three consecutive distichs throughout having the same initial letter, but the poem contains no regular system of verse-paragraphs,[1] and where something approaching a verse-paragraph emerges it as often as not does not coincide with an alphabetic section.

The real conclusion suggested by the alphabetic poems of the Old Testament, then, appears to be this : some Hebrew poems were divided into larger sense-divisions consisting of the same number of distichs throughout the poem, and some were not.

The other feature of some Hebrew poems that has often been regarded as pointing to a strophic division is the occurrence of refrains. This, again, does clearly mark off successive sections of a poem from one another, and more directly and naturally than an alphabetic scheme leads to a division of the poem into sections corresponding to the greater sense-divisions of the poems. In some of these poems the refrain occurs at equal, or approximately equal, intervals (e.g. Isa. ix. 7–x. 4, Ps. xlii.-xliii.), in others at irregular intervals (Ps. xlix.). I am, of course, referring to the intervals in the present Hebrew text, or of that text as it may be emended by

---

[1] The spaces in the R.V. of Lamentations iii. and the lack of spaces in Lamentations i., ii., and iv. suggest the exact opposite of the actual facts.

the help of the ancient versions ; I am not for
the moment considering whether the practice of
some modern scholars in making conjectural
deletions from the text so that the refrain shall
always occur at *exactly* equal intervals is sound
or not.

Some Hebrew poems consist largely or even
entirely of a succession of very loosely connected
lines or distichs ; now and again one or two
distichs may be more closely connected than the
rest, but for the most part we cannot speak of
greater sense-divisions in such poems at all ;
and then nothing that can with any degree of
propriety be termed a strophe disengages itself.
But other poems do develop a theme in such a
manner that greater sense-divisions necessarily
result ; in this case it seems to me convenient
in a translation to distinguish the verse-paragraphs resulting from these greater sense-divisions
by spacing between them : otherwise we fail
to mark externally, though we should do so in
prose, the distinction between paragraph and
paragraph.   This, however, is merely a question
of translation, and has nothing to do with any
intention of the writer to give to the expression
of his thought any further artistic form beyond
the distich with its rhythm and parallelism.
But we may fairly detect the intention of the
writer to submit to such further artistic form,
if we find, though his poem contains no refrain

and is fitted to no alphabetic scheme, that the
greater sense-divisions occur throughout the poem
at regular intervals. But this raises the further
important question : What are regular intervals ?
How ought the paragraphs to be measured ? By
lines ? or by distichs ? How are tristichs to be
treated if they interchange irregularly with
distichs ? In discussions of strophe, Psalm ii.
has often been selected as a clear example of
regular strophic structure ; and so it is, if we
count by Massoretic verses. The articulation of
the poem is perfectly clear ; the greater sense-
divisions occur, and are correctly indicated in
the Revised Version by the spacing, at the end
of every third verse. But the author of Psalm ii.
was certainly innocent of the Massoretic verse-
division, and of this mode of counting. Now,
if we count by lines the four parts are not equal,
for while the first, third, and fourth parts contain
each seven lines, the second contains only six.
If we count by distichs and assume that a tristich
was a legitimate substitute for a distich, the poem
falls into four well-marked sense-divisions, each
containing three distichs (or tristichs).

I will not here examine this aspect of the
question in further detail, but merely record my
opinion that groups of two, three, four, and
occasionally, as in Isaiah ix. 7–x. 4, of a larger
number of distichs, occur in many poems with
such exact or approximate regularity as to make

it probable that the writer deliberately planned and carried out this division into *equal* verse-paragraphs or strophes.

But if a writer might deliberately distribute his poem into equal strophes, might he not also distribute it into unequal strophes ? The occurrence in some poems of a refrain at unequal intervals might seem to indicate that he did. Yet even this is doubtful : the regular recurrence of *equal* sections in any considerable poem cannot easily be attributed to accident ; on the other hand, sections of unequal length are precisely what would naturally result from a writer expressing his thought free from any further restraint beyond that imposed by the distich : unless, therefore, we can detect some method in the irregularity, poems in which the greater sense-divisions, though well marked, consist of a varying number of distichs must be considered to have been written free from the restraint of any strophic law ; in this case, if we use the term strophe, it must mean simply a verse-paragraph of indeterminate length uncontrolled by any formal artistic scheme.

Attempts have from time to time been made, however, to discover method in the irregularity of poems divided into unequal paragraphs, and so to make good the claim that strophe is as constant as parallelism. Köster, in the year 1831, first offered an elaborate examination of the Hebrew strophe ; [1] he reached the conclusion that parallelism of verses is as regular as parallelism of lines, and consequently that all Hebrew poetry is more or less strophic in nature. The " more or less " is an important saving clause ; but a still more important one follows, and this secures Köster's accuracy of observation at the expense of his theory ; he claims that no one can point to any poetical passage of the Old Testament which does not, *within the same degree of license that is permitted in parallelism within the distich,* follow to some extent a symmetrical plan. But since Köster has previously admitted that the parallelism between verse-groups is generally synthetic, and since, as I have maintained, synthetic parallelism is really not parallelism, all that Köster succeeds in maintaining is that in every Hebrew poem there is between verse-groups a parallelism that is generally of the type that is, strictly speaking, not parallelism at all. And this is only a roundabout way of saying that in Hebrew poems there are greater sense-divisions than those of the successive single distichs ; and this, as I have suggested above, though scarcely true of all, is true of very many Hebrew poems.

One other point in Köster's discussion may be briefly indicated : in some of his specimens he

---

[1] " Die Strophen, oder der Parallelismus der Verse der hebräischen Poesie untersucht " in *Theologische Studien und Kritiken*, vol. iv.

claims that the sense-divisions, though not equal, are regularly or symmetrically unequal; he claims, for example, that Psalm xxvii. divided according to the main sense-divisions falls into two groups of three (Massoretic) verses each, followed by two groups of four verses each, the scheme being accordingly $3+3+4+4$. This kind of hypothetically intentional scheme was later discovered everywhere by D. H. Müller, who is the author of perhaps the most extensive work on the strophe in Hebrew poetry; [1] Müller also claimed to be able to find not only symmetrical inequality in the verse-groups, but also repetition of the same words in corresponding positions of such verse-groups, as, for example, in the second lines of the first and fourth verse-groups, or in the first and last lines of the same verse-group. Such symmetrical arrangements and correspondences would remain as impressive as are the remarkable arithmetical formulae by means of which Müller claimed to represent them, if on examination these formulae proved to rest on any exact and probable basis of calculation. What is all-important for such schemes to be anything more than the self-delusions of a modern student is that the unit of reckoning should be clearly defined and consistently maintained; and this neither with Köster nor Müller is the case. The

[1] *Die Propheten in ihrer ursprünglichen Form* (1895); *Strophenbau und Responsion* (1898). For a severe criticism of Müller's and kindred theories, see Ed. König, *Stilistik, Rhetorik, Poetik*, pp. 347 ff.

Massoretic verse not only rests on a division of the text made long subsequent to the composition and writing of the poems, but it is anything but a clear and consistent unit, for it consists sometimes of a single line, oftenest of a single distich or tristich, but not infrequently of two or more distichs. Yet the Massoretic verse is made the basis of Köster's reckoning, with the result that the symmetrical formulae $3+3+4+4$ can have no relation to any intention of the author of Psalm xxvii. ; and any scheme based either on the line or on the distich as the unit would give a different and much less remarkable result.

Müller avoids the error of making the Massoretic verse the unit of reckoning, but he is not constant to any single real unit. König[1] has sufficiently criticised Müller's strophic division of Amos i. 2–ii. 5. I select here as another example of the arithmetical symmetry of Müller's formulae and the unreality which they express his treatment of Amos iv. According to Müller this chapter opens and closes with a strophe of 8 lines ; between the initial and final strophes are strophes consisting successively of 5, 4, 3, 2, 1 lines, and the arithmetical formula given for the whole poem is $8+(8 \times 2)+8$. This looks symmetrical enough, but how is it obtained ? Müller divides the chapter as follows :—

---

[1] *Stilistik*, p. 348.

vv.   1-3 said to contain 8 lines.

    4-6   „   „   5 lines and a refrain.

    7-8   „   „   4   „   „

    10   „   „   3   „   „

    9   „   „   2   „   „

    11   „   „   1   „   „

  12, 13   „   „   8 lines.

It will be observed (1) that *vv.* 10 and 9 are transposed to secure the exact arithmetical progression ; (2) that $5+4+3+2+1$ only amount to 15, while if we add to this all five occurrences of the refrain the sum is 20 ; but neither 15 nor 20 is a multiple of eight ; so the symmetrical figure $16=8\times2$ is obtained by reckoning five occurrences of the refrain as one line only ! But this is only part of the capriciousness that underlies the formula.   When we examine the " lines " we find some to be true lines, while others are a large number of Hebrew words constituting, or consisting of a quantity equivalent to, at least a distich.   In verse 9,

הכיתי אתכם בשדפון ובירקון

I have smitten you with blasting and mildew,

is reckoned a single line, but in verse 11, which the arithmetical progression requires shall contain one line and no more, this *single* " line " consists of הפכתי בכם כמהפכת אלהים את סדם ואת עמרה ותהיו כאוד מצל משרפה, " I have overthrown some among you as when God overthrew Sodom and Gomorrah,

and ye were as a brand plucked out of the burn-
ing," which is somewhat more in quantity than
הרגתי בחרב בחורים עם שבי סוסיכם ואעלה באש מחניכם
ובאפכם, " I have slain your young men with the
sword together with your captive horses, and I
have made the stink of your camps to come up
into your nostrils " (v. 10), which counts, and with
good reason, as *two* lines !

With the breakdown of the arithmetical part
of Müller's scheme there breaks down also the
significance of the correspondences. In strictly
measured sections it might be significant of
intention if the same word should occur, say, in
the first line and the last of two corresponding
sections ; but as soon as the measurement ceases
to be exact the mere recurrence within a few lines
of such frequently recurring words as Yahweh
becomes entirely insignificant.

There may be here and there a certain artifice
in the repetition at given intervals of particular
words, and to such an artifice is probably to be
attributed the almost regular recurrence, even
in the present text of Psalm cxix., of the same
eight different words for law ; but such artifices
are scarcely more frequent than the use of
alphabetic schemes, and have just as little power
to create real strophes or verse-paragraphs.

CHAPTER VI

THE BEARING OF CERTAIN METRICAL THEORIES
ON CRITICISM AND INTERPRETATION

CHAPTER VI

THE BEARING OF CERTAIN METRICAL THEORIES
ON CRITICISM AND INTERPRETATION

HITHERTO our discussion has been confined to the forms of *parallelistic* poetry. I have endeavoured to keep, as they should be kept, distinct, the two forms, parallelism and rhythm, while pointing out the intimate connexion that often exists between them. Yet that connexion is not so intimate but that either form *may* exist apart, even in literatures that employ both. Arabic " rhymed prose," which is not bound by the strict laws of Arabic metre, often employs parallelism as freely as any Hebrew poem; [1] on the other hand much of the strictly metrical Arabic poetry is totally lacking or exceedingly deficient in parallelism,[1] and few Hebrew poems maintain complete parallelism throughout.[2] If it is customary, as it certainly seems to be, for non-parallel couplets in a Hebrew poem to fall into the same rhythm as the parallel couplets,

[1] See above, pp. 40-43.   [2] See above, pp. 59 ff.

can a Hebrew poem entirely dispense with strict parallelism ? We cannot rule this out as impossible, nor should we be wise to treat it as very improbable ; but, even if parallelism were entirely absent, a very essential characteristic of the poetry would still remain, if it continued to be parallelistic throughout, in spite of the total absence of parallelism of terms.

But the question has recently been forced to the front : Is there a Hebrew rhythmical poetry that dispenses not only with parallelism, but also with the parallelistic structure that is an essential characteristic of all the Hebrew poetry of which we have yet taken account ?

Lowth, by his analysis of parallelism, brought to light the fact that this parallelism was as conspicuous in much of the prophetic writings as in Psalms or Job : he thus extended the then recognised boundaries of what is poetry in the Old Testament. By his analysis of rhythm Sievers claims to have carried this extension of the still generally recognised boundaries of Old Testament poetry very much further : what, till the publication of his first work on Hebrew metre,[1] had been universally regarded as prose has under his hands come to wear the appearance of regular metrical composition ; he has detected

---

[1] E. Sievers, " Metrische Studien," i. " Studien zur hebräischen Metrik " in the *Abhandlungen der phil.-hist. Classe der königlich sächsischen Gesellschaft der Wissenschaften*, xxi. (1901). See especially ch. x. pp. 371 ff.

in it some of the same types of rhythm (yet with a difference) that occur in books or passages of the Old Testament generally recognised to be poetry, and also some types or rather some combinations of types of rhythm that are not found there, but are yet no less strictly rhythmical than the rest.

Lowth's discovery that the prophetic writings were in large part poems could not but have had, and has actually had, a very considerable effect on the criticism, in the broadest sense of that term, of those writings, on our conceptions of their inspiration, origin, composition, and interpretation. Just as little, if they succeed in establishing themselves, can Sievers' theories of the rhythmical forms of the books of Genesis and Samuel, two books which he has subjected to an exhaustive metrical analysis,[1] fail to affect the criticism of these books and others of the same general character. For this reason I propose to give some account of Sievers' theory of the metres of Genesis, to suggest certain objections, and to indicate one possible result that follows. After that I will return to the consideration of the parallelistic poetry and consider the legitimacy of certain theories of its rhythm. I refer more particularly to Duhm's theories, which have exercised very considerable influence not only

---

[1] E. Sievers, " Metrische Studien," ii. " Die hebräische Genesis " ; iii. " Samuel " (*Abhandlungen* . . . , xxiii.).

in Germany but also in this country, where the results of the theories are beginning to be presented uncriticised even in books intended for popular use.[1] Sievers' developed theory of the metrical character of the texts commonly supposed to be prose has not, I think, yet commanded much assent,[2] but this working out of his theory must obviously affect in some measure any judgment as to the soundness of its fundamental principles. An examination of these two influential, or potentially influential, theories, will furnish a number of illustrations of the way in which theories with regard to the forms of Hebrew poetry may affect the criticism and interpretation of Hebrew literature.

In his first volume (pp. 397 ff.) Sievers, in order to test the rhythmical character of simple narrative style, examined the inscription of

[1] See e.g. M. G. Glazebrook, Studies in the Book of Isaiah ; B. Duhm, The Minor Prophets translated in the Rhythms of the Original (English translation by A. Duff).

[2] O. Proksch, however, in his recently published commentary, Die Genesis übersetzt u. erklärt, 1913, gives a general adherence to Sievers' theory, though frequently and greatly differing from him in the detailed application of it.   In illustration of these differences, I quote a sentence or two from my review of the commentary in the Review of Theology and Philosophy, ix. 200-204 : " Proksch divides Gen. iii. 1-19 into 32 metrical units, all seven-stress lines : Sievers divides the same passage into 33 metrical units, of which 27 are seven-stress lines, the others examples of various rhythms.   Considerably less than half of Proksch's ' sevens ' are identical with Sievers' ' sevens ' : to be exact, 12 of Proksch's lines are identical with Sievers', and 20 are not. Even more remarkable is the difference in xxix. 2-14 a.   Here both Proksch and Sievers agree that we have a continuous use of ' sevens ' throughout the passage ; nevertheless not a single one of Proksch's first fifteen lines is identical with one of Sievers'."

Mesha, selecting this as an ancient text that had not been subjected to accidents of transcription. He analysed it into 37 rhythmical periods, claiming that " the metrical structure " of this poem was all the easier to seize, and the better secured, by the fact that the ends of the verses were marked by a vertical line, which was but rarely used to indicate a mere pause within the verse. If it were certain that the vertical line used in Mesha's inscription was really intended to mark off *metrical* periods, the fact would be of the utmost importance ; for, if the Moabite king recorded his exploits in metre, and used this line to make the metre clear, a strong presumption would be created that Judges, Samuel, and Kings, large parts of which closely resemble the Moabite inscription in style, were also originally in large part metrical ; and the use of this line might be expected to cast even more direct light on Hebrew than the marking of the scansion in the Assyrian inscription to which I have previously referred.[1] But that the vertical line in Mesha's inscription has a metrical significance is anything but clear : what is certain is that it occurs at places where *punctuation* is required, generally a full stop, more rarely a semicolon, or a comma. Thus the line occurs twenty-five times at points where Dr. Cooke [2] in his translation punctuates with a full

---

[1] See above, pp. 140 ff.
[2] G. A. Cooke, *A Text-book of North Semitic Inscriptions*, pp. 2-4.

stop, five times where he punctuates with a
semicolon, three times where he punctuates with
a comma. In three other places the line occurs
where the inscription cannot be clearly read.
Even in the three cases where the line corresponds
to a comma, the pause is considerable, *e.g.* in
line 7, " I saw my desire upon him and upon his
house, and all Israel perished utterly for ever."
We may compare with this the relation of the
line to Sievers' metrical periods : it occurs at the
end of twenty-eight out of thirty-seven of these,
and thrice in the middle of one of them.   Inas-
much as Sievers' periods are made to end with a
real pause in the sense and are not " run on "
lines, it would be inevitable that a mark of
punctuation should generally stand at the end
of them ; but the absence of the mark at the
end of nine of his periods is much more unfavour-
able to the theory that the mark has a metrical
significance than its presence at the end of
twenty-eight is favourable ; for there may well
have been difference of opinion among Moabite,
as there notoriously is among English, writers
as to the frequency with which punctuation
should be expressed ; there could have been
none as to the point at which a metrical period
ended.   It is also to be observed that according
to Sievers' metrical analysis, the metrical periods
in the inscription are of five different lengths—
of three, four, five, six, and seven stresses ; and

that more than two successive periods of the same length never occur, and often immediately contiguous periods are of different lengths.

We pass now to the consideration of Sievers' *Hebrew Genesis Rhythmically Arranged* (1904–1905). As compared with his analysis, contained in the first volume of his metrical studies, of Mesha's inscription and a few specimens of Hebrew narratives, viz. Genesis ii., xli., Judges ix., Ruth i., Job i., ii., Sievers' treatment of Genesis shows two prominent differences : (1) he has abandoned the attempt to make the metrical periods and the sense-periods coincide : if he is correct in regarding Genesis as metrical, then the distinguishing feature of this narrative poetry is that it largely consists of " run-on " lines ; (2) the same metre is discovered running uninterruptedly through long consecutive passages.

The rhythms alleged to be of most frequent occurrence are (1) the six-stress period ; (2) the seven-stress period—the rhythm which, as we have seen (pp. 173 ff.), probably occurs in Psalms ix., x., but is rare in what have commonly been regarded as the poetical parts of the Old Testament. With these two simple rhythms, as we may call them, though the term is not employed by Sievers himself, there alternate the more complex rhythms produced by the *constant* alternation with one of these of a shorter period, viz. (3) sevens alternating with a short verse of three

or four stresses : *e.g.* Genesis ix. 1-4 (P), xxvi.
1-13 ; (4) sixes alternating with a short verse
of three or four stresses : *e.g.* Genesis xxvi. 14, 15.

Of these rhythms the simple sevens is by far
the most frequent : long passages in which
Sievers discovers it are, for example, Genesis i.,
i.e. P's account of creation ; xi. 1-9, J's account
of the building of the tower of Babel ; xxiv.,
J's account of Eliezer's mission to find Isaac a
wife.

The same rhythm, it will be seen, occurs in
more than one of the main sources discovered
by literary criticism. This is not regarded by
Sievers as an argument against the general
validity of that criticism ; quite the reverse :
he finds his metrical analysis constantly confirming it, and also furnishing a clue through a
labyrinth with which criticism was already
familiar, but through which it had hitherto
failed to find a way. The compositeness of
J, E, and P has been very commonly admitted,
but the attempt to analyse these sources into yet
earlier sources has hitherto led to but relatively
meagre or insecure results. Sievers claims
through metre to lead us to a detailed and secure
analysis of these sources of J, E, and P. As this
promise of valuable assistance in the analysis of
sources is made not by some amateur in the
study of metre, but by a great and recognised
master of the subject, Sievers' *Genesis,* if for no

other reason, might well claim the attention of critical students of the Old Testament.

Briefly stated Sievers' conclusions with reference to the sources are these : J, E, and P were not derived direct from free oral tradition, but one and all from *earlier literary sources which were metrical.* These earlier sources can be recovered by observing the changes of metre within the present text. J rests on four principal sources, a source written in seven-stress periods, another in six-stress periods, another in seven-stress periods alternating with a short verse, and a fourth in six-stress periods alternating with a short verse. J also contains fragments of a source written in four-stress periods. E rests on three main sources, one written in sevens, one in sixes, and one in sixes alternating with a short verse. P is analysed into six sources ; the main source is written in sevens ; the other sources include one written in sixes, one in sevens alternating with a short verse, and another in which every two seven-stress periods are followed by a short verse. The main source in simple sevens admitted of an *occasional* short verse.

It is difficult to judge of this complicated theory from passages where there is much mixture of J, E, and P, or of Sievers' sources of these sources. It is better to take what appears even to Sievers to be a long continuous passage from a single source, and to see by what means and

P

with what results the theory is carried through. Genesis xxiii., which Sievers with every one else refers to P, and he in particular to his " sevens " source of P, may serve as the first illustration.

In this chapter Sievers discovers twenty-eight periods of seven stresses and three short verses of three stresses. The three latter are obtained without any textual change from the present Hebrew text ; of the twenty-eight longer periods, sixteen are obtained from the present text, the remaining twelve rest on alterations of the Hebrew text which, it is claimed, remove transcriptional error and the results of the more frequent·disturbing activity of editors who both changed and added words.   In three of these twelve cases the LXX more or less clearly supports the change ; in another Sievers makes both an addition and an omission which metrically cancel one another. More or less can doubtless be said for several of the alterations [1] requisite to reduce the remaining eight lines to regularity ; but that all the changes are required by anything but the exigencies of the metrical theory will seem to most who examine them improbable.

In Genesis xxiv. 1-52 (J) Sievers finds eighty seven-stress periods interrupted by eight glosses

[1] In v. 6 Sievers omits אלהים, regarding נשיא אלהים as an editorial amplification of נשיא : at the end of v. 7 he omits לבני חת, and in v. 8 מלפני ; in v. 9 he substitutes המערה for המכפלה אשר לו ; in v. 15 he omits ארץ (with LXX) and שקל ; in v. 16 שקל and לסחר ; in v. 17 the clause שרה (with LXX) and שקל ; in v. 16 שקל and לסחר ; in v. 17 the clause שרה עפרון אשר במכפלה אשר לפני ממרא ; in v. 19 he omits אברהם, inserts אשר עפרון, and alters במכפלה to המכפלה.

of from three to nine words, and another line of different rhythm. Of the eighty seven-stress lines, twenty-two depend on departures from the present text ; but several consecutive seven-stress lines [1] are discovered without any alteration of the Hebrew text.

As a last example of Sievers' metrical analysis I select Genesis i. on account of the peculiar interest of the reconstruction of the text involved in it : at the same time it is right to add that Sievers expressly states that his analysis of this particular chapter is one of the most uncertain and tentative of his results. According to the analysis the chapter contained forty-nine seven-stress periods interrupted by one line (in v. 20) of three stresses and by what is regarded as a gloss of two lines in v. 16. Of the forty-nine seven-stress periods no fewer than thirty-two rest on textual alteration—a far larger proportion than in either of the previous examples that have been given here. But a large number of the textual changes are of one type : in order to obtain rhythmical regularity Sievers found that, in every case where אלהים, *God*, occurred, rhythm required either one word less or one word more : in the former case he omits אלהים, in the latter he prefixes יהוה, *Yahweh* ; so that in respect of the use of the divine names, Genesis i.

---

[1] *E.g.* eight such lines occur in v. 42 (from אם ישׁ) to v. 46 (to שׁתה) ; seven such lines in v. 47 (from בתי־מי) to v. 51.

would agree with the present text of Genesis ii., iii., though not, according to Sievers, with the original text of all the sources incorporated in ii. and iii.

It would be unwise to condemn the whole of Sievers' analysis of Genesis on account of the improbably large amount of conjectural emendation needed to carry through the rhythmical reconstruction in Genesis i. and some other passages : the strength of his case is seen rather in such facts as that, for example, in chapter xxiv. eight *consecutive* similar rhythmical periods may be found *in the present text*.

Nevertheless Sievers' results in general seem to me insecure, and their insecurity due to these considerations : (1) the vocalisation on which they depend is, as I have pointed out in a previous chapter,[1] hypothetical, some elements in it being probable, others most uncertain ; (2) the number of conjectural emendations required solely in the interests of the theory is very large ; (3) the analysis of narratives in Genesis and Samuel requires a constant recurrence of " non-stop " lines and enjambed clauses. Not only are the lines " non-stopped," so that, *e.g.*, a verb may stand at the end of one, its accusative at the beginning of the next line, but the well-marked caesuras within the lines, so prominent in the parallelistic poetry, frequently disappear, while

[1] See above, pp. 147-149.

in others a full-stop may appear at the caesura and virtually no stop at all at the end of the line. Sievers, it is true, still points his " sevens " with spaces for the two caesuras, but the space frequently divides construct and genitive, or other words as closely connected with one another. Two lines at the beginning of Genesis xxiii. may serve as examples of the points just referred to ; I add a translation to bring out the striking difference between this kind of metrical composition, if it be such, and parallelistic poems :

מאה ועשרים שנה   חיי שרה   ויהיו שני
בקרית ארבע היא   ותמת שרה   ושבע שנים
חברון

And were the years   of the life of Sarah   one hundred and twenty years
And seven years.   And Sarah died   in Kirjath-Arba, which is Hebron.

And in the following lines from Genesis i., as reconstructed by Sievers, a full-stop occurs in the middle of the first line, though the same line ends with a verb the accusative to which begins the second line :

ידהי אור   ויהי אור   וירא יהוה אלהים
את־האור כי־טוב   ויבדל יהוה   אלהים בין־האור ובין־החשך

Let there be light :   and there was light.   And Yahweh Elohim saw
The light that it was good.   And divided Yahweh   Elohim between the light and the darkness.

Now no doubt there can be found analogies

to most of these phenomena in English blank
verse : but there remains this surely relevant
and fundamental difference between English and
Hebrew poetry : the foot in Hebrew, according
to Sievers' theory, is much more elastic than the
foot in English blank verse : the Hebrew foot, it
will be remembered, consists, according to the
theory, of a stressed syllable either by itself, or
preceded by one to three unstressed syllables,
and in certain cases followed by one but not more
than one unstressed syllable ; briefly, whereas
the foot in English blank verse is dissyllabic, or
by resolution trisyllabic, the foot in Hebrew
may consist of one, two, three, four, or five
syllables. There is a further point : Hebrew, as
contrasted with English, has far fewer prepositions, conjunctions, and other short independent
words unlikely to be stressed : the consequence
is that any passage in Hebrew must consist most
largely of words that can quite appropriately
receive a stress : if then a rhythmical line consists
of so many stressed syllables combined with a
very elastic number of unstressed syllables, and
is subject to no other law such as that of the
stopped lines and the distich, it becomes almost
impossible for any passage not to be rhythmical.
For the number of the words in any or almost
any passage will divide either by 3, 4, 5, 6, or 7
with, if necessary, a few words at the end, to
appear as a broken line. To what other law,

then, does Sievers conceive his lines to be subjected ? It is difficult to discover any, though
it is obvious that he still *prefers* that his caesuras
and line-ends should coincide with some sense-
pause if possible, and this apparently is why he
distributes his texts among several metres, though
if we utterly disregard sense-pauses, and allow
ourselves an equal liberty of textual emendation,
most of the lines could be redivided into blocks
of a different number of feet. It appears to me,
therefore, that the analogy of English blank
verse with its freedom from line-bondage is a
bad ground for assuming a similar free epic
or narrative verse in Hebrew : the analogy of
Semitic poetry is against the assumption : and
we seem driven back on to the stopped line and
the distich as the normal basis of Hebrew poetry
of all kinds.

There remains one further consideration : it
is brought forward by Sievers himself, and he
attempts to turn the force of it : the redactors
and interpolators who often, by their additions,
destroyed the metre of their sources, themselves
wrote in metre ; the glosses attributed to them
are for the most part " metrical." " I cannot,"
writes Sievers,[1] " otherwise account for this
than by the supposition that in a period not yet
accustomed to free prose the tendency to bring
everything that had to be said into verse form

[1] *Die hebräische Genesis*, p. 216.

may have been so strong that such redactors involuntarily composed verses when the extent and substance of what they wanted to say in any way permitted of this. At the same time they had so little artistic intelligence or experience that they thrust their own products of a moment unconcerned into the older texts without troubling much about the mess (*Unheil*) they thus made of them."

In view of the various considerations which I have now brought forward I am not prepared, on the one hand, to admit the metrical analysis of Genesis as confirming the analysis into J, E, and P, nor, on the other hand, out of regard for hypothetical metrical requirements, to insert Yahweh in Genesis i., and thereby abandon the well-grounded conclusion that P made no use of the divine name Yahweh in his narrative, till he reached the point at which he records the revelation of the name to Moses.

But though the theory that the *whole* of Genesis is derived from metrical sources must be dismissed as unproved, the question yet remains whether, in addition to such obvious poems as Lamech's song (Gen. iv. 23, 24) and Jacob's Blessing (xlix. 1-27), traces can still be discerned, within or behind the narratives, of *any* metrical passages or sources. And here we may first observe that certain speeches introduced into the narratives differ in style from the prose of the narratives themselves, in virtue of some use of

parallelism or some approximation, even in the
present stage of the text, to rhythms familiar
from their occurrence in what are generally
recognised to be poems. Such speeches are the
curses pronounced by Yahweh on Adam and
Eve and the serpent (Gen. iii. 14-19), the blessings
pronounced by Isaac on Jacob and Esau (xxvii.
27-29, 39, 40), and Jacob's speech to Laban
(xxxi. 36-42). To justify the statement that
these show some use of parallelism and some
approximation to metre, let it suffice to point out
that the closing words of the curse on the serpent
form, as a matter of fact, an unmistakable
distich 3 : 3, the lines of which are completely
parallel to one another (a . b . c | a′ . b′ . c′); that
Isaac's blessing on Jacob closes with three
distichs in each of which the lines are completely
parallel to one another, the schemes being
a . b | a′ . b′, a2 . b | a′ . b′2, and a . b | a′ . b′; and
that xxxi. 38 b, c is a perfectly clear example of
a distich 3 : 3 with the lines completely parallel
to one another (a2 . b | a′2 . b′). Yet in none of
the passages quoted is it possible to discern in the
present text metrical regularity. Such metrical
regularity can be obtained with least alteration
of the present text in the curse on the serpent.
If we omit in *v.* 14 the words ו הבהמה מכל, *of all
cattle and* — an omission which was originally
suggested by Stade [1] quite irrespective of metrical

---

[1] In the *Zeitschr. für die alttestamentliche Wissenschaft*, xvii. 209.

considerations—and in *v.* 15 the words וּבֵין זַרְעֶךָ, *and between thy seed,*[1] and if, with Sievers, we are prepared to include וְאֵיבָה אָשִׁית under a single accent, we have left four successive six-stress periods, the first three being divided into three two-stress lines, the last into two three-stress lines, a method of varying the treatment of six-stress periods within the same poem that has already been referred to (p. 182, n. 2).   With the two omissions just defined the Hebrew text and English translation read as follows :

כִּי־עָשִׂיתָ זֹּאת | אָרוּר אַתָּה | מִכָּל־חַיַּת הַשָּׂדֶה
עַל גְּחֹנְךָ תֵלֵךְ | וְעָפָר תֹּאכַל | כָּל־יְמֵי חַיֶּיךָ
וְאֵיבָה־אָשִׁית בֵּינְךָ | וּבֵין הָאִשָּׁה | וּבֵין זַרְעָהּ
הוּא יְשׁוּפְךָ רֹאשׁ | וְאַתָּה תְּשׁוּפֶנּוּ עָקֵב

Because thou hast done this,
    Cursed art thou
    Above all the beasts of the field ;
On thy belly shalt thou go,
    And dust shalt thou eat,
    All the days of thy life ;
And enmity will I put between thee
    And between the woman,
    And between her seed :
He shall crush thee on the head,
    And thou shalt crush him on the heel.

---

[1] For the omission of these words there is little, if anything, to be urged apart from metrical considerations. It is true that the last lines contrast the woman's seed and " thee," *i.e.* the serpent, and take no account of " thy seed " : but *per contra* they refer only to the woman's seed and do not mention the woman independently. With the threefold repetition of בֵין in the emended text, cp. Gen. xvii. 7, וַהֲקִמֹתִי אֶת בְּרִיתִי בֵּינִי וּבֵינְךָ וּבֵין זַרְעֲךָ ; but in this passage the addition of וּבֵין זַרְעִי to בֵּינִי would of course have been impossible.

We seem to be left, then, with these alternatives—that certain speeches, especially curses and blessings, were originally metrical, but that their metrical character has been destroyed or obscured by additions and alterations, or that the speeches in question, while differentiated from the simplicity of the prose of ordinary narrative, were not subjected to regular metrical form. In favour of the first alternative, so far at least as the curses and blessings are concerned, is the fact that the blessings of Jacob (Gen. xlix.), Moses (Deut. xxxiii.), Balaam (Num. xxiii., xxiv.) are all unmistakable poems, and that an important function of the early Arab poets was to compose and recite curses.[1] At the same time most of the passages cited are in their present form considerably removed from metrical regularity.

Even if, however, we admit that the speeches referred to in the last paragraph are metrical, they could reasonably be explained as instances of the same writer passing from the prose of narrative to poetical form in the speeches of the persons of his story—a transition which is clearly

---

[1] See particularly I. Goldziher, *Abhandlungen zur arabischen Philologie*, " Über die Vorgeschichte der Hiǧā' Poesie," referred to and briefly described in my note on Num. xxii. 6 (*Commentary on Numbers*, p. 328). See further G. Hölscher, *Die Profeten* (1914), pp. 92 ff., 120 f., where examples are given. It must be observed, however, that many of these early curses are not composed in the classical Arabic metres, but in *saj'* (see above, p. 44 f.) ; an example of a curse in this " rhymed prose " is Sura cxi. of the Ḳur'ān.

marked and obvious in the book of Job, unless prologue and speeches are there referred to different writers.

But a rather different question arises when we turn to the narratives of Creation; for here we shall find ourselves dealing not with differences between narrative and speeches, but with a question of differences between different parts of what is alike narrative. The question we have to put here is this : Are these narratives in their present form, or do they rest on Hebrew sources that were, entirely prose ? or are there sufficient traces of rhythm even now left to suggest that these narratives rest in part at least on Hebrew sources that were written in poetical form ? If the narratives are prose, and if the sources on which they rested were also all prose, then, although the Hebrew *story* of Creation shows the well-known resemblances to the Babylonian *story*, the literary form given to the story by the Hebrews was at all times different : it was prose, whereas the Babylonian story was told in verse. And even if Sievers were right, and the whole of the Creation narratives in Genesis were metrical, there would still be a difference ; the Babylonian poems are cast in the old parallelistic 4 : 4 rhythm, the Hebrew narratives, according to the hypothesis, mainly in Sievers' non-parallelistic " sevens." But Sievers has also drawn attention, and this time

I think rightly, to the appearance in small
quantity of the 4 : 4 rhythm in Genesis ii. : he
recognised more of it in the first volume of his
metrical studies than in *Die hebräische Genesis,*
and his earlier is perhaps preferable to his later
view. Delete the superfluous אלהים after יהוה
in Genesis ii. 4 b, and it is a fact that ii. 4 b-6 can
easily, and most of it must, be read as periods
of four stresses equally divided by a slight
caesura, as follows :

ביום עשות־יהוה	ארץ ושמים
וכל שיח־השדה	טרם יהיה־בארץ
וכל עשב־השדה	טרם יצמח
כי־לא המטיר	יהוה על־הארץ
ואדם אין	לעבד את־האדמה

In the day when Yahweh made	heaven and earth,
No plant of the field	was yet in the earth,
And no herb of the field	had yet sprung up ;
For Yahweh had not sent	rain upon the earth,
And man there was none	to till the ground.

Not only is this *possibly* metrical, but (1) the
second and third, and in some measure the
fourth and fifth lines, are certainly parallels ;
(2) the hypothetically metrical periods are certainly sense - periods ; (3) the anarthrous ארץ
ושמים without את stands in striking contrast to
the את השמים ואת הארץ of Genesis i. 1. Not only,
then, have the lines of the Hebrew,

> No plant of the field was yet in the earth,
> And no herb of the field had yet sprung up,

a close material parallel in the Babylonian,

No reed had sprung up, no tree had been created,

but the rhythm of the Hebrew, if correctly seized as 4 : 4 (=2 + 2 : 2 + 2), is identical with the rhythm of the Babylonian.

I cannot here pursue the remaining traces, for the most part less clear, of the same rhythm in subsequent parts of the chapter, and still less the various interesting questions which are raised by this apparent formal as well as material resemblance of some of the Hebrew with some of the Babylonian stories of Creation ; but the probability that behind Genesis ii. lay at least one Hebrew metrical story of Creation seems to me sufficiently strong to be worth consideration.

If Genesis ii. 4 b-6 is metrical, it is an example not of the hypothetical non-parallelistic metrical poetry which Sievers finds everywhere in Genesis and Samuel, but of that same parallelistic poetry which has so long been recognised in Psalms and Job and much of the prophetical books. But if Sievers' theory that the narratives of Genesis are metrical is rightly judged to be unproven and improbable, ought we at this end of our discussion to question the *metrical* character even of parallelistic poetry ; was Hebrew poetry of any kind subject to metrical laws ? Have we a right to adopt such a system as Sievers' to explain the metre of parallelistic poetry, and then to deny

the soundness of his application of his system
to Hebrew narratives ?

It must suffice at this point to recall some
positions previously reached : in parallelistic
poetry the lines are in general well defined, and
where there is much parallelism of terms the
limits of the lines are certain ; to secure a
rhythmical balance, or other relation, which
would be immediately perceived between these
parallel lines, a far greater elasticity could safely
be given to the rhythmical foot than if a really
perceptible rhythm were to be imparted to a
long passage in which there were no regularly
recurring pauses. Even after an examination
of Sievers' attempt to extend so greatly the
amount of metrical composition in the Old Testament, it seems to me possible and useful to
return to parallelistic poetry and to insist (1) that
this consists primarily of distichs ; (2) that these
distichs fall into two broad classes according as
the second line balances or echoes the first ;
and (3) that the lines of these distichs can also
be more accurately classified according to the
number of the stressed words that they contain.

The uncertainties in dealing with parallelistic
poetry arise rather when we raise these questions :
Must a single type of distich be maintained
throughout the same poem ? if not, what types
and what extent of variation are permitted ?
Again, are all poems strophically arranged, and

are all strophes of equal length ?　I have already given my reasons for answering these questions in the sense that the laws of Hebrew poetry did not require either that a single type of distich must be used throughout the same poem, or that all poems must be divided into equal strophes : and that as a matter of fact some Hebrew poems are perfectly, or nearly, consistent in the use of a single type of distich and strophes of the same length, and that others are not.　But the contrary opinion is held and enforced with far-reaching critical results :　single words are rejected from lines in order to reduce all the distichs to a single type, and whole distichs in order to reduce all the strophes to the same length.　More rarely equality is restored or invented by addition of words or distichs.　Dr. Briggs in his commentary on the Psalms so emended the text that most of the Psalms divide into exactly equal strophes, strophes that each contain exactly the same number of lines, distichs, or tristichs as the case may be.　Duhm has done much the same for Isaiah, Jeremiah, and the Twelve Prophets, not to speak of his work on Psalms and Job. I am, of course, far from maintaining that either these scholars, or others with the same devotion to regularity, have failed to put forward many valuable suggestions : if some poems, though not all, were regular, a scholar who attempts to make all regular may succeed in divining the real regularity of those that were regular at the same time that he is imposing an unreal regularity on a poem that never was actually regular.

In illustration of the far-reaching effects of the determination to impose regularity at all hazards on all poems, I will now confine myself to some examples of Duhm's methods and results. I premise that there is a far stronger *prima facie* case for questioning the originality of the text of the books with which Duhm deals than that of the book of Genesis ; and that there is far more reason in the case of these books than in Samuel for suspecting that even the LXX fails as a sufficient corrective of the Hebrew text ; so far then an editor of the prophets or of Job or of many of the Psalms ought to suspect more corruption which must be treated, if treated at all, by conjecture, than an editor of Genesis or Samuel. But there is need for the greatest possible caution in using a metrical theory as the sole reason for emendation ; for one Hebrew metre can be changed into another with fatal ease ; drop the verb, or some other parallel term that the sense will spare from the second line of a 3 : 3 distich, and the result is the very dissimilar 3 : 2 ; and, conversely, in a 3 : 2 distich prefix an infinitive absolute to the verb of the second line, and a distich 3 : 3 is the result. For example Isaiah xiii. 11 c, d,

Q

והשבתי גאון זדים

וגאות עריצים אשפיל

And I will make the pride of the presumptuous cease,
And the haughtiness of the awe-inspiring will I bring low,

is as it stands an excellent 3 : 3 distich of completely parallel lines; it can be very simply
reduced to a distich of 3 : 2 lines incompletely
parallel by omitting, with Duhm, the overlined
word. But what is the probability that the
conversion of one metre into another would
take place accidentally several times in the same
poem without affecting the sense? Or what the
probability that a scribe would intentionally
convert 3 : 2 into 3 : 3 by such additions in some
distichs of the poem, while leaving others in the
original 3 : 2 ?

If the ease with which every Hebrew text can
in some manner be adapted to Sievers' anapaestic
system should make us slow to accept such
applications of it as his metrical analysis of
Genesis, the ease with which, if we treat the
rhythm merely as so many stresses to a line,
one metre can be converted to another should
warn us against the seductive regularity which
Duhm places, for example, upon Isaiah xiii.
This chapter, says Mr. Box, who, in common
with some other English scholars, reproduces
Duhm's assertions, consists of seven-lined strophes
in the rhythm of the Hebrew dirge; and in this
resembles the poem in chap. xiv. Yet it is

really difficult to believe that any one could have reached this conclusion except under the dominance of a theory of regularity or the spell of a great master; and the false conclusion here happens to be of some critical significance, for, if Isaiah xiii. consists of six seven-lined strophes in *ḳinah* rhythm, and chapter xiv. contains a poem consisting of five exactly similar strophes, confidence in the unity of xiii. and xiv. may receive an utterly untrustworthy support. The actual fact with regard to Isaiah xiii., as I have shown elsewhere,[1] is that the *ḳinah* rhythm is all but confined to the first eight verses of the chapter, and in the remaining fourteen verses, which contain twenty-five distichs, there are but three or four distichs at most of the *ḳinah* type : the rest are 3 : 3 ; Duhm reduces these 3 : 3 distichs to 3 : 2 by two exceedingly simple devices : either a word is arbitrarily dropped from the second line of the distich, or, if this is not convenient, it is *assumed* that the second and shorter line of a 3 : 2 distich has dropped out. Corruptions of both kinds certainly occur ; but it is exceedingly improbable that accidents of the same kind happened several times over within a few verses and yet so as to leave excellent 3 : 3 rhythm.

Another passage where difficult critical questions arise has been similarly treated by Duhm.

---

[1] *Isaiah*, pp. 234 ff.

He asserts that in Isaiah xxxiv., xxxv. the same metre is maintained throughout, and he represents the whole as disposed in four-lined strophes ; but he also makes this significant remark : " The text has suffered a remarkable number of mutilations, especially at the ends of the *stichoi*." Yet as a matter of fact the metre is not the same throughout : some of the distichs are certainly 3 : 2, most are certainly 3 : 3, but, just as in xiii., xiv., the 3 : 2 distichs are massed together ; they are almost confined to xxxiv. 1-10. A difference between the rhythm of xxxiv. 1-10 and 11-17 is, I believe, certain : and, if so, it is critically important ; for the arguments which have led many scholars to abandon the earlier view that Isaiah xxxiv. and xxxv. were written in the exilic period in favour of the view that they are a late post-exilic prophecy rest mainly on xxxiv. 11-17—which is metrically different from xxxiv. 1-10. The critical questions are complicated and difficult, and cannot be discussed here : but Duhm's judgment on these chapters seems to me to illustrate a second unfortunate result of the theory that Hebrew poetry was absolutely regular : on the one hand it leads to much unnecessary correction of the text ; and, on the other, to a certain obtuseness to real difference of rhythm. The 3 : 2 distich is something really different from a 3 : 3 distich, even though both occur in the same poem : and if one type of distich is exclusively used or dominant in one part of a passage, and another in another, a question may always arise whether the two parts are of the same origin : that even such a change as this *necessarily* implies difference of origin in all cases I am not prepared to assert : as a matter of fact, though I pointed out the difference of rhythm between Isaiah xiii. 1-8 and 9-22, which Duhm and others had attempted to conceal by groundless emendations, I refrained from asserting that the two parts in question were of different origin.

But it is in his criticism of the Book of Jeremiah that Duhm's rhythmical principles have proved most dangerous ; here, as is well known, he works with the principle not only of regularity of distich and strophe, but also of one man, one metre. Though we owe to Duhm himself one of the warmest appreciations of Jeremiah as prophet and poet, we are yet asked to believe that this great prophet and poet confined himself throughout his long career to one metre ! Working on this principle Duhm not only rejects the larger part of the poems attributed to Jeremiah, but he violates parallelism and shows obtuseness to rhythmical differences in order to retain much even of what he does retain, but which, if his critical theory that Jeremiah wrote only in " *ḳinah* " rhythm were correct, ought to be rejected. I have shown elsewhere [1] with what violence, and even with what ridiculous results at times, as in his strophic division of Isaiah xi. 1-8, Duhm tears asunder the things that parallelism most evidently intended to be kept together. I must here confine myself to two examples of Duhm's treatment of the text of Jeremiah. The first example is Jeremiah iv. 3, 4 : the present Hebrew text reads, and may be divided, as follows :—

כי-כה אמר יהוה | לאיש יהודה ולירושלם

נירו לכם ניר | ואל תזרעו אל-קצים

המלו ליהוה | והסירו ערלת לבבכם

איש יהודה | וישבי ירושלם

פן-תצא כאש חמתי | ובערה ואין מכבה

If we approach this passage without a theoretical prejudice, is it not obvious that the marked tendency of the clauses is to balance one another, not to echo one another, as, according to Duhm, if genuine, they should do ? A further feature of the passage is the prominence of parallelism :—

> For thus saith Yahweh
>   To the men of Judah and Jerusalem,
> Break up your fallow ground,
>   And sow not among thorns ;
> Circumcise yourselves to Yahweh,
>   And take away the foreskin of your heart,

---

[1] *Isaiah*, pp. 211 ff., and *Zeitschrift für die AT. Wissenschaft*, 1912, pp. 193-198.

Men of Judah,
  And inhabitants of Jerusalem ;
  Lest my fury go forth like fire,
  And burn with none to quench it.

The rhythm for the most part is actually 3 : 3 ;
I will not stay to inquire what grounds there may
be for believing that that rhythm was originally
maintained throughout : what I have to do is
note how Duhm turns it into 3 : 2 and with what
results :—

(1) He rejects the words " to the men of
Judah and Jerusalem " in *v.* 3 (line 2 of the above
translation) and also the similar words (lines 7
and 8 above) of *v.* 4 ; the latter omission is,
perhaps, right.

(2) Having rejected line 2 above, he has to
tear asunder lines 3 and 4 which are most obviously parallel to one another : line 3 is tacked
on to line 1 to form a distich, and it is then
assumed that the first line of the distich, of which
line 4 above is the second line, has disappeared.

(3) Very interesting and specious is the treatment of the first part of *v.* 4 : Duhm divides as
follows :—

המלו ליהוה והסירו | ערלת לבבכם

Circumcise yourselves to Yahweh, and take away
  The foreskin of your heart.

Now there is no doubt that the object of a verb
may form the second part of a 3 : 2 line (or
distich) : I recall as examples two lines in
Lamentations ii. 6 :—

שכח יהוה בציון | מועד ושבת
וינאץ בזעם אפו | מלך וכהן

Yahweh hath caused to be forgotten in Sion
Festal meeting and Sabbath;
And hath spurned in the indignation of his anger
King and priest.

Judge the line from a grammatical point of view only, and Duhm's division of Jeremiah iv. 4 seems to be at least a legitimate alternative to the division of the line after יהוה; but once the sense and parallelism are considered, how improbable does such a division appear. המלו and הסרו ערלת together are parallel terms, a clause of two terms being parallel to a single term, according to a practice which I have abundantly illustrated in a previous chapter:[1] what Duhm does is to chop this second parallel into two, giving one half to the line that has already expressed the whole idea, and leaving to the second line a mere lifeless fragment.

My other example of Duhm's methods is taken from the fine apocalyptic vision in Jeremiah iv. 23-26.   I give it first exactly as it stands in the Hebrew text, the divisions of the text being of course my own :—

23 ראיתי את הארץ | והנה תהו ובהו | ואל השמים ואין אורם
24 ראיתי ההרים | והנה רעשים | וכל הגבעות התקלקלו
25 ראיתי והנה | אין האדם | וכל עוף השמים נדדו
26 ראיתי והנה | הכרמל המדבר | וכל עריו נתצו מפני יהוה

[1] See above, pp. 70-82.

In translating these lines I adopt two emendations noted in the next paragraph, and for convenience of printing throw the sections of the long Hebrew lines into separate lines :—

23 I beheld the earth,
   And, lo, 'twas formless and empty ;
   And the heavens, and they had no light.
24 I beheld the mountains,
   And, lo, they were trembling,
   And all the hills moved to and fro.
25 I beheld [the ground],
   And, lo, there was no man,
   And all the birds of the heaven were fled.
26 I beheld the garden-land,
   And, lo, 'twas wilderness,
   And all the cities thereof were broken down before
                                          Yahweh.

Two emendations suggested by Duhm and essential to his rhythmical scheme, though they are not *essential* to what I believe to be the correct view of the rhythm of the passage, seem to me probable : he reads האדמה after ראיתי in *v.* 25, and transposes והנה and הכרמל in *v.* 26 : this gives an exact similarity of structure to all four verses.

Once again, if any one will read these verses, whether emended as just suggested or not, without any prepossession as to what metre Jeremiah must have used, or as to the general desirability of attaching the term *ḳinah* to as much prophetic poetry as possible, he cannot, I believe, feel that they have any real rhythmical resemblance to

the prevailing rhythm in Lamentations i.-iv. :
these four similar periods are neither *four* lines of
ḳinah-like character as Cornill [1] describes them,
nor *eight* lines of alternately three and two
stresses, *i.e.* strict *ḳinah* lines, as Duhm will have
it : they are four periods of the rarer rhythm
4 : 3.[2] What Cornill says is worth quoting :
" The metre here assumes a somewhat different
form. The characteristic of the *ḳinah* strophe,
the short second member, to be sure remains ;
but the whole is weightier and tends more towards
the gigantic : the first members have mostly
four, the second three full stresses." The last
remark is correct so far as it goes, but omits the
very important additional fact that the first
members are equally divided by a strongly
marked caesura : this caesura gives to the entire
period the rhythmical value 2 : 2 : 3 rather than
4 : 3, and *an effect which is the very opposite of
the ḳinah* : there is no rhythmical echo, but two
short balanced clauses are rounded off with a
longer clause ; the period swells out to its close
instead of echoing off.

Thus Cornill's remarks seem to me an apt
illustration of the disadvantages and the risk
of confusion involved in working with too restricted a rhythmical nomenclature.

Instead of trying to compress the four periods

---

[1] *Das Buch Jeremia*, p. 53. Cf. the note in *The Century Commentary*
(A. S. Peake) on Jeremiah.   [2] See above, pp. 171-176.

into four *ḳinah* lines or distichs, Duhm goes to
the opposite extreme and endeavours to squeeze
eight ḳinah lines (or distichs) out of the present
text amplified by a few additions which are
really far too slight for the purpose. It is a
question whether here the textual changes, or
the rhythmical results, due to the necessity of
making everything attributed to Jeremiah *ḳinah*
rhythm, are the more improbable; of the *ḳinah* (!)
lines that result this is one : [1]

את כל הגבעות | התקלקלו

and the additions to the text, besides that already
mentioned (האדמה in *v.* 25), are these : four
times over, in order to convert two stresses into
three, Duhm inserts את ! and that in a poetical
passage ! [2] and in another place (*v.* 25) he resorts
to the favourite device of inserting an infinitive
absolute—נדוד. These five changes represent a
hypothetical loss of eleven letters : how often

[1] To judge how far Duhm's lines resemble real 3 : 2, or *ḳinah*, lines,
it is best, however, to read them entire. Duhm's lines are as follows :—

ראיתי את הארץ | והנה תהו

ופנה אל השמים | ואין אורם

ראיתי את ההרים | והנה רעשים

ואת כל הגבעות | התקלקלו

ראיתי את הארמה | והנה אין האדם

וכל עוף השמים | נדוד נדדו

ראיתי את הכרמל | והנה מדבר

וכל ההרים נתצו | מפני יהוה

[2] In the present text את occurs but once (in *v.* 23), and may there
be an error for אל (so Rothstein in Kittel's *Biblia Hebraica*) : note אל
in the clause, also dependent on ראיתי, at the end of the verse, and the
ἐπί of the Greek version (=על).

does the text of a short passage accidentally lose in transcription eleven letters distributed over five places without the sense being in the slightest degree affected ?

It is by such methods as these, which could be illustrated by an abundance of other examples, that Duhm succeeds in imposing regularity of line and strophe on Old Testament poetry. And it is on results so obtained that Duhm and others build up far-reaching critical and exegetical conclusions.

I will in conclusion briefly summarise some of the facts and some of the inferences drawn from them to which I have endeavoured to draw attention in these discussions, and briefly refer to one or two points which it has not been my purpose to discuss more fully.

The main forms of Hebrew poetry are two—parallelism and rhythm, to which, as a third and occasional form, we may add strophe. Rhyme, so common in many languages, and a constant and necessary form of all strictly metrical poetry in Arabic, as well as a characteristic of that other type of composition in Arabic known as *saj* (" rhymed prose "), is in Hebrew, as in Assyrian, merely occasional. Curiously enough it is conspicuous in one of the earliest existing fragments of Hebrew poetry, the song of Lamech (Gen. iv. 23, 24), and yet it never developed into a form [1] of Hebrew poetry till poetry of the Old Testament, or parallelistic, type had long become extinct, and there came, under the influence of the Moslem culture and Arabic poetry, a renascence of Hebrew poetry in the Middle Ages.

Of the two main forms of Hebrew poetry, parallelism and rhythm, parallelism is most intimately associated with the sense, and can and should be represented in translation. In its broader aspects and general differences of types it was analysed once for all by Lowth : but a more accurate and detailed measurement of parallelism is required. Such a more exact measurement of parallelism enables us more readily to classify actual differences in different poems and different writers ; and in particular to disentangle the very different types of incomplete parallelisms and merely parallelistic distichs grouped by Lowth under the single term " synthetic parallelism." A study, more especially of the different incomplete parallelisms, also affords an opportunity of watching the intimate connexion between parallelism and at least a certain approximation to rhythm.

Merely judged from the standpoint of parallel-

[1] For examples of rhyme in Hebrew, as also for evidence that it was too occasional and irregular to constitute a form of Hebrew poetry, see E. König, *Stilistik*, 355-357 ; G. A. Smith, *The Early Poetry of Israel*, 24 f. ; C. F. Burney, " Rhyme in the Song of Songs " in the *Journal of Theological Studies*, x. 554-557.

ism, rhythms fall into the two broad classes of balancing and echoing rhythms. Further metrical analysis is in detail frequently most uncertain : but while recognising this uncertainty, it is important, in order to avoid confusion, to adopt a method of measurement that is capable of giving us a clear and sufficient nomenclature. This is to be found in defining lines or distichs by the number of the stressed syllables in them. The exact number of unstressed syllables that may accompany a stressed syllable may be uncertain, but is certainly not unlimited.

A single rhythm need not be maintained throughout a poem, though there were probably limits to the degree of mixture that was tolerated. But in particular the elegy, though it commonly consisted of 3 : 2 distichs, was not limited to these : it certainly admitted along with these in the same poem 2 : 2. Mere change from a longer to a shorter distich of the same class, or even occasionally from a balancing to an echoing rhythm, is no conclusive evidence, and in many poems (for poems differ in the degree to which they are regular) is scarcely even a ground for suspecting corruption of text or change of source. On the other hand, a change in the dominant rhythm should raise a question whether or not a new poem has begun.

Finally the question remains whether, though parallelism in Hebrew seems commonly to have concurred with certain rhythmical forms, it may not in some cases, as in the Arabic *saj*, have been used in a freer style more closely allied to ordinary prose.

Of the history of parallelism and rhythm I have been able to say little. Did parallelism in Hebrew create rhythm, or was it added to an existing type of rhythm ? This is an interesting if an obscure question of origins. As to the lifetime of parallelism, we saw that it runs back to the earliest poetry preserved in the Old Testament, and that it was still a form of Hebrew poetry in the second century A.D., but was not to be clearly traced later : nor did it wake to new life with the revival of Hebrew poetry in the Middle Ages. An interesting episode is the transference of Hebrew parallelism to poetry composed by Jews in Greek, as *e.g.* in the Book of Wisdom.

If we speculate as to the historical development of rhythms, we shall perhaps most safely select as the earliest the 4 : 4 (or 2 : 2) rhythm, which Hebrew has in common with Assyrian, but which at a later time in Hebrew was outstripped by 3 : 3 and 3 : 2.

The best service to the future of Old Testament studies, so far as these can be affected by the examination of those formal elements with which alone these discussions have attempted to deal, will be rendered, I believe, by those who combine

with that further study of Hebrew metre which
is certainly needed, for it is a subject which still
presents many obscurities and uncertainties, an
unswerving loyalty to the demands of that other
and more obvious form or characteristic of
Hebrew poetry which is known as parallelism.

CHAPTER VII

THE ALPHABETIC POEM IN NAHUM

CHAPTER VII

THE ALPHABETIC POEM IN NAHUM

[The following discussion first appeared in the *Expositor* for September 1898. It was written to establish a position which has since been generally conceded, viz. that Nahum i. contains at least part of an alphabetic poem, or acrostich. But once this position is conceded it is reasonable enough to endeavour to rediscover the whole acrostich; and since 1898 fresh attempts have been made in this direction. But it still remains true that the argument that the whole acrostich and not merely part of it lies latent in Nahum i., ii. is much less cogent than the argument that chapter i. contains the first half of such a poem; it is also true that the emendations necessary to restore the last half of the poem are altogether more speculative and uncertain than those required to restore the first half. For this reason, and because the recognition of the fact that at least part of an alphabetic poem is present in Nahum i. has a very important bearing on the criticism of the Book of Nahum, I here reproduce what I wrote, without substantial alterations beyond additions which are inserted in square brackets, and the omission of a paragraph on Psalms ix. and x., which is rendered superfluous by the fuller discussion of those Psalms in the next chapter.

To have discussed all that has been written on this poem since 1898 would have been alien to the purpose of this discussion: it would also be unnecessary; for the history of the criticism of Nahum i. and the many suggestions that have been made with a view to restoring the original text are very fully and admirably reviewed by Dr. J. M. Powis Smith in the "International Critical Commentary" on Nahum.]

THE Old Testament contains a number of acrostich poems. The two laws of such acrostichs are that the initial letters of the several sections should follow the order of the alphabet, and that the sections devoted to each letter should be of (at least approximately) the same length. Different poems differ in the length of the section, but within the same poem the length must be the same. Thus in Psalm cxix. the length of each section is sixteen lines,[1] in Psalm xxxvii. four lines, in Lamentations cc. i., ii., iii.[2] three long (" ḳinah " [3]) lines, in Lamentations c. iv. two " ḳinah " lines, in Psalms xxv., xxxiv., cxlv. [Prov. xxxi. 10-31, Ecclus. li. 13-30] two lines, in Psalms cxi., cxii. one line. Slight deviations from each of these two laws occur in the present text of the poems. In some cases the deviation

---

[1] In this example every other line [*i.e.* every distich] within each section begins with the same letter. The verse in English most frequently contains two lines of the original ; but as it sometimes contains more, sometimes less, the relation between different acrostichs can only be satisfactorily described by reckoning lines. The English reader will find the structure of the acrostich Psalms indicated by marginal letters in the recently issued English translation of the Book of Psalms (*Sacred Books of the Old Testament*) by Wellhausen and Furness [1898].

[2] In Lamentations c. iii. each of the three lines of the several sections begins with the same letter.

[3] Cf. Driver, *Introduction*[6] [[9]], pp. 457 f. [See, now, pp. 116-120 above.]

is clearly due to textual corruption. As a
generally recognised instance of this, the absence
of a word beginning with ם in Psalm xxxvii. 27 c
may be instanced. Whether the absence of the
ו verse in Psalm xxv., of the נ verse in Psalm
cxlv., or the fact that in Psalm xxv. only a single
line is devoted to א be original or the result
of transcriptional error cannot be said with
certainty. But even if the originality of the
irregularities in question be admitted, the few
exceptions simply serve to prove the two general
laws already stated.[1] [More difficult and complicated questions of text in relation to a
partially obvious alphabetic scheme arise in
connexion with Psalms ix. and x., which are
made the subject of special study in the next
chapter.]

It is a matter of more recent observation, and
at least in England [it was down to 1898 [2]   a

---

[1] [A special study of alphabetic poems—"Alphabetische und alpha-
betisierende Lieder im Alten Testaments," by Max Löhr—will be found
in the *Zeitschr. für die AT. Wissenschaft*, 1905, pp. 173-198.]

[2] [But since 1898 the situation has entirely changed. Dr. Driver
subsequently admitted more decisively than he had done previously
that Nahum i. rested in part on an alphabetic poem (see below, p. 247 *n.*).
And several scholars who have written since, both in England and
America, have recognised parts of an acrostich in this chapter : see *e.g.*
A. R. S. Kennedy, " Nahum " in Hastings' *Dictionary of the Bible*, iii.
475 ; Karl Budde, " Nahum " in *Encyc. Biblica*, 3261 ; Paul Haupt,
" The Book of Nahum " in *The Journal of Biblical Literature*, xxvi.
(1907), 1-53 ; W. R. Arnold, " The Composition of Nahum i. 1–ii. 3 "
in the *Zeitschr. für die AT. Wissenschaft*, xxi. 225-265 ; C. F. Kent, *The
Sermons, Epistles, and Apocalypses of Israel's Prophets* (1910), 155-157 ;
J. M. Powis Smith, " International Critical Commentary," 287-297. The
sceptical judgment of A. B. Davidson referred to in the text has found
no recent support.]

matter] of much less general recognition that the Book of Nahum, like Psalms ix., x., contains in whole or in part a mutilated acrostich. Following up earlier suggestions by a German pastor of the name of Frohnmeyer and by Franz Delitzsch, Bickell [1] and Gunkel [2] have ventured to reconstruct out of Nahum i. 1–ii. 3 a complete acrostich in which each stanza consists of two lines ; and Nowack, in his excellent commentary on the Minor Prophets published last year [*i.e.* in 1897], has indicated the structure of the poem in his translation, and defended the requisite emendations in his notes. Three of the leading Old Testament scholars in our own country have recently [*i.e.* within the years 1896–1898] had occasion to refer to the subject. It has received at once the fullest and the most sceptical discussion from Dr. Davidson,[3] who appears to doubt the existence of any intentional alphabetic arrangement in Nahum c. i., and certainly discountenances any attempt to restore the latent acrostich, if such exist. Dr. Driver's judgment is expressed as follows in the last [*i.e.* the 6th] edition of his *Introduction* [1897] : " In Nahum

---

[1] In the *Zeitschr. d. Deutschen Morgenländischen Gesellsch.*, 1880, pp. 559 f. ; *Carmina Vet. Test. metrice* (1882), p. 212 f. ; and " Beiträge zur sem. Metrik " in the *Sitzungsberichte* of the Vienna Academy (Phil. Hist. Series), vol. 131, Abhandlung V. (1890).

[2] In the *Zeitschr. für die AT. Wissenschaft*, 1893, pp. 223-244, and *Schöpfung und Chaos* (1895), pp. 102 f.

[3] *Nahum, Habakkuk, and Zephaniah* (Camb. Bible for Schools), 1896, pp. 18-20.

i. 2–ii. 2 . . . traces of an acrostich . . . seem
to be discernible." In a subsequent review of
Nowack's commentary he has expressed himself
somewhat more fully, but not more approvingly.
After admitting that "undoubtedly there are
traces of an alphabetic arrangement in the
successive half verses," he expresses great doubts
" whether this was ever intended to be carried
systematically through, or whether it is due to
anything more than the fact that the author
allowed himself here and there, perhaps half
accidentally, to follow the alphabetical order." [1]
Dr. G. A. Smith,[2] while agreeing with the two
scholars whose views have been just cited that
much of the reconstruction of Bickell and Gunkel
is arbitrary, quite decisively admits that the
traces of an acrostich are real. To cite his own
words : " The text of chapters i.-ii. 4 has been
badly mauled, and is clamant for reconstruction
of some kind. As it lies, there are traces of an
alphabetical arrangement as far as the beginning
of ver. 9 " (p. 82). At the same time Dr. Smith
minimises, as it appears to me, the force of the

---

[1] *Expository Times*, Dec. 1897, p. 119. Compare also *Introd.*,[6] p. xxi.
[But in the Addenda (p. xxii f.) to the 7th ed. of the *Introduction* the
originally acrostich form of Nah. i. 2-9 is definitely admitted. In the
last edition of the *Introduction* (1913) the note (p. 337) runs : " In
Nah. i. 2–ii. 2 (Heb. 3) traces of an acrostich are discernible which,
though the restoration of the whole can be effected only with great
violence, can be recovered with probability for *v.* 2-9 " ; and reference
is made to the discussion which is now republished here, and to his
own further discussion of the subject in the *Century Bible : Minor
Prophets*, ii. (1906), pp. 25-28.]

[2] *Book of the Twelve Prophets*, vol. ii. (1898), pp. 81-84.

evidence and fails to take full account of what he himself admits.

Under these circumstances a fresh discussion of the subject will hardly be considered uncalled for. It may be true of the last part of the poem that the restoration of the acrostich " can never be more than an academic exercise " (Davidson) ; but the establishment of the fact, if fact it be, that parts or the whole of a regularly and consciously constructed acrostich poem lie latent in the Book of Nahum cannot remain without effect on the exegesis of the passage and on certain not unimportant critical problems.

Where too much is attempted it frequently happens that too little gains recognition. Both Bickell and Gunkel have attempted to reconstruct an entire acrostich. Much of the detail is of necessity uncertain. The consequence is that, as we have seen, it is still [*i.e.* in 1898] doubted whether the chapter contains even any fragments of an acrostich. We must therefore distinguish between the proof that Nahum contains traces of an acrostich, which, when the evidence is duly presented, is cogent, and certain details of reconstruction, which are requisite if an entire acrostich is to be restored, but for which the evidence is in one or two cases strong, in many slight, and in some *nil*.

The proof that Nahum contains at least parts of an acrostich must be based on the phenomena presented by the Hebrew text and the versions of the first nine verses of chapter i. Any one who is unconvinced by these will remain unconvinced by the much less conspicuous and significant phenomena of the following verses. The influence of the two laws of the acrostich— alphabetical succession of initial letters and equal lengths of the several verses or sections— can best be made clear to those unfamiliar with Hebrew by a translation arranged in parallel lines. Variations from the Hebrew consonantal text are printed in italics. The initial letters are printed on the left hand together with a numeral indicating the position of the letter in the Hebrew alphabet; and these are inserted in brackets when they are only gained by rearrangement of the order of words or lines. For convenience of reference in the subsequent discussion, the number of the lines of the translation are placed on the right hand. [The verse numbers are indicated by superior figures in the text.]

1. א [2] A God jealous and avenging is Yahweh,
　　　Yahweh taketh vengeance and is full of wrath;[1]

---

[1] [There can be no question that the dominant rhythm of this poem is 3 : 3; but the first distich is 4 : 4. The occurrence of 4 : 4 in a poem mainly consisting of 3 : 3 is not impossible; nevertheless this distich was probably not 4 : 4 in its original form. For, (1) except by unnaturally dividing it, so that it should be rendered, *God is jealous, and Yahweh is avenging*, the first line does not fall into two equal divisions as is commonly the case in 4 : 4 rhythm (see pp. 168 f.); (2) the use of the same term *avenging* in both lines is improbable; (3) the Greek version appears to rest on a text that had only six words (*i.e.* 3 : 3

[Yahweh taketh vengeance on his adversaries,
And retaineth anger for his enemies.

3 Yahweh is longsuffering and great in strength,   5
But [1] Yahweh will not wholly acquit.]

2. ב   In whirlwind and storm is his way,
And clouds are the dust of his feet.

3. ג   4 He rebuketh the sea and drieth it up,
And parcheth all the rivers.   10

(4. ד)   Bashan and Carmel *languish*,[2]
And the growth of Lebanon withers.

5. ה   5 Mountains quake because of him,
And *all* the hills melt.

6. ו   So the earth becomes desolate [3] before him,   15
The world and all that dwell therein.

(7. ז)   6 Before his indignation who can stand ?
And who can endure the heat of his anger ?

8. ח   His wrath pours out like fire,
And rocks are *kindled* [4] by him.   20

9. ט   7 Good is Yahweh to *those who wait for him*,[5]
A stronghold in the day of distress.

---

rhythm). The exact form of the original may remain a matter of some
uncertainty ; most probably it was :

A jealous God is Yahweh,
One that avengeth, and is full of wrath.

Powis Smith prefers, *A jealous and avenging God is Yahweh, and filled
with wrath* : and it is true that the period of six accents may divide
into 4 : 2 (see p. 182 f.) ; but in that case, too, the four-stress section is
generally divided by a secondary caesura into two equal parts (p. 182),
whereas the longer line in the verse as taken by Powis Smith does not
so divide.]

[1] I follow the Syriac in connecting Yahweh with this line ; cf. LXX
as punctuated in Swete's edition : MT., and consequently E.V., connect
it with the following line.

[2] See below [where דלל is suggested in place of אמלל].

[3] Point ותשׁא (the word used of desolate cities in Isa. vi. 11) instead of
ותשׂא. The R.V. rendering of the latter word is hazardous. In favour of
the emendation, cf. Targ. וחרובת. Vulg. *contremuit* is at least no support
of MT.

[4] MT. נִתְּצוּ means " are thrown down," not " are broken asunder "
(R.V.) ; by a transposition of the second and third letters we get
נצּתו = are kindled.

[5] LXX τοῖς ὑπομένουσιν αὐτόν = לקֹוָיו (cf. *e.g.* Isa. xlix. 23). It has
sometimes been supposed that לקויו is a simple misreading of למעוז

(10. י)   He knoweth those who trust in him,
           [1] And in the overflowing flood *delivers them*.[1]

(11. כ)   An utter end he maketh of *them that rise against*
                                              him,[2] 25
           And he *thrusts* [3] his enemies into the darkness.

(12. ל)   [4a] *Not twice does he take vengeance on his adversaries*,[4]
           [9b] *An utter end he maketh*.

(13. מ)   [9a] *Why do ye plan against Yahweh?* [5]

The foregoing translation represents to the
eye the original structure of the poem, which is
quite obscured by the unoriginal and indeed
very late verse division found in E.V. The fact
that any of the alphabetic letters occurs in the
middle of a *verse* is a matter of entire indifference
to our argument. The question is : How frequently and with what regularity do they occur
at the beginning of *lines*? The main and
indisputable facts can be seen by a glance at the
marginal letters accompanying the translation.
Before discussing some of the more ambiguous
phenomena it will be well to point out that the
lines are, for Hebrew poetry, remarkably regular
in length. The case for the reality of metre in

(Hebrew text) or *vice versa*. But this is unlikely. The individual
letters are not very similar. More probably the present Hebrew and
Greek texts have each arisen by the intentional or accidental omission
of one of the two words. The Targum is too free to afford convincing
evidence ; but the translation would be easily explained by the text
assumed above. It runs thus : " Good is Yahweh to Israel that
they may stay themselves upon him in time of distress "—Israel = לקוי ;
that they may stay themselves upon him = למעוז.

[1] Supply יַצִּילֵם.   [2] [Reading בקמיו for מקומה.]

[3] Reading יהרף for ירדף ; cf. Job xviii. 18.

[4] Reading יקום and בצריו for תקום and צרה, after LXX ἐκδικήσει, ἐν θλίψει.

[5] The *order* of these [three] lines is different in MT. Otherwise the
text is unchanged except as indicated in n. 4.

Hebrew poetry does not appear to me to be made out.[1] But there is no question that in many poems the lines consist of approximately the same number of words. This is the case with the present passage. The regular length of the line is three or four [2] independent words. In one case only (l. 14) the number of words is only two.[3] In line 5, which, as we shall see below, is probably part of a gloss, the number is five. Unless the emendations adopted in lines 22, 25 be accepted, two other lines also extended to five words.[4] The effect of the emendations is in each case to make out of a single line of five words two lines of three words (ll. 21, 22 ; 24, 25). With the exceptions mentioned the emendations adopted do not effect the length of the lines. Even in the Hebrew text as it stands, out of twenty-seven lines all but four consist either of three or four independent

[1] [This statement is now, of course, to be modified in accordance with Chapters I.-VI. of the present work.]

[2] [The lines, except as indicated above, regularly consist of *three* stressed words : the only examples, even in the present text, of lines clearly containing four stresses are *v.* 2 a, b ; and these also, as pointed out above (p. 249, n. 1), were both originally lines of three stresses.]

[3] *I.e.* in the Hebrew text. In the translation I have adopted Gunkel's suggestion. He inserts כל before הגבעות (cf. Ps. cxlviii. 9 ; Jer. iv. 24 ; Amos ix. 13). [Though line 23 contains three *words*, it is most naturally read as a line of two *stresses*, חסי בו falling under a single stress. Probably enough, therefore, a word has fallen out, though whether that word was *Yahweh* and we ought, as many think, to read *Yahweh knoweth* for *He knoweth* is uncertain. The repetition of Yahweh so soon after line 21 is not required.]

[4] The dissimilarity in length of these lines to the others appears in Prof. Smith's translation, *Book of the Twelve*, ii. p. 93, 4th and 2nd lines from bottom.

words.   A great tendency to approximate regularity of length must therefore be admitted.

Turning now to the occurrence and position of the acrostich letters, it will again be well to proceed from the certain to the uncertain.

As the Hebrew text stands apart from any, even the slightest emendation, the 2nd, 3rd, 5th, 6th, 8th, and 9th letters of the Hebrew alphabet stand at the beginning of the 7th, 9th, 13th, 15th, 19th, and 21st lines respectively ; in other words, they stand separated from one another by precisely the same *constant* interval which would separate them in an acrostich poem so constructed that two lines should be given to each successive letter ; actual instances of similarly constructed and virtually unmutilated poems are, as we have seen, Psalms xxv., xxxiv., cxlv., and Proverbs xxxi. 10-31. This single fact, when duly considered, appears to me to necessitate the conclusion that we have in this passage the result of fully conscious design, and in these lines, as in those that intervene, parts of an acrostich.   Previous [1] English presentations of this subject, so far as known to me, have not brought into sufficient relief the evidence of the influence of both laws of the acrostich — the occurrence of the letters of the alphabet in regular succession *at regular intervals*.

In the Hebrew text as it now stands the 11th

---

[1] [Previous, that is to say, to 1898.]

and 17th lines do not begin with ד and ו respectively, as they should do if they formed part of
an acrostich. Nor, again, does the 23rd line
begin with ר, as it should do if the acrostich or
the fragment thereof extended so far. Is there
anything apart from the acrostich theory which
suggests that at these points the Hebrew text
is corrupt ? Or failing that, can the acrostich
theory be satisfied by simple and probable
conjectural emendation ? If this should be so,
the evidence of the uncorrected Hebrew text,
in itself so strong as to be almost irresistible,
receives some further support.

In the case of what should be the *daleth* verse
(ll. 11, 12), but which in our present text begins
with an *aleph,* the versions are certainly interesting and suggestive. In the two parallel lines
(11, 12) the Hebrew text has the same verb
(אמלל) ; in *all* the early versions (LXX, Syr.,
Targ., Vulg.), the verbs in the two lines are
different.[1] Thus the double occurrence of the
same word in the two parallel lines is on
grounds of textual criticism open to grave
suspicion.[2] On the same grounds, however, it

---

[1] LXX, ὀλιγώθη . . . ἐξέλιπεν ; Syr., ܐܠܐ . . . ܡܚܒ ; Targ.,
נתרו . . . צדי ; Vulg., " Infirmatus est . . . elanguit." This cannot
well be attributed to a mere desire for variation, for just below, in lines
17, 18, both Syr. and LXX translate *different* Hebrew words by the
same Greek (ὀργή) or Syriac (ܡܚ ܘܓܙ).

[2] I question whether the mere fact of the repetition of the same
word in the second line could reasonably be regarded as suspicious.
There are too many similar instances in our present Hebrew text for
it to be safely assumed that a Hebrew poet never used the same verb

must be admitted that all these versions read
אמלל with initial *aleph* at the beginning of the
former of the two lines,[1] where the acrostich requires a word beginning with *daleth*. This is a fact
which ought to be frankly faced and duly considered in deciding to what extent Nahum i. 1–
ii. 2 preserves an acrostich poem. But it must be
noted further that the verbs used by the LXX
and Syriac versions in the second line of the same
parallel (l. 12 in the above translation) never
occur elsewhere as translations of אמלל, although
in each of these versions several equivalents of
אמלל are found [2] one of which might have been

in two parallel lines. [Such repetitions as occur in the Hebrew text
here do, however, appear to me now to be in themselves open to *some*
suspicion, though not of course to be *certainly* due to textual corruption.
Some may be original; others, like the repetition of אמלל here, are
due to the accidental repetition of the term in the first line of a distich
driving out the parallel, but different, term in the second line. Other
more or less certain examples of such accidents may be found in Isa. xi.
5, xvi. 7, xxvi. 7, and are pointed out in the notes on those passages
in the "International Critical Commentary." See further, below,
pp. 295 f.]

[1] In each case the words, used by the versions in this place, occur
elsewhere as translations of אמלל : thus ὀλιγοῦν in Joel i. 10, 12 ; ܐܟܠ
in the Pesch. of Isaiah xxiv. 4, 7, Jeremiah xv. 9, Hosea iv. 3 ; צדי
(in the Targums as printed in Walton's Polyglot) in Isaiah xix. 8,
xxiv. 4, Jeremiah xv. 9 (cf. 1 Sam. ii. 5 ; and the Pesch. use of ܝܘܪ in
1 Sam. ii. 5, Jer. xiv. 2, Lam. ii. 8) ; *infirmatus* (or *infirmus*) *est* in the
Vulgate of 1 Samuel ii. 5, Isaiah xxiv. 4 (*bis*), 7, Jeremiah xv. 9, Hosea
iv. 3, Psalm vi. 3.

[2] In addition to the words mentioned in the last note but two, the
LXX uses ἀσθενής (or verb) Psalm vi. 3, Lamentations ii. 8, 1 Samuel
ii. 5 ; πενθεῖν Isaiah xvi. 8, xix. 8, xxiv. 4, 7, xxxiii. 9 (?) ; κενοῦσθαι
Jeremiah xiv. 2, xv. 9 ; μικρύνεσθαι Hosea iv. 3 ; and the Syriac uses
ܝܘܪ 1 Samuel ii. 5, Jeremiah xiv. 2, Lamentations ii. 8 (cf. also the
usage of צדי in the Targ.—see preceding note) ; ܒܚܝܠ Psalm vi. 3
and (Ethpeel of verb) Isaiah xix. 8 ; ܡܫܚ Joel i. 10, 12, Isaiah xvi. 8.

used had the translators merely desired variant renderings in the two lines of the same verb.

It is, therefore, improbable that אמלל stood in the Hebrew text of line 12 at the times when the LXX and Syriac versions were made.[1] On the other hand there is reason for believing that the actual reading of the Hebrew text which lay before at least the Greek translators was דלל (dālal). For (1) this verb is translated by the same Greek word that is found in line 12 in Isaiah xxxviii. 14, and probably also in Isaiah xix. 6 ; compare also Isaiah xvii. 4 ; (2) the two final letters of דלל are the same as of אמלל; this would have facilitated an accidental copying of the verb of the previous line. The chief question that remains is whether the verb דלל would be appropriate. Certainly there is no other instance of its being used of foliage, but in Isaiah xxxviii. 14 it is used of languishing eyes, in Isaiah xvii. 4 (Niphal) of the glory of Jacob, and in Post-Biblical Hebrew (Hiphil) of thinning out vines or olives.[2]

But beyond this not unimportant suggestion the versions do not help us. Already when they were made lines 11, 17, 23 began with other

---

[1] It is less improbable that the Targ. and Vulg. read אמלל here as well as in the preceding line, though of course the difference in the translations still constitutes a considerable [?] presumption against identity in the original. But both words used in Targ. and Vulg. also appear elsewhere as translations of אמלל. On צדי and *infirmatus est* see preceding note ; for נתר cf. Joel i. 10, 12, and for *elanguit* Joel i. 10, 12, Isa. xxxiii. 9.   [2] See *Peah.* iii. 3, vii. 5 ; *Shebi'ith* iv. 4.

letters than those required by the acrostich. In line 23, however, the initial word is וידע ; the acrostich is at once satisfied by the simple omission of ו, which leaves ידע. That ו was constantly added through dittography or overlooked before another ו or י, with which latter letter it is frequently confused, becomes clear from a comparison of the LXX and Hebrew texts. In assuming then that the ו at the beginning of line 23 is intrusive, we are simply assuming what we know for certain frequently happened in similar cases.

The recovery of the initial ד and ז requires us to assume two [1] cases of transposition of words in the course of the transcription of the Hebrew text prior to the Greek translation. Once again no one questions that transpositions have taken place in the course of transcription. That the three initial letters wanting in the present text

---

[1] In lines 11, 12 we must assume that the verbs of the two lines became transposed [see p. 296] and that the original Hebrew ran דלל בשן וכרמל ופרח לבנון אמלל.   In line 17 the fourth word of the line (לפניו) became transposed (having lost its final letter) to the beginning ; for the present text לפני זעמו מי יעמד read therefore וזעמו מי יעמד לפניו.   The sense remains the same, but the Hebrew becomes more idiomatic ; cf. Driver, *Tenses*, §§ 196 f. [The last clause is an overstatement.   I should have said : the sense remains the same, and the Hebrew quite grammatical.   The order of the emended text is rather, as Driver puts it (*Minor Prophets*, p. 26, n. 7), " less easy and natural than the existing order." The author of the acrostich adopted a possible, though less easy, order for his words in the interests of his alphabetic scheme, just as the author of Ps. cxix. uses אתה in *v*. 4, and places את־חקיך at the beginning of *v*. 8, to satisfy the conditions of his alphabetic scheme rather than because he wished to express any real emphasis.   An objection taken to the emendation by Arnold is entirely lacking in force, and is completely answered by Powis Smith.]

S

reappear by means of such comparatively simple emendations, thus giving us nine successive letters of the alphabet as initial letters at remarkably constant intervals, turns a prior great probability into virtual certainty.

If then the case is made out that lines 7-24 are nine successive stanzas of an acrostich poem which has suffered in three cases at the beginning of lines, and at least three or four times elsewhere from transcriptional error, how much may we infer with regard to the rest of this poem, of which at least this considerable fragment has survived without serious mutilation ? Is the rest of the poem to be found in the remainder of the passage ? Has it also suffered merely from the chances and accidents of transcription ? Or has it been in parts obliterated, in parts interpolated ?

That it has received some interpolation no one will question. The prophetic formula, " Thus saith Yahweh " (v. 12), never formed part of an acrostich poem ; and its presence can hardly help suggesting that the latter part of the poem, even if it survive in the main, has been to some extent recast by the inserter of these words. We have then to reckon with the probability of intentional as well as transcriptional changes in such parts of the poem as may be discovered after these words.

As it is the purpose of the present chapter to

distinguish what is certain or very probable
from details which are uncertain and only gain
what varying degrees of probability they may
severally possess in the light of that which is
more certain, it will be sufficient from this point
on to make brief notes on some of the more
uncertain details and some of the questions
which a careful study of Nahum i. 1–ii. 3 must
necessarily raise.

(1) In the translation I have ventured to
indicate the acrostich letters of the next three
stanzas to those already discussed. Their restoration involves greater assumptions than did the
restoration of the initial ד, ז, and י. But the
emendation which gives the כ stanza (ll. 25, 26)
seems to me very probable, and the transposition
that places the ל stanza (ll. 27, 28) in its right
place and gives us a first line of the מ stanza
(l. 29) probable. The כ stanza immediately
appears if we assume that a single word (יצילם =
he delivers them) has dropped out after the
words " with an overflowing flood." Not only
so ; the same emendation gives us two parallel
lines of three words each instead of a single line
of five words—a length which we have seen
above in itself raises suspicion. The ל stanza
and the first line of the מ stanza reappear on a
mere rearrangement of lines. Lines 27, 28, 29
in the above translation stand in the Hebrew
text in the order 29, 28, 27. On exegetical

grounds the rearrangement appears to me an improvement, and thus far gains independent support.[1]

(2) From the first line of the מ stanza onwards the acrostich can only be restored by much more radical alterations, and any particular suggestion can be regarded as little more than a possibility. At the same time the general fact that at least parts of the remainder of the poem lie embedded in the following verses appears probable. It is just in this part of the passage that the text is frequently so corrupt as to be unintelligible. It is, for instance, difficult to believe that any one can seriously consider *v.* 10 in its present form to have been written by an intelligent Hebrew.[2] Of details, the most probable appears to me that the מ stanza began with the סירים of *v.* 10. In *v.* 12 the sense almost requires us to omit the ו of וענתך, so that we may translate " I have afflicted thee, but will afflict thee no more "; עבתך might then be considered the commencement of the ע stanza. Transpositions and omissions can seldom be dismissed as impossible ; for apart from any acrostich theory it is very

---

[1] The translation adopted by Dr. G. A. Smith and Prof. Nowack of line 29, " What think ye of Yahweh ? " is, to say the least, hazardous—more especially if with the former scholar we regard *v.* 11 as genuine. Partly on this ground, partly on others, I am not inclined to follow Prof. Nowack in transposing lines 3, 5, 4 so that they follow line 29, and form the answer to the question.

[2] " These [? *read* there] are parts of Nahum i. (as *vv.* 10-12) in which the text is desperately corrupt " (Driver, *Expos. Times*, p. 119, footnote). Cf. also Davidson's notes on i. 10, 12, 15.

difficult to believe that the sudden transitions from Judah to Nineveh (?) as the person addressed in i. 8, 15 (Heb. i. 8, ii. 1) is original. Professor G. A. Smith, who never suffers himself to be controlled by the acrostich theory, nevertheless finds it necessary to " disentangle " i. 13, ii. 1-3, from the rest, and print these verses by themselves as an address to Judah.

(3) The first line of the translation begins in the Hebrew, as it should do, with an *aleph* ; it and the following line constituted the first section of the poem. But as the section must not exceed two lines, lines 3-6 cannot be original— at least in their present position. I have little doubt myself that Gunkel is right in regarding them as a gloss intended to limit explicitly the absolute assertion of the preceding lines.[1] It is worth noticing that line 5 is suspiciously long, consisting as it does of five words.

(4) Lines 1, 2, and 7-29 thus constitute the first 25 lines or the first 12½ sections of an acrostich poem of 44 lines or 22 sections ; some of the remaining 17 lines may survive mutilated and in disorder in chapters i. 10–ii. 3. The translation as given above (with the omission of ll. 3-6) in all probability approximates very

---

[1] " This is not obvious, and would hardly have been alleged apart from the needs of the alphabetic scheme " (G. A. Smith, p. 83). Perfectly true ; but if the alphabetical scheme in parts be independently proved a reality, the view of *v.* 1 taken above, though not immediately obvious, becomes the most probable.

closely to the sense and form of the first half of
the original poem.

(5) Nahum i. 1–ii. 3 is at most only in part the
work of the prophet Nahum. The main alternatives are these : (*a*) Nahum recast and in
places expanded an existing acrostich poem.
(*b*) Nahum composed an acrostich poem which
has suffered much in transcription and has been
in places expanded by some subsequent editor.
(*c*) Some fragments of Nahum (? part of i. 11–
ii. 3) have been combined with parts of an
acrostich poem. (*d*) An acrostich poem which,
either before or after, suffered transcriptional
corruption and interpolation has been incorporated in the book of Nahum by an editor, just as
a short psalm (Isa. xii.) was incorporated in the
book of Isaiah, and a longer psalm in the book
of Habakkuk (c. iii.). Alternative (*a*) is very
improbable ; nor is (*b*) likely. But if either of
these be adopted, this poem would be the earliest
Hebrew acrostich of certain date, the next
earliest being chapters i.-iv. of Lamentations.

(6) In view of the doubt that attaches to the
chapter, evidence for the date of Nahum drawn
from chapters ii. and iii. should be allowed to
outweigh any counter evidence in chapter i.
The effect of this is to strengthen the strong
arguments which have induced recent writers [1]

---

[1] Davidson, *Nahum, Habakkuk, and Zephaniah*, pp. 13-18 ; G. A.
Smith, *Book of the Twelve Prophets*, ii. pp. 85-88. Cf. Driver, *Introduction*, p. 335 f.

to assign the prophecy to the year 608 rather than *circa* 660 or 623.

The present discussion contains, I am well aware, comparatively little that will be new to those who are acquainted with the German discussions to which I have referred, and to which I have throughout been greatly indebted, although I hope that my suggestion, based as it is on the evidence of the LXX, that the verb of the *daleth* stanza is דלל, may find acceptance.[1] But I shall have achieved my purpose if I have succeeded in proving that it must henceforth be accepted as a fixed point for the criticism and interpretation of Nahum that the position of certain initial letters in the first chapter is not fortuitous, but the result of a fully conscious design ; and, therefore, that this chapter contains at least considerable parts of an acrostich poem.

---

[1] [Among those who have accepted דלל are Driver, Duhm (*Zeitschr. für die AT. Wissenschaft*, 1911, p. 101), and Powis Smith (" International Critical Commentary "). It is not obvious that those who still prefer one of the alternative emendations (ראב or רכאו) have fully considered the evidence of the versions as given above.]

CHAPTER VIII

THE ALPHABETIC STRUCTURE OF PSALMS IX. AND X.

CHAPTER VIII

THE ALPHABETIC STRUCTURE OF PSALMS IX. AND X.

[The following discussion first appeared in the *Expositor* for September 1906. It is here republished substantially unchanged except by the addition of one long note on Ps. ix. 6-9 (pp. 271 f.), and a few words or shorter notes elsewhere. These additions are enclosed in square brackets.]

SOME few years since [1] I attempted to prove afresh (for at the time it was not generally admitted by English scholars) the existence in the first chapter of Nahum of part of an alphabetic poem ; in recoil from certain over-elaborate and inconclusive attempts to prove that an *entire* alphabetic poem lay concealed there, several writers had expressed scepticism of the existence of even a part of such a poem, for which nevertheless the evidence, rightly considered, was really, and is now more generally admitted to be, irresistible.

I here propose to rediscuss the question of the

---

[1] The *Expositor*, 1898 (Sept.), pp. 207-220. [Now appearing as Chapter VII. of the present work.]

alphabetic structure of Psalms ix. and x. In this case it is agreed that we have to do with parts of an alphabetic poem (or of two); but opinion remains divided as to the extent of these parts. In the interests alike of the criticism of the Psalter, the history of the Hebrew text, and the interpretation of the particular psalm (or psalms), it is important to narrow down the legitimate differences of opinion to the utmost.

In the present Hebrew text, and consequently in modern versions, Psalms ix. and x. form two distinct poems. On the other hand, in the Septuagint, probably also in the later Greek versions of Aquila, Symmachus, and Theodotion, certainly also in Jerome's version, which was made direct from the Hebrew, Psalms ix. and x. formed a single undivided whole.[1] Is the unity of the poem as presented in the versions accidental or fictitious ? or does the division into two psalms in the Hebrew text correspond to original diversity of origin ? These questions, which are of first importance for the interpretation of the poem (or poems), are intimately connected with the question of the alphabetic structure.

The unity of the two psalms has been maintained chiefly by those who also hold ,that the incompleteness of the alphabetic scheme, which marks the text in its present condition, is mainly due to textual corruption. This theory has been

---

[1] See Baethgen, *Psalmen*,[3] p. 22.

presented (with many differences in detail) by
Bickell, by Dr. T. K. Abbot, whose valuable
article,[1] dependent in the main on Bickell, but
with important independent suggestions, seems
to have exercised less influence than it deserved,
by Dr. Cheyne in the second edition of his *Book
of Psalms*, and by Duhm. It is, I believe, substantially correct, and its failure to gain more
general support from English writers is probably
due to the numerous and, in some cases, necessarily uncertain conjectures with which its
presentation has been connected. My more
particular purpose is to show that the alphabetic
arrangement certainly extends *further* than has
been generally admitted except by those who
have argued that it extended throughout. If
this can be established, it will invalidate the most
attractive of the theories that deny the unity of
the poem, that of Baethgen, which I shall describe
below, and it will establish at the least a considerable presumption that the alphabetic arrangement, where it now fails to appear or appears
less clearly, once existed, and consequently that
the two psalms are a unity whose integrity has
been impaired mainly, if not exclusively, by the
ordinary accidents of textual transmission.

To facilitate the discussion I give first a
translation with some notes on the text, chiefly

[1] In *Hermathena*, 1889, pp. 21-28 ; also in *Essays chiefly on the
Original Texts of the Old and New Testaments*, pp. 200-207.

on those parts of the text which are of importance in the present examination. In order to concentrate attention on my main point, I have left unadopted, and generally, too, unnoticed, many emendations suggested more especially by Dr. Cheyne and Duhm which otherwise would unquestionably deserve attention, if not acceptance. But the result of my examination, as I point out at the close, appears to me to render certain types of these emendations improbable.

In the translation all departures from the Hebrew consonantal text, whether justified by the ancient versions or not, are printed in italics. Words which are unintelligible (either in themselves or in their context), and yet cannot be satisfactorily emended, are left untranslated and represented by . . . ; in some cases where a lacuna may be suspected I have used the signs + + +. Words or letters omitted are represented by ʌ. So far as the alphabetic strophes are clear, I have printed them as strophes with the initial letter at the head, following the method adopted in the Authorised Version and Revised Version of Psalm cxix. and by Dr. G. A. Smith in his translation of Lamentations ii. and iv. [which appeared first] in the *Expositor* for April 1906, pp. 327-336, [and subsequently in *Jerusalem from the Earliest Times*, ii. pp. 274-283]. Those initial letters which do not occur in the present Hebrew text I have given in brackets alongside

of the immediately preceding initial, at the
head of a section extending (without subdivision
into strophes) down to the next initial occurring
in the text.   In this way I hope that I may
bring the problem presented by the present
state of the text somewhat clearly before the
reader's eye.   In Psalm ix. the verses are
numbered according to the Hebrew enumeration,
which, beginning with 2, is one in advance of
the English throughout.   In Psalm x. the Hebrew
and English enumerations agree.

א

IX.   ² I will give thanks unto *Thee*, Yahweh, with my
whole heart,
    I will recount all Thy wonders ;
  ³ I will rejoice and exult in Thee,
    I will make melody to Thy Name, O Most High.

ב

  ⁴ Because mine enemies shall turn backward,
    Shall stumble and perish at Thy presence ;
  ⁵ For Thou hast maintained my right and my cause,
    Hast sat upon the throne as a righteous judge.

ג, (ד), (ה)

  ⁶ Thou hast rebuked the nations + + +,
    Thou hast destroyed the wicked + + + ;

---

²ᵃ *Thee* with LXX (*i.e.* אודך for אודה of the Hebrew text), and in
agreement with the address to Yahweh in the following verses.

⁶⁻⁹ [These verses should contain what survives of the three
strophes which began with the letters ג, ד, and ה.   Of these initials
only ג appears in the present text.   In spite of the loss of its initial
letter, ה, the third of these strophes seems still to be almost complete ;
for ויהי (*v.* 10), the beginning of the ו strophe, is preceded by two
distichs, with lines parallel to one another and of normal length, which

Thou hast wiped out their name for ever and aye,
7 The enemy (?) + + +.
Silent (?) are the ruins for ever,
  And the cities Thou didst uproot—perished is their memory.

---

are closely connected with one another in thought : Yahweh is on the
point of giving judgment (*v.* 8), which he will give in justice and
righteousness (*v.* 9).   In the first line of *v.* 8, which should begin with
the initial ה, the term ישב is parallel to the three terms of the second
line, and the two words ויהוה לעולם are non-parallel terms (cp. p. 76 f.) :
of these יהוה seems the more needed ; לעולם may or may not be
original ; if the distich was, as some of the distichs in this poem
certainly appear to be, 4 : 3 (p. 173-176), the original may perhaps be
recovered by simply substituting הנה יהוה for ויהוה ; if the distich was
3 : 3, by making this substitution and omitting לעולם.

Verses 6 and 7 contain only about one line, or at most four or five
words, more than the normal length of one strophe, whereas two
strophes, beginning with נ and ד respectively, must originally have
stood here.   Is the loss of between two and four lines, or, say, six to
ten words, spread evenly over the two strophes, or has the ד strophe
wholly dropped out in the same way that whole strophes have disappeared from Ps. xxv. and cxlv. (see p. 245) ?   In the latter case
v. 6 might be the first distich, and *v.* 7 a corrupt and slightly expanded
form of the second distich of the נ strophe ; and what is printed above
as two mutilated lines in *v.* 6 was in reality a single line with secondary
parallelism (cp. p. 104) between its two clauses—a feature which appears
elsewhere in this poem (see ix. 14 a ; x. 11 b, 12 a, 17 b).   Be this as
it may, I am, on the whole, inclined now to think that לעולם ועד at
the end of *v.* 6 and לנצח in *v.* 7 a were originally parallel terms in
the final distich of the נ strophe ; I suspect that this distich was 4 : 3,
that האויבתמו conceals a noun with the 3rd pl. masc. suffix parallel to
שממ, and חרבות a 2nd sing. pf. form of a vb. parallel to מחית.   Instead of
the last line of *v.* 6 and the first two of *v.* 7 given above, I should now
suggest :

> Thou hast wiped out their name for ever and aye,
>   Their . . . hast thou . . . for evermore.

If this view be correct all that survives of the ד strophe is וערים נתשת אבד
זכרם המה, of which the last word may be a corrupt form of the first word
of the ה strophe ; *i.e.* of twelve to sixteen words of the ד strophe, but
four or five survive : under these circumstances to guess what the
initial word was seems to me fruitless.]

6 ab Duhm, perhaps rightly, sees here fragments of two parallel
lines (for the thought is certainly parallel) rather than the whole of a
single line (R.V. and most).   [But see preceding note.]

7-8 These verses are certainly corrupt, but the above emendations
(like others that have been proposed) are little more than makeshifts.

Silent : reading דמו for חמו ; [yet this is very doubtful ; see the

Behold (?) [8] Yahweh sitteth (enthroned) for ever,
He hath established His throne for judgment ;
[9] And 'tis He will judge the world in righteousness,
He will pass sentence on the peoples with equity.

ו

[10] So may Yahweh be a high retreat for the crushed,
A high retreat in seasons of extremity;
[11] And let them that know Thy Name trust in Thee,
For Thou hast not forsaken them that seek Thee,
O Yahweh.

ז

[12] Make melody unto Yahweh, who sitteth (enthroned)
in Sion,
Declare among the peoples His doings ;
[13] For he that requireth blood hath remembered ∧,
He hath not forgotten the cry of the afflicted.

ח

[14] Be gracious to me, Yahweh, behold my affliction ∧,
O Thou who raisest me up from the gates of Death ;
[15] In order that I may recount all Thy praises,
(And) in the gates of Sion's daughter exult in Thy
salvation.

---

discussion on *vv.* 6-9]. The Authorised Version (=R.V. marg.) is sufficiently criticised by Kirkpatrick, but the Revised Version is also very questionable ; literally the Hebrew text runs, *The enemy* (singular) *are* (plural) *ruins for ever.*

Behold : reading הנה יהוה for המה ויהוה of the Hebrew text. The Revised Version again substitutes for a wrong translation of the Authorised Version a wrong one of its own. In rendering *their very memorial has perished*, it emphasises *memorial* which the Hebrew text does not, and omits the emphasis which (doubtless owing to textual corruption) actually falls on the pronoun. The only correct rendering of the present text is *their memorial, even theirs, has perished.*

[13a] *Remembered:* Hebrew text adds *them ;* but the position of the pronoun is suspicious.

[14a] *Affliction:* Hebrew text adds משנאי which the Revised Version renders, (*which I suffer*) *of them that hate me.* But the construction is

T

ט

16 The nations have sunk down in the pit they made,
   In the net they hid their own foot has been caught;
17 Yahweh hath made Himself known in the execution
                                              of justice,
   The wicked has been trapped in the work of his
                                              own hands.

י

18 The wicked shall return unto Sheol,
   (Even) all the nations that forget God;

כ

19 For the poor shall not be forgotten for ever,
   (Nor) the hope of the afflicted perish for aye.
20 Arise, Yahweh, let not frail man be strong,
   Let the nations be judged before Thy face;
21 Appoint terror for them, O Yahweh,
   Let the nations know they are frail men.

(מ) ל

X. 1 Wherefore, Yahweh, standest Thou afar off,
      Hidest Thou (Thine eyes) in seasons of extremity?
    2 In arrogance the wicked hotly pursues the afflicted;
      Let them be caught in the devices they have
                                              imagined.
    3 For the wicked praiseth *his* desire;
      The greedy getter blesseth *his appetite*.

---

harsh, and the presence of the word overloads the line. Not improbably
משנאי has arisen from מנשאי, the participle originally used in the next
line, which was subsequently explained by the synonymous מרוממי (so
Lagarde, and many since).

³ The last two words of the Hebrew text of this verse belong to
verse 4 : see next note. After their removal, there remains :—

כי־הלל רשע על תאות נפשו
ובצע ברך

These lines are obviously ill-balanced ; הלל רשע in the first is parallel
to בצע ברך in the second, but the object in the first line consists of two

נ (ס)

4 The wicked [3] contemneth Yahweh (saying)—
    4 " According to His full anger He will not punish " ;
" There is no God " is the sum of his thoughts ;
    5 Stable are his ways at all times.

---

words parallel in sense, while the second contains no object at all.
Apparently, then, the missing object of the second line has accidentally
shifted up to the line above. If so, תאות once immediately preceded
ובצע ; by a wrong division of words the ו appears to have become
detached from an original תאותו and prefixed to ובצע. In line one
the על is probably derived from an original ל by reading the final ע
of the preceding word twice. The two lines now balance and parallel
one another perfectly. For the phrase *to bless one's own soul* or *appetite*,
used of the godless, cf. xlix. 19. This is Duhm's emendation, and, to
quote his words, the thought is : " The godless man praises not God,
but his own belly (cf. Luke xii. 19) " ; cf. also Phil. iii. 19. The lines,
thus restored, read as follows :—

כי־הלל רשע לתאותו

ובצע ברך נפשו

4 In the Hebrew text the last line of *v.* 3 and the first of *v.* 4 stand
thus :—

ובצע ברך נאץ יהוה

רשע כנבה אפו בל־ידרש

But the citation from this verse in *v.* 13 (על מה נאץ רשע אלהים, *Wherefore*
" *hath the wicked contemned God* ") clearly shows that נאץ יהוה רשע
originally stood here as an independent sentence ; and so it does
stand in the earliest form of the text, to wit, in the LXX. Consequently, what precedes נאץ belongs to *v.* 3 ; what follows רשע begins
a new line and a new sentence. These positive reasons for the division
of sentences adopted above are supported by strong negative considerations, viz. that the last line of *v.* 3 as it stands in the Hebrew text and
R.V. admits of no satisfactory and natural explanation, and that
those who follow the Hebrew sentence-division are driven to a highly
questionable translation of the words כנבה אפו—*the pride of his
countenance* (R.V.), or *the loftiness of his looks* ; but *countenance* in
Hebrew is פנים, *not* אף. אף means *nostril*, *nose*, and then, metaphoric-
ally, *anger* ; that in Hebrew (or Arabic) it ever acquired the sense *face* is,
to say the least, unproven. It is customary (and idiomatically correct)
to render אפים ארצה—*with the face to the earth* ; but there is no reason
to question that the Hebrew thought of the *nose*, rather than the whole
face, touching the ground.

In the height (?) are Thy judgments from before him ;
As for all his adversaries, he puffeth at them ;
6 He saith in his heart, " I shall never be shaken,"
. . . . 7 . . .

5b *In the height :* questionable, but, if correct, to be paraphrased
as in R.V. Abbot happily suggests מרו for מרום, and renders, *Removed
are Thy judgments from before him.*

6 This verse originally included the first word of *v.* 7 (see next note).
The smooth translation of the R.V., with its excellent parallels, completely conceals the really desperate character of the Hebrew text.
Presumably the Revisers treated אשר as = ὅτι recitative, and therefore left it untranslated. This is a rare usage, but sufficiently established to justify invoking it, if אשר really *introduced* the speech here ;
but it does not : it stands nearly at the end of the words spoken (after
all generations) ! The A.V., *He hath said in his heart, I shall not be
moved : for (I shall) never (be) in adversity*, is, perhaps, a less illegitimate
translation, but the sense is self-condemnatory—I shall not be moved,
because I shall not be moved. Tautologous, too, is Dr. Driver's
translation (*Parallel Psalter*), " I shall not be moved, I who to all generations shall not be in adversity." Other attempts have been made to
render and explain the verse as it stands, but these may suffice to show
that the present text is really impossible. We might, indeed, render—
He hath said in his heart, I shall never be moved who is not in adversity,
i.e. He who is now prosperous is confident that his prosperity will
continue, but for three considerations : (1) The two lines would be
exceedingly ill-balanced ; (2) the *order* would be as awkward in Hebrew
as I have intentionally made it in English ; and (3) it takes no account
of אלה which has to be included from *v.* 7.

Duhm's treatment of the words אשר לא ברע, together with אלה of
v. 7, may be in the right direction, but it is not free from some of the
objections urged against the present text. He points אלה of *v.* 7 אֻלָה
(=אֻלַי Gesenius-Kautzsch's *Grammar*, 91 e), the word found in a
similar context in lxxiii. 4 (wrongly rendered in R.V.), and renders,
He whose paunch is not ill (fed), i.e. the godless " in fair round belly with
good capon lined " forgets God, and is quite happy about his own fate.

7 Again the R.V. conceals the strange order of the Hebrew text as
at present divided. To visualise the argument for the division adopted
above, I give the R.V. altered only in so far as to restore the Hebrew
order :—

Cursing | his mouth is full of | and | deceit and oppression,
Under his tongue is | mischief and iniquity.

A mere glance at the lines suggests the strong probability that the words
cursing and *and* in the first line are intrusive, and have spoilt a very
fine and perfect parallelism. But, further : (1) The position of אלה,
cursing, before the verb throws on it a strong emphasis, for which,
nevertheless, no reason can be discovered, and the real object consisting

פ

His mouth is full of deceits and oppression,
    Under his tongue is mischief and trouble ;
⁸ He sitteth in places of ambush in the villages,
    In secret places he slayeth the innocent.

ע (צ)

His eyes watch privily for the hapless,
⁹ He lieth in ambush in a secret place as a lion in
                              his covert;
He lieth in ambush to snatch away the afflicted,
    He snatcheth away the afflicted, dragging him off
                              in his net.

¹⁰ [The righteous] . . . sinketh down,
    And the hapless fall by his strong ones (?).
¹¹ He saith in his heart, " God has forgotten,
    He hath hidden His face (and) seeth nevermore."

---

like its parallel, in the next line of a *pair* of qualities, comes limping awkwardly in at the end as an afterthought. Why is there a stress on cursing ? Why, so much more stress on cursing than on deceit or oppression ? Why, perhaps we may further ask, is cursing somewhat incongruously coupled with " deceit and oppression " ? These are questions which commentators who follow the traditional division of the text have never answered, if they have even considered them. (2) The inclusion of אלה in the first line would overload it, giving it five word-accents against the four of its parallel : this lack of balance is only aggravated when Baethgen removes אשר from *v.* 6 and prefixes it to *v.* 7 !

Read, then, in 7 a פיהו מלא מרמות ותך, *i.e.* omit the ו before מרמות (necessarily introduced when אלה had been connected with *v.* 7), or less probably the waw of ומרמות may have shifted from an original מלאו, lit. *Deceit and oppression fill his mouth.*

⁹ *In a secret place :* The omission of these words, which may have been accidentally repeated from 8 b, improves the vigour and rhythm of the line.

¹⁰ Again, the attempt to render the existing Hebrew text has reduced commentators to the most desperate straits. R.V. renders,

    He croucheth, he boweth down,
    And the helpless fall by his strong ones.

But to whom does the pronoun refer ? Many, since Ewald, have

ק

12 Arise, Yahweh, O God, lift up Thine hand :
Forget not *the cry of* the afflicted ;
13 Wherefore hath the wicked contemned Yahweh ?
Hath he said in his heart, " Thou wilt not punish " ?

ר

14 Thou hast seen ∧ ∧ mischief and vexation,
Thou lookest (upon them) to place them in Thy hand ;
The hapless committeth his cause unto Thee,
Thou hast been the helper of the orphan.

---

referred it to the lion, and have quite gratuitously explained " his strong ones " to mean his claws. But this involves the extremely improbable supposition that the pronoun refers to a subject introduced *allusively* three lines before (9 a) and *dismissed*, for 9 b, c cannot refer to the lion, since the lion does not hunt with a net, nor insist that his meal shall consist in particular of the poor. As the text stands, the subject of 9 b, c, that is, the wicked man, can alone be reasonably regarded as the subject of 10 a. But, then, why should the wicked man be described as *crushed* ? for this, and not *to crouch* (R.V.), is the sense of דכה. As a matter of fact, 10 a must be interpreted by its parallel 10 b; both lines must refer to the poor : but, then, a term referring to the poor is as badly needed in 10 a as in 10 b—indeed, more so. Thus exegetical considerations point strongly to the loss in 10 a of a term parallel to חלכאים in 10 b. Rhythmical considerations point strongly in the same direction. For (1) 10 a (two words) is shorter than its parallel (three words) ; and (2) it is abnormally short in relation to the entire poem : it is the only real and unambiguous case (even in the present text) of a line of two words. The obscure דכה (or ידכה ḳ're) I have left untranslated above, but to bring out the sense I have tentatively made good the loss of the term parallel to *hapless* in 10 b. Whether that term was *righteous* or one of a dozen others must be determined, if determined it can be, by other arguments [see page 283] than those here adduced to prove that *some* word, be it what it may, has fallen out of the text at this point.

12ab The lines are ill-balanced ; perhaps אל (O God) in *a* is an editor's substitute for Yahweh : in line *b* עצקת has been supplied in accordance with ix. 13.

14a The Hebrew text is scarcely tolerable. Duhm (followed above) omits כיאתה as a corrupt duplication of ראתה. Even so perhaps the original text is not exactly recovered.

ש

¹⁵ Break the arm of the wicked and evil,
    Though ∧ wickedness be sought for, it shall not
                      be found ;
¹⁶ Yahweh is King for ever and aye,
    The nations are perished out of His land.

ת

¹⁷ Thou, Yahweh, hast heard the desire of the humble,
    Thou directest their heart, makest Thine ear
                      attentive ;
¹⁸ To do justice to the orphan and the crushed,
    That frail man of the earth may terrorize no more.

The two laws of an alphabetic poem are (1) that the initials of successive strophes follow the order of the alphabet, and (2) that these initials should follow one another at regular intervals. This regular interval in Psalms ix. and x. is four lines, as may be seen by a glance at the strophes beginning with א, ב, ו, ז, ט, ק, ר, ש, ת, not at present to refer to others.

The lines throughout the poem are of equal or approximately equal length, the normal length being three or four accented words.[1] Of the eighty-three lines into which the Revised Version

---

^{15a} The LXX, which connects *the wicked and the evil,* is preferable to the Massoretic interpretation of the Hebrew text, which begins a fresh sentence with the second term (so R.V.).

^{15b} The meaning is clear: Exterminate wickedness; but how precisely this was expressed is uncertain. I have read רשעה for רשעו, and both verbs as Niphals.

^{18b} The line is over long. Duhm omits the last three words, and renders, *that they may be in dread no more.*

[1] [That some of the lines contain three, some four stresses is due to the fact that the author makes use of 4 : 3 rhythm : see pp. 171-176.]

divides the two Psalms, fifteen are abnormally long or short, *i.e.* they contain more than four or less than three accented words. Of these, eight in the Hebrew text contain only two accented words, six contain five, and one contains seven. But the line of seven words (x. 14 a) should certainly be read as two lines (and probably of three words each, one word being dittographic) as in the above translation, x. 14 a, b. On the other hand, the Revised Version wrongly makes two lines (each of two accents) out of one in the case of ix. 14 b, c = ix. 15 b in the above translation. In this case the mis-division of the Revised Version spoils the parallelism. The case is similar, though less obvious, with ix. 13 a, b (R.V.) = ix. 14 a above (one line of four accents ; see note above). With this corrected division of lines the ה strophe, like the nine strophes enumerated above, contains four lines, each of normal length, instead of four abnormally short lines and two normal lines, giving in all, in the Revised Version, six lines to the strophe which would be altogether abnormal.

We have still to consider five lines each containing in the Massoretic text two word accents, and six lines each containing five. Of the five lines of two accents, four become of the normal length of three accents, if we simply delete the makkeph : these are ix. 2 b, 4 a, 14 b, x. 12 b ; in the last case, however, the shortness

is more probably caused by the loss of a word
(see note above). The only remaining instance
of a line of two accents is x. 10 a, and there, as
I have shown above, there are very strong
exegetical reasons for suspecting the loss of a
word.

Two of the lines of five accents contain a word
which there are strong reasons (already given),
apart from rhythmic considerations, for transposing in the one case (ix. 7 b) to the following,
and in the other (x. 7 a) to the preceding line.
With the removal of the intrusive words these
lines become of the normal length of four words.
If in x. 6 a לדר ודר be makkephed, as in Psalm
cxxxv. 13, and in ix. 19 a לא לנצח, as in Psalm
ciii. 9, these lines also are of normal length.
There remain x. 12 a and x. 18 b, where reasons,
other than rhythmical, for reducing the length
of the lines are less cogent.

This survey may suffice to show that the text
of lines containing less than three or more than
four accents is open to grave suspicion.

The most crucial question in dealing with the
structure of Psalms ix. and x. is this : How far
back from the end of the Psalm does the alphabetic arrangement extend ? It is generally said
that the strophes beginning with the last four
letters (ת, ש, ר, ק) remain ; but it is also commonly stated or *implied* that the immediately
preceding strophes have been lost and their place

taken by others, or that these strophes, though as they stand they are original, were never brought into the alphabetic scheme. But what are the facts ? I turn first to the twelve lines immediately preceding the ק strophe, for here are facts which have been overlooked or not appreciated.

1. The eighth line (x. 8 c) before the ק strophe begins with ע, *i.e.* ע occurs as an initial letter *at the exact interval* from ק at which it should occur in an alphabetic poem following the order observed in Lamentations ii., iii., iv.[1] where the פ strophe precedes the ע.

Even if this fact stood by itself and so might possibly be due to accident, it ought to be taken account of ; but it does not stand alone, for

2. If we read back three lines and four words (*i.e.* the normal length of a line), in all therefore four lines, from the point where the initial ע occurs, we find the word פידו : *i.e.* פ stands *at the exact interval* from ק and ע at which it should stand by the well-established laws of this poem. I have stated the fact thus, for thus stated it is indisputable. It is true that according to the traditional verse division פידו does not stand at the beginning of the line, but I have shown in the note on the passage above that there are the

---

[1] The same order (ע before פ) was found by the Greek translators in their Hebrew text of Prov. xxxi. It was probably also found in the original form of Ps. xxxiv., for sense seems to require the transposition of *vv.* 16 and 17 (=15, 16 R.V.).

strongest reasons (entirely independent of alphabetic considerations) for holding that the line originally began with this word, and that the traditional division of the text gives bad sense, bad rhythm, and bad parallelism.

3. Although the fourth line (x. 10 a) before the initial ק does not begin with צ, there are, as I have already shown, the strongest independent reasons for believing that this abnormally short line has lost a word in the course of textual transmission.

I submit that this combination of facts—the abnormal shortness and strangeness of the fourth line before initial ק, the occurrence of initial ע at the beginning of the eighth and of initial ס at the beginning of the twelfth line—is not accidental, but is due to the fact that Psalm x. concludes not merely with the last four but with the last seven strophes of an alphabetic poem.

Working back afresh from the initial ק in x. 12 we find at the beginning of the twentieth line before it the letter נ (in x. 3 b),[1] *i.e.* נ stands *at the exact interval* before ק at which it should stand in an alphabetic poem of four-lined strophes. On the other hand, if we count downwards from the initial י in ix. 18, or the ל in x. 1, it occurs two lines too soon. Moreover the initial ס,

---

[1] For the justification of following the Greek as against the Hebrew tradition in beginning the line with נאץ, see note above, p. 275.

which should precede it, and the ס, which should follow, are not found in the present text. Having regard to these facts alone, we might consider the position of נ in relation to ק accidental. But when we connect this with our previous conclusion, such an explanation becomes difficult; for נ occurs at the correct interval before not only ק but also before ס and ע. I recall further at this point that the fifth line after the נ (x. 5 b), where initial ס should stand, is suspicious, though perhaps not impossible, in style, and that the substitution of a similar word beginning with ס appears to be a considerable improvement. The case of the missing initial מ may be taken with a consideration of the first part of the poem; and this may be brief, for opinion differs less seriously here.

Of late it has never been seriously questioned that Psalm ix. was originally alphabetic, and this being so it is unnecessary to discuss at length whether the ד and ה strophes were shorter than the rest in the original poem. No reason or sound analogy can be given for such abbreviation, and we have not the slightest ground for assuming that the author was such a bungler as without reason to have failed in the very simple art of writing an alphabetic poem. It follows that the equivalent of about four lines has fallen out of the text between ix. 6 and ix. 10.

But if this has certainly happened at one point

in the poem, it is not improbable that it has happened elsewhere. If, therefore, the alphabetic structure can be traced down to the ל strophe and from the נ strophe to the end, the most probable explanation of the facts that in the present text six lines only instead of eight stand between initial ל and initial נ and that initial מ is absent must surely be that two lines have fallen out of the text, one of which contained the missing initial.

The only strophes now left for consideration are those with the initials י and כ. The י strophe clearly begins with ix. 18, for the initial י occurs here and at the correct interval after ט; but where did it end? The data appear to me somewhat ambiguous. But the question is obviously connected with another : Does the original כ occur in the present text; if so, where? One suggestion may be decisively dismissed, for it too implicitly charges the author with bungling. It has been said that the ק with which ix. 20 begins was intentionally substituted for כ because the two letters had some resemblance in sound ! This is as if the composer of an English acrostic should find it beyond his powers to discover a suitable word beginning with C and should use instead a word beginning with G !

If the original כ survives, it most probably survives in the first word of ix. 19; then the present text would present a י strophe of two

followed by a כ strophe of six lines. In that
case we must suppose that a couplet has shifted
from the י into the כ strophe, and we may, with
Duhm, place ix. 21 immediately after ix. 18.
But this, though a possible, and indeed a not
improbable solution, is not certain, for though
ix. 21 follows ix. 18 well enough, its connexion
with ix. 18 is by no means obviously better than
with ix. 20.

Others have suggested that ix. 20, 21 do not
belong to the original alphabetic poem but are
an independent close to Psalm ix. This theory
would be more probable if the verses were absent
from the Greek text ; but they are not, and the
theory requires the assumption that verses intended to form an independent close to Psalm
ix. after it had been separated from Psalm x.
are present in a text which still treats Psalms ix.
and x. as continuous.

One curious fact must not be concealed.
Psalm ix. 20 begins with ק and the third line
following (ix. 21 a) with ש. In this sequence
Baethgen detects the continuation, after a gap
of several strophes, of ix. 19. He also assumes
the loss of two lines after ix. 20. This particular
assumption is invalidated, if it be shown that the
original ק strophe really occurs in Psalm x. It
is just possible, however, that, if ix. 20, 21 are
intrusive, they were derived from an alphabetic
poem of two-lined strophes ; but the sequence

may quite well be accidental; to be sure of
alphabetic structure we need a sequence of at
least three letters, for only so can we determine
the fixed interval between the letters which
gives the sequence its significance.

I conclude my discussion with a brief criticism
of certain theories as to the literary and textual
history of Psalms ix. and x.

Professor Kirkpatrick's ultimate conclusion
is that Psalm ix. "appears to be complete in
itself, and it seems preferable to regard Psalm x. as
a companion piece rather than as part of a
continuous whole." This appears to me highly
improbable, and it certainly does nothing to
alleviate the grave exegetical difficulties which
Baethgen attempts to remove; but I will not
discuss it here, for it does not depend on any
conclusion as to the completeness of the alphabetic structure, since it would not be safe to
deny that a writer may have chosen to compose
two separate poems, one following the alphabetic
scheme to the eleventh letter, the other from the
twelfth to the twenty-second and last.

Some other theories which deny the unity
of Psalms ix. and x. have proceeded from the
assumption that parts of the two Psalms are
alphabetic, and parts non-alphabetic; and that
x. 1-11 or x. 3-11 are the non-alphabetic part,
which is of different origin from the rest. Now
such theories must be so modified as to be scarcely

worth maintaining if my argument that even
in the present text the alphabetic structure can
be clearly traced back to x. 7 is sound ; and
they fall completely to the ground if my further
argument that the original initial נ survives in
its original position in x. 3 is also admitted.

Baethgen's theory may be considered at
greater length, for it is based on weighty exegetical
considerations. I will cite his remarks somewhat
fully. After indicating the reasons for considering that Psalms ix. and x. were originally connected, he continues : " The reason for the
division adopted by the Massoretes lies in the
difference of subject ; but the conclusion of
Psalm x. refers to the same circumstances that
form the subject of Psalm ix. ; moreover the
alphabetic scheme does not reach its close till
the end of Psalm x. Psalm ix. is a song of
thanksgiving and triumph over the defeat of
heathen foes. . . . With x. 1 ff. there begin
bitter complaints about the absence (*Ausbleiben*)
of divine help. But the oppressors are not the
same as in Psalm ix. ; they are not heathen,
but godless Israelites. . . . Corresponding to this
remarkable change from triumph to bitter complaint and to the entirely different historic
background which is presupposed is a break
in the alphabetic arrangement." Baethgen then
points out, as I have already done, how the
alphabetic scheme survives down to the י strophe

in ix. 19 and then continues, " After this everything is lost till ק ix. 20, שׁ ix. 21.   In x. 1-11 there
is no alphabetic arrangement.   In x. 12, 13 again
ק, in x. 14 ר, in x. 15 f. שׁ, and x. 17, 18 ת.   Since
x. 16-18 agree most excellently with the beginning,
and indeed with the entire contents of Psalm ix.,
but not in the slightest with the rest of Psalm x.,
the conjecture that x. 1-15 formed no original
part of the poem cannot be dismissed.   The
verses x. 12-15 follow, it is true, an alphabetic
arrangement, but their subject matter and language connect them with x. 1-11 ; cf. x. 13 with
x. 3, 4, 11, x. 14 with x. 8-10 (חלכה), x. 15 with
x. 4.   The language of x. 1-15 is harder and more
peculiar than that of ix. 1-21, x. 16-18 ; yet
between both parts there are links, cf. x. 1
and ix. 10 (לעתות בצרה) :   x. 12 with ix. 13, 19.
It is no longer possible to explain satisfactorily
all these remarkable phenomena.   The interpolation of x. 1-15 and the loss of the strophes from
כ to צ between ix. 19 and ix. 20 may have been
accidental and perhaps due to a leaf getting
misplaced in binding. . . . But it is just as likely
that a later editor intentionally gave the Psalm
its present form by removing a section and
substituting another for it."

Certainly Baethgen's strongest argument is
drawn from the apparent difference of subject
in the present text—in ix. and x. 16-18 the
nations, in x. 1-15 the wicked.   Both Dr. Cheyne

U

and Duhm, who maintain the substantial unity of the whole, feel this so strongly that they assimilate ix. and x. 16-18 to x. 1-15 by reading where the term *nations* (גוים) occurs either *the treacherous* (בגדים ; so Cheyne) or *the proud* (גאים ; so Duhm).

Baethgen's argument from difference of style I believe to be fallacious ; the style of x. 1-15 only appears harder when we treat what has suffered corruption and become unintelligible as the original style of the writer. Doubtless parts of x. 1-15, particularly x. 6-10, are in the present text harder than most of Psalm ix. ; but they are corrupt ; and in turn ix. 6, 7, which are also corrupt, are harder than, for example, x. 1, 2 or x. 7 (after אלה) to x. 9.

But the theory breaks down owing to the improbabilities which it implies in connexion with the alphabetic sequence. It will be sufficient to consider what Baethgen, in common with every one else, admits, that x. 12-18 constitute a perfect sequence of four alphabetic strophes (ת, ש, ר, ק). Yet on Baethgen's theory this perfect sequence is the result of accident. The last strophe and a half belonged to one poem, the remaining two and a half to another ; in binding, a leaf fell out of place and with it the original alphabetic order was broken, and yet, marvellous to relate, the leaf which accidentally took its place contained part of another alphabetic poem of precisely the same structure which exactly dovetailed into the end of the poem. The last lines of the lost leaf should have contained the four lines of a ק strophe, followed by four lines of a ר strophe, followed by two lines of a ש strophe: the leaf which on the hypothesis was accidentally substituted for it actually contained four lines of a ק strophe, followed by four lines of a ר strophe, followed by two lines of a ש strophe. Moreover the accidentally substituted leaf so well dovetails into the leaf that preceded that it commences with ל at the exact and correct interval of eight lines from the initial .

The case is scarcely better if we accept Baethgen's alternative suggestion that x. 1-15 were *intentionally* substituted for a section of the original alphabetic poem. For are we to suppose that the editor selected these verses in particular because he noticed that they contained the suitable sequence ש, ר, ק ? Are we to suppose that in the passage thus chosen (x. 1-15) this sequence of these three letters at the same fixed interval was mere accident ? The latter supposition becomes even more improbable, impossible indeed, when account is taken of the further sequence פ, ע, which connects, as shown above, with the sequence ש, ר, ק.

The only modification of Baethgen's theory which seems to me tenable is that x. 1-15 was

throughout alphabetic, and was deliberately
written to be interpolated between ix. 21 and x.
16 by a later editor, who for some reason found
the verses thus replaced unsuitable. This would
account for the admitted sequence ש, ר, ק, for the
further traces of alphabetic structure, for the
exact dovetailing of the inserted section, and for
the points of connexion in thought and style
between x. 1-15 and ix. + x. 16-18. But in this
form the theory cannot of course derive any
argument from the present alphabetic phenomena.
It must depend on the difference, apparent
certainly if not original, of subject. But why
should an editor, who thought it necessary to
interpolate a long section, have failed to make
the further slight changes necessary to assimilate
the subject throughout ?

Several of those who attribute the present
incompleteness of the alphabetic structure to
textual corruption have sought to restore the
original text by transpositions. Some of these
transpositions are certainly questionable. For
the remnants of the alphabetic structure testify
not only to the fact of textual corruption, *but
also to certain limitations within which that corruption has occurred* ; they must therefore be treated
as regulating factors in any reconstruction of
the text. Thus treated, they go far to invalidate
not only theories of large interpolation of foreign
matter, but also theories of extensive transposi-

tion and omission. In so far, therefore, as they
involve such transpositions I find the theories
of Bickell, Cheyne, and, in a less degree, of Duhm,
improbable. For example, on Bickell's theory,
among the textual corruptions are the following :
(1) ix. 20, 21 have been added to the original
poem ; (2) the original ב strophe consisted of
x. 3 (now somewhat expanded) + x. 4 + x. 5 a,
and has shifted from its original position so as
to follow the ל strophe, x. 1, 2 ; (3) the נ and ס
strophes have fallen out clean after x. 5 b (from
מרום), x. 6 which constitute the original מ
strophe. But all this involves this rather improbable combination of accidents : (1) the position of initial נ in the present text at the correct
distance before initial פעקרשת is pure accident,
for on the theory it is not the original initial נ ;
(2) the ל of x. 1 is the original initial, but it has
only retained its position at the correct interval
after initial י by a lucky combination of changes :
the assumed interpolation of ix. 20, 21 would
have removed it four lines too far from initial י,
but this was neutralised by four lines exactly
of the ב strophe getting misplaced after the ל
strophe ; (3) by accident eight consecutive lines
(the נ and ס strophes) drop out between x. 6 and 7
without any such break in the sense as would
indicate so considerable a loss.

Dr. Cheyne's reconstruction assumes frequent
expansion of the text through the intrusion of

variant readings of the same line and corresponding losses of lines. With regard to the addition of ix. 20, 21, the transpositions at the beginning of Psalm x., and the loss of exactly the eight lines of the נ and ס strophes he nearly agrees with Bickell. But further, on his theory, the occurrence of initial פ and ע at the correct interval before the initial ק is due to a lucky combination, within the twelve lines concerned, of addition and omission ; two lines have fallen out between x. 10 and x. 11, but just this quantity of matter by a curious freak of fortune has been added within the same section by the expansion of two original lines into the four lines 9 b and 10 a, d of the present text.

The text of Psalms ix. and x. has certainly suffered corruption. The LXX contains a few more correct readings than the Hebrew text, and preserves the correct division of lines in one case where the Massoretic text has destroyed it. But even conjectural emendation is justified and indeed demanded, and that to a somewhat greater extent than I have admitted in the provisional translation given above for purposes of this discussion. Exegesis that fails to take account of this, that insists on interpreting everything in the present text as the actual words of the author, must go wrong. In addition to this general conclusion, the results, briefly summarised, which an examination of the structure of the poem appears to me to offer as the starting-point of sound exegesis, are these : Psalms ix. and x. are a single poem; the original poem consisted of eighty-eight lines of three or four accented words; the equivalent of four or five of these lines has been lost—the equivalent of two or three between ix. 6 and ix. 10, two lines exactly between x. 1 and x. 4. On the other hand, at no point between ix. 2-5 or ix. 10-17 or x. 6-18 has the text received addition or suffered loss to the extent of more than a word or two, but several such small losses or additions or corruptions of words are indicated by the abnormal length of the lines or the impossibility of the style.

ADDITIONAL NOTE ON THE REPETITION OF TERMS IN PARALLEL LINES

[See page 254, note 2.]

THE clearest proof that some instances at least of repetition (in the present Hebrew text) of the same term in the two parallel lines of a distich are due to scribal error is furnished by the double text of Psalm xviii. = 2 Samuel xxii. Thus in *v.* 7 in Samuel the verb אקרא, *I call*, occurs in both lines; but the second אקרא is an error, and probably a relatively late error, for the LXX in Samuel has different verbs—ἐπικαλέσομαι in the first, βοήσομαι in the second line. The original Hebrew text is preserved in the Psalm, which has אקרא, *I call*, in the first, אשוע, *I cry for help*, in the second line. Similarly in *v.* 32 מבלעדי, *save*, occurs in Samuel in both lines, in the Psalm in the first line only, זולתי, *except*, being used in the second line. Here the LXX has πλὴν both in the Psalm and Samuel in both lines; nevertheless the Hebrew text of the Psalm, with different prepositions in the two lines, is the original text. A somewhat similar error to the two just considered occurs in *v.* 47 : here the Psalm has in the two lines as synonymous terms צורי, *my rock,* and אלהי ישעי, *the God of my salvation* : through erroneous repetition of the term of the first line Samuel agrees with the Psalm in the first line, but in the second line has the conflate phrase, *the God of the rock of my salvation.* In *v.* 29 Samuel has *Yahweh* in both lines ; the Psalm, *Yahweh* in the first, and *my God* in the second line : the text of Samuel is wrong, but is perhaps not due to mere extrusion of a differentiated term by a repetition of the same term. Somewhat different, too, but worthy of consideration in this connexion, is the loss of the undoubtedly correct משברי, *billows,* of 2 Samuel xxii. 5 in the Psalm through the substitution for it in the latter passage of חבלי, *snares,* which occurs in the next distich.

At times parallel terms in parallel lines suffered transposition : where accidents of this kind have taken place, they cannot generally be detected. It has been suggested that such an accident befell the text of Nahum i. 4 (see p. 257, n. 1); and there is one certain example of such an accident in the poem that occurs both in Isaiah ii. 2-4 and Micah i. 1-4 : in Isaiah ii. 2 e, 3 a = Micah iv. 1 e, 2 a the parallel terms, גוים, *nations,* and עמים, *peoples,* occur in this order in Isaiah, in the reverse order in Micah.

A few further examples may be given of repetitions in the present Hebrew text which there is some reason to suspect was not in as original fact. In Job ix. 10 עד־אין occurs in both verses ; but in the earlier occurrence of the verse in v. 9 we find the versation ואין . . עראין. In Job xii. 23 לגוים is repeated, but five MSS. give לאמים in the second line. In xiii. 7 תדברו is repeated, but the Lχρ has λαλεῖτε . . φθέγγεσθε ; the letters v b never renders דדר, except perhaps in Eccles. xiii. 22, but it renders הביע in Ps. lxxvii. 2, lxxiii. 4 : or should perhaps read תביעו for the second תדברו. Similarly the repeated יעות in Job viii. 3, שר in Amos v. 9, ימוחו in Jer. xi. 22 are all represented by different words in the Lχρ.

ERRATA

Page 296, last paragraph.

Lines 2 and 3, *for* was not in as original fact *read* were not in the original text.

Line 3, *for* verses *read* lines.

  „ 4, *for* verse *read* line.

Lines 4 and 5, *for* versation *read* variation.

Line 5, *for* עראין *read* ער־אין.

Lines 7 and 11, *for* Lχρ *read* LXX.

Line 7, *for* letters v b *read* latter verb.

  „ 7, *for* דדר *read* דבר.

  „ 8, *for* Eccles. *read* Ecclus.

  „ 9, *for* lxxiii. 4 : or *read* xciv. 4 ; we.

INDEX I

OF PASSAGES OF SCRIPTURE

[The references are according to the enumeration of the Hebrew text: in one or two cases the different English enumeration is given in brackets; in the Psalms, the English enumeration is generally one verse behind the Hebrew.]

INDEX II

OF MATTERS

301

THE END

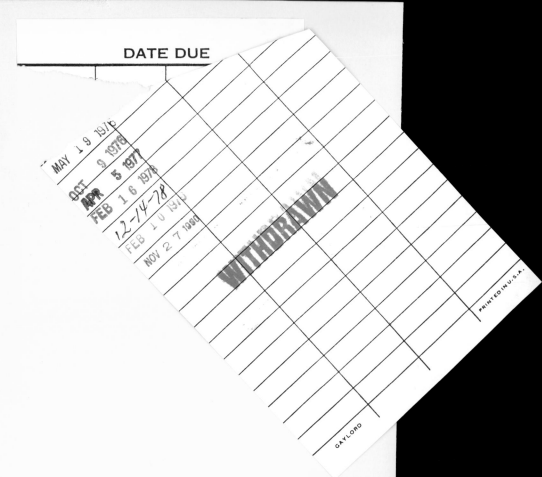